THE DIASPORA OF BELONGING

WOW! MY GUY! THANKS SO MUCH FOR
EVERYTHING ADAM. FOR REAL.
HOPE YOU ENJOY!

THE
DIASPORA OF
BELONGING

GENTRIFICATION, SYSTEMS
OF OPPRESSION, AND WHY OUR
CITIES ARE OUT OF PLACE

~~JAY SHARMA~~

Jay
12/2020

NEW DEGREE PRESS

COPYRIGHT © 2020 JAY SHARMA

All rights reserved.

THE DIASPORA OF BELONGING

Gentrification, Systems of Oppression, and Why Our Cities are Out of Place

ISBN   978-1-63676-565-5 *Paperback*
               978-1-63676-154-1 *Kindle Ebook*
               978-1-63676-155-8 *Ebook*

For my Thai.

CONTENTS

PART I

HOW WE SETTLED
(OR BASE FARE)

AUTHOR'S NOTE

"Excuse me."

"Oh, my bad," I say as I duck around the stanchion, clearing the way out.

"'Preciate it."

"NORTH STATION. CHANGE HERE FOR GREEN LINE. BUS SERVICE."

Exhaling, I return to my original stance, with my back to the door. This way, I can survey the rest of the train car. If I wanted to, I could turn around to watch the city of Boston fade behind me, but I like looking around the train. I like observing the different characters and interactions. I like catching the eyes of a stranger, or even striking up conversation with some old ass townie. I like seeing who I get to share this space and time with.

"NEXT STOP: COMMUNITY COLLEGE. DOORS OPEN ON BOTH SIDES. COMMUNITY COLLEGE, NEXT STOP."

Growing up, it became easier and easier to take the train. It also became more fun. I spent less time studying the routes and worrying about my stops, and more time thinking about the people, their days, and what a train did for us. It was like directing a movie: Any type of character I needed would simply appear. If not now, then maybe in a few stops. What made the train even better was that every rider directed their own movie, which allowed me to be a side character. In this anonymity, I could bury myself in a book, bust a quick nap, or listen to my iPod. No one really knew what I was thinking or where I was going. And they didn't really care.

"NEXT STOP: SULLIVAN. BUS SERVICE. DOORS OPEN ON BOTH SIDES. SULLIVAN, NEXT STOP."

I grew up a few blocks from here. I remember the whole block was lathered with South Asian families. I remember running to the park behind our street. I remember my barber Miguel, who still works just a few blocks away, dancing Merengue as he cuts my hair.

Recollecting myself, I prepare a relocation strategy, this is the stop that sees the most foot traffic coming from Downtown. On the platform, there's almost always a chance you'll see a young couple with a stroller, a cyclist, a rider on their phone, a college student, or a twenty-something-year-old security guard. Playing it cool, I dissolve into a crowd, ending up next to a businesswoman reading her Kindle.

"SULLIVAN. CHANGE HERE FOR BUS SERVICE."

Taking the train in and around the city was—and still is—liberating. There's always been a certain sense of independence that consumes me; I never needed permission from anyone to ride. All I needed was my CharlieCard, and I could access virtually any part of the city I wanted.

Taking the train was the most leveled playing field there was. You could be a banker, a veteran, an engineer, a construction worker, houseless, a chef, or even a government official, and it didn't matter. You had to wait for the same train, sit in the same seats, and exist in the same space as everyone else. Here is where our lives intersected. To see this scene uncover itself was to see the magic of cities.

"NEXT STOP: WELLINGTON. BUS SERVICE. DOORS ON BOTH SIDES. NEXT STOP: WELLINGTON."

I plan my escape route from the train car, as if I'm a running-back reading the defense. I survey the faces one last time, and make a mental note of where the vacant seats are. I scout for riders I think will get off next, wondering if they're wondering the same. I shift my weight onto the balls of my feet. The train stops. The right side opens first and, after a few seconds, the left one does too.

"WELLINGTON, DOORS OPEN ON BOTH SIDES. BUS SERVICE."

If I had stayed on, more folks would start closing their books, calling their rides, and packing their things. The next stop was Malden Center, which means I'd see a good amount of the Asian riders get off. Just like there was a noticeable amount of Black and Latinx folks who lived by Sullivan, or the mix of white people who lived by Oak Grove; I had noticed where folks were usually getting off.

When I noticed these patterns, others stood out too. Some were baseless, some were not. Stops were more frequent closer to the city than outside it. Minorities typically lived near other minorities. Different groups of riders boarded at different times of the day, visited different parts of the city.

Noticing these things jump-started my love for cities. I realized that I was lucky to see such trends in real life, and even luckier to have this exposure just by sitting in a single train car. I got to see a spectrum of races, cultures, fashion, behaviors, personalities, and occupations. Without realizing it, my awareness of my surroundings and my spacial understanding were being polished every time I tapped my CharlieCard.

* * *

I remember my pops driving my mom and me to South Station to catch a Fung-Wah bus to Queens, NY (which, at times, feels more like "home" for me). Sometimes it'd be early in the morning, and I'd see a sea of suits, sunglasses, and Dunkin' cups. Sometimes it'd be in the evening, and employees who worked there had already skedaddled, catching a train home or bouncing to a post-work work event. Every night, these single-use areas looked like a cross between a movie set and a ghost town: eerie, desolate, and overshadowed.

One thing about cities in particular that always amazed me was how quickly places could change from one moment to the next. How could such vibrant places feel so stark and cold? Why did some areas only come alive at night? What brought that feeling of familiarity and relief when I got off at "my" train stop? How could a single train car weave together so many parts of the urban fabric? How do cultures and spaces unite and define a city? How do cities get their feel? Why do some cities remind us of other cities? Why do some cities feel like home? What does it mean to belong?

* * *

The feel of a city is embedded in its public spaces, architectural styles, and neighborhoods. It leaks through slang and dialect, stains local restaurants, and is characterized by locals themselves. Some cities feel charming or ethereal. Others feel historic or outdated. Some cities didn't distinguish themselves until the late twentieth century; others have been around since European colonialization efforts.

But cities hold the hearts of many. Efforts to measure and quantify their impacts have been a topic of interest for ecologists, economists, geographers, sociologists, historians, and more. The idea of "hometown pride" is permeated across America. A look into Instagram's hashtag data found that cities like San Francisco, Seattle, Tulsa, New Orleans, and Buffalo were being consistently appreciated for their beauty, architecture, and food.[1] A 2017 survey conducted by Gallup and the US Census Bureau compiled public opinion about city pride and found that in the thirteen most proud metropolitan areas, over 74 percent of residents reported being proud of their city—a 10 percent increase compared to the national average.[2]

What's more persuasive is that all these areas were under 650,000 people, and included small cities like Asheville, North Carolina and Green Bay, Wisconsin (which goes to show that big cities aren't always the ones instilling a sense of community and pride). Despite attempts by researchers to pinpoint the source of this pride, it's still unclear whether or not there is a singular overriding factor responsible for our pride. Safety, economics, a sense of community, and the presence of colleges have all been linked to pride, but those, too, vary by city.

It still remains a fact, however, that some of our greatest cities have terrible stories. Many of these revolve around political, racial, and economic atmospheres in the nation at the time. Given this country's malicious history and its seemingly inexorable treatment of Indigenous folks, immigrants, women, and people of color, associations between the character of people and their cities have been called into question.

---

1   "The Most Loved Cities on Instagram," LendingTree, accessed September 1, 2020.
2   Cheyenne Buckingham and Joseph Gideon, "13 Cities Where People Are Proud of Their Communities," 24/7 Wall St, last modified March 20, 2020; "2016 Community Well-Being Rankings," Gallup-Healthways Well-Being Index, March 2017.

Here's a tiny example: Almost every time I share that I'm from Boston, I am met with enlarged eyes, followed by an ominous, "Isn't Boston, like, really racist?" I usually respond one of two things: either "What parts of Boston have you visited?" or "Who told you that?"

But it's true. Racism, like many other things, exists on a geographic spectrum. We know racism is entrenched in our systems and institutions, but what about our buildings and public spaces? It doesn't matter where in America you are— the liberal Northeast, the deep South, the ambiguous Midwest, or the laid-back West Coast—there are injustices baked into our built environments that communicate decades of hate and discrimination.

This is to say, many of our cities have been formed as reactions to social, political, economic, or geographic challenges. And in the process of developing those cities, the ruling class has managed to implement and uphold prejudiced design and zoning practices. Boston, despite being smaller than other major cities, still has suburbs and an urban core. But could they all be considered part of the same city? What does it mean to live in an urban setting? What counts as urban anyway?

It turns out that patterns of settlement have dictated what an "urban area" actually is. The phrase has, at different times, been used to refer to places with 8,000 people (in 1880), 4,000 people (1890), and 2,500 people (1900). Adjustments and refinements in urban categorization were made because the initial thresholds were set too high to obtain an accurate distinction between urban and rural areas.[3] In 1920, for the first time, the US Census Bureau recorded over half of the US population as living in an urban setting.[4]

By 1950, an urban area was defined as a built-up area with more than 50,000 inhabitants—the definition that remains in use today. The 1950 census, as a result of suburbanization, solidified the concept of urbanized areas, which is used to describe densely settled communities outside of urban cores.

Today, over 80 percent of Americans live in urban areas, more than double what it was a hundred years ago. Not only did folks move into existing cities, but new cities started popping up between others, forming urban corridors and ultra-connected stretches of lands. By 2050, the share of folks living in cities is expected to reach 90 percent.[5]

People play a huge role in the formation and continued success of a city, and cities are likewise responsible for supporting and sustaining the people. The symbiotic relationship between the two entities has become so interlinked that, at times, they become indistinguishable. As such, the composition and feel of a city is more fluid than we like

---

3   Michael Ratcliffe, "A Century of Delineating A Changing Landscape: The Census Bureau's Urban and Rural Classification, 1910 to 2010," U.S. Census Bureau, accessed July 28, 2020.

4   "Urban and Rural Areas," U.S. Census Bureau, accessed July 28, 2020.

5   Center for Sustainable Systems, "U.S. Cities Factsheet," University of Michigan, Pub. No. CSS09-06 (September 2020).

to think. Perhaps it's because people are transient beings, and our feelings are largely a reaction to our surroundings.

Cities, like the physical markers in them, are not permanent. Waves of people and capital moving in, out, and around cities show the magnetic characteristics of places. The attraction of diversity and culture brings people into cities. The repulsion of monotonous landscapes and unaffordability forces others out. The strive for a proper work-life balance pushes folks around cities and to different neighborhoods. These pursuits undeniably displace aspects that give our cities their character and inexorably change the way cities feel. Despite troubled histories of discrimination and oppression, cities can intentionally manage their infrastructure, feel, and reputation to usher a sense of inclusivity and belonging.

Seattle is a great example. Named after a Chief from the Duwamish Tribe, Seattle is now a beacon, of sorts, for inclusivity and community. But on February 7, 1865, the Board of Trustees of Seattle passed Ordinance No. 5, which called for the expulsion of all Native Americans from the city, a stark difference from the city we know today.[6] Detroit is another example. Once regarded as the automotive capital of the world in the early twentieth century, Detroit (like many Rust Belt cities) saw a sharp decline in population, economic GDP, and livelihood, and ended up filing for bankruptcy back in

---

6   "Reflecting on an Act of Discrimination: County Council Recognizes Native American Expulsion Remembrance Day," King County, February 4, 2015.

2014.[7] But with active city management and dedication, both cities were able to change for the better. Today, the 7th of February is the Native American Expulsion Remembrance Day for Seattleites, and Detroit managed to pull itself out of bankruptcy just a year after filing.

* * *

Housing, understandably, is a critical component of the constantly evolving, symbiotic relationship between cities and people. The balance between affordability and opportunity has created tensions among residents and with their governments. Recently, parts of this tension have manifested themselves into a process known as gentrification.

Gentrification is a complex subject, with many causes and effects. It is typically a combination of decades-long economic segregation and divestment, displacement of long-time residents, and a shift in community dynamic and character. It can be seen in increasing rents, property taxes, bursts of chic bars and eateries, rebranding, or an increase in public services. It can be measured by changes in educational attainment, median home values, median household incomes, or resident demographics.[8] Displacement is central to gentrification, but that doesn't mean it is required to raise the same concerns and attitudes surrounding the process. Gentrification, displacement, and neighborhood change occur across the world. But colonialism, slavery, and

---

7   Pete Saunders, "Detroit, Five Years After Bankruptcy," *Forbes*, July 18, 2018.
8   Michael Maciag, "Gentrification Report Methodology," Governing, January 31, 2015.

institutional segregation in America make its occurrence particularly pertinent, devastating, and alienating.

Some folks have accepted "gentrification" as an embedded step in the life cycle of all cities and neighborhoods; it is not. This premature acceptance of "gentrification" is oftentimes a mere observance based on a few criteria in a limited time-frame (such as looking solely at out-migration to surrounding neighborhoods over a long period of time). Data and research by some of the nation's leading experts demonstrate that actual gentrification is limited to a handful of neighborhoods in a handful of cities. Lastly, gentrification only reaches gentrifiable neighborhoods—those that are "good enough" for prospective residents—and tends to bypass neighborhoods of extreme poverty.

But just so we're clear: America doesn't have a gentrification problem; it has a poverty problem.

And when we speak of gentrification, we're just choosing the cherry atop a sundae of economic segregation, ignoring the foundational toppings of disinvestment, neglect, resource scarcity, disenfranchisement, and persistent, systemic barriers to economic mobility.

* * *

I spent the past year researching, thinking, and learning about what goes into the tricky topic of gentrification (and economic segregation). In the process, I consulted a number of experts from across the country and in different areas of expertise. This book is not designed to be a detailed encyclopedia, but rather an introduction to the complexity of urban systems and the role of communities in our lives. But questions remain: How can we maintain the livability of our cities and prioritize the care for the people around us? How can we move toward a regenerative economy—using social justice as a design framework—to create equitable and connected communities?

Having been in urban settings my entire life, I've witnessed the magic of cities. There's the suspense of interactions. The thrill of city shenanigans. The characters. The unexpectedness. The choice of having a passive experience versus an active one. There's the wide canvas covered by buildings, bridges, nature, and art. The system of roads, highways, trains. The flow of people, goods, and information. It's all stimulation to the unrestful mind. It's all a giant maze, waiting to be explored.

But from what history tells us, the cities that will thrive are those that work *with* the people; cities that are revolutionary, inclusive, and supportive. These cities are dynamic, well-positioned, and imperfect. Cities must craft their delicate character and reputation around their resources and bandwidth. Cities, and the people who live and work in them, must be willing to understand the ways policies and design affect all types of people. They have a huge opportunity to foster inclusion and diversity by creating and maintaining spaces for connection, both with residents and within built and natural environments.

This book is not about why designers should have to fix the problems created by the government and politicians. It is a bridge for folks to come together and reevaluate existing infrastructure and systems in place today, as a means to make our cities and communities more equitable, inclusive, and livable. This bridge is for architects, planners, engineers, residents, developers, politicians, immigrants, business owners, historians, thinkers, doers, travelers, students, techies, public health experts, and more. The bridge is where we convene. It is where we will teach, heal, and learn. And it must be a place we are willing to leave better than we found it.

In order to truly have democratic and equitable cities, people need to be empowered. Those in positions of power need to listen and embrace change. A focus on community, starting with public ownership, accessible design, and better education, needs to characterize our cities. A focus on connection—between people, spaces, and ideas—needs to be the defining pillar for a redefined way of life in the city.

Tag along as we visit twelve of the most interesting cities in America. We'll start in the Northeast and make our way across the country as we explore our history and the different facets of gentrification. We'll learn how food patterns mimic larger sociopolitical movements, the difference between places and spaces, the development of urbanized areas, and among many other things, how racism has shaped our urban landscapes. But perhaps more importantly, this book will help you become a more educated, aware, and involved resident.

1

MOBILITY IN SPACE

———

"Whatever good things we build end up building us."

JIM ROHN

———

It's well past six on a Sunday night. Which means we finna be late.

My brother and sister and both of my parents are already waiting outside. I grab my headphones, lock the door behind me, and hop in the backseat. We're going to a temple that my parents frequent, nestled in a Victorian-styled townhome in the city. Going to this temple means going to Back Bay, which, by default, means going for a walk in the Commons. We cruise along the Charles, past the Garden, Mass General, and the Museum of Science. I see bricks. I see steel. I see stone. I see glass.

I see the remnants of Boston's colonial history through its infrastructure, but I also see hints of Boston's evolution, especially when we park off of Comm Ave. I see the giant mirror that is the John Hancock Tower and the Trinity Church beside it, with its many steeples and columns. While this unabridged juxtaposition is an eyesore for some, it's refreshing and revealing to me. Refreshing because it's a disruption in space, and revealing because it encapsulates the history of Boston. Cities are like a movie series; no matter what frame you look at, you could draw some type of conclusion. The best part of these movie series is that are tons of them scattered across the country, and even more across the world.

My inclination for history sparked my interest in the ways cities evolve at the intersection of the built and natural environments; this led me to complete a degree in civil engineering, where I learned about buildings and materials and design. But I graduated with more questions than I came in with. Why do cities look different? Why do they look the same? Why are Americans so dependent on cars? Is there a Chinatown in every city? Why do people move to be near other people? How and why do cities grow?

I learned that these last two questions could be answered by understanding that throughout human history people have gathered together for safety, survival, and convenience.

* * *

The story of humans in the modern world starts with hunter-gatherers, originally organized in family groups of ten to twelve adults, plus children. These family groups occupied a territory large enough to supply them with fruits, nuts, and plants to forage, as well as wild animals to hunt for meat. Their territories featured regular landmarks, which served as shelters and vantage points. Groups often belonged to "clans," which were no larger than one hundred adults. These clans shared common values, myths, beliefs, and ancestors.[9]

The emergence of agricultural methods and small-scale villages eventually led to communities of three to five hundred individuals. These communities were mostly self-contained and self-governed; villagers often viewed residents from another village as hostile and ill-intentioned. Over time, higher population density set the stage for both increased conflict and increased cooperation. Shared and common-pool resources, such as rivers and farming land, required management between villages to ensure equal access. This cooperation stimulated the advent of technology, such as dams and dikes, which soon allowed for better agricultural practices and eventually, food surpluses. Surpluses then allowed villagers to divert their focus to other industries, such as government, art, manufacturing, and trade.[10] Naturally, cooperation between villages and community groups led to the first ancient civilizations.

Scattered predominately throughout the current-day regions of the Middle East, these civilizations all had a few things in common: an organized social hierarchy, a form of centralized government, a division of labor, a form of communication (either written or verbal), and a form of local trading and monetized economy. These settlements were agricultural civilizations and drew much of their livelihoods from nearby

9   *Encyclopaedia TimeMaps*, Academic ed., s.v. "Hunter-Gatherers," accessed May 25, 2020.

10 *Encyclopaedia TimeMaps*, Academic ed., s.v. "Origins of Civilization," accessed May 25, 2020.

rivers. This strategic practice allowed for an array of benefits—namely water for drinking, fertile soil for farming, and fish for consuming. Access to rivers also facilitated trade and transportation.

A few examples of these River Valley Civilizations include the widely-known civilizations of Mesopotamia (situated between the Tigris and Euphrates Rivers), Egypt (on the Nile River), the Indus Valley (on the Indus and Ganges Rivers), and the Huang He (on the Yellow River). Other city civilizations include the Norte Chico civilization (in present-day Peru) and Mesoamerica (in present-day Mexico). All were established between 4000 and 1500 BCE.

Now if we zoom out, we can already see some similarities between ancient civilizations and today's cities. Most are located by a body of water (to facilitate trade). Shared resources (reservoirs for drinking water, recreational areas, commercial shopping areas, etc.) require cooperation between neighboring cities. And rivalries between high schools and townships have now married tribalism and patriotism, akin to ancient villager attitudes.

* * *

The period between 1500 BCE and 1500 CE saw an increase in food production, trading networks, the spread of information, and an increase in population across all ancient civilizations. This growth made way for subsequent establishment of empires and geographical expansion, and with this expansion came an onset of cities—each with a different purpose.[11] Some cities were significant religious centers (like Constantinople), trading ports (like Amsterdam), or commerce centers (like Alexandria), while others remained political centers (like Athens).

Sometime between fifteen and twenty thousand years ago, the American continents began the peopling process, via the Bering Land Strait.[12] These peoples became known as Paleoamericans and Mesoamericans, and included groups such as the Chan-Chan, Mississippians, Mayans, and Aztecs. Indigenous groups incorporated their way of life into the layout of their cities and structures, and planned for things like travel routes, city centers (for festivals and markets), and even astrological events (as part of a larger astro-archaeological approach to design). Groups during this period shared a tribal component, similar to ancient hunter-gatherer groups, as a form of social bonding. This social structure helped serve as a measure of protection from other groups but, perhaps more importantly, it also formed a basis of identity.

As these groups and civilizations expanded, they shared a handful of fundamental design components: road networks, distinct residential and market areas, sanitation/drainage systems, and a central square or religious center. Most ancient civilizations—both here and abroad—used local topography and geography for military advantages. These are seen in things like moats, portcullises, border walls, and fortresses.

---

11   "Urbanization and the Development of Cities," Lumen Learning, accessed May 25, 2020.

12   Laura Geggel, "Humans Crossed the Bering Land Bridge to People the Americas. Here's What It Looked Like 18,000 Years Ago," LiveScience, February 15, 2019.

As civilizations expanded in population, economic activity, and military and political power, cities began to form more organically. The need to transport people and goods spurred development of roads and streets in many settlements. One particularly notable example can be seen in the ancient Roman Empire where engineers ensured roads had proper drainage, maintenance, and signage, and even constructed tunnels, bridges, and highways. This intricate system helped enable the movement of messengers, soldiers, and horse-drawn wagons for merchants.[13]

The rise and fall of different empires produced reconstruction and remodeling in many European cities. Roads were optimized for military processions and large, open centers developed as a way to display a country's pride and power. Across most civilizations, the presence of open spaces allowed the merchant class to form informal markets to sell their goods and crafts, providing convenience and a sense of camaraderie within cities. In Mesoamerican civilizations, public plazas served as a place for religious ceremonies, markets, traditional rituals, and other celebrations. Unsurprisingly, as development and economic activity picked up in Europe, so too did greed and colonization efforts.

Eventually, rulers started sending merchants to establish commerce with other countries. The fruitful returns of trading expeditions—spices, jewels, minerals, foods, textiles, and more—lured countries to expand their global reach. Africa (the continent) became a target for these European countries;

---

13   Evan Andrews, "8 Ways Roads Helped Rome Rule the Ancient World," *History.com*, last modified August 29, 2018.

its location as well as share of natural resources and minerals enticed the colonizers. Soon explorers started to kidnap and enslave African peoples, and established colonies to generate more wealth. Eventually, this plague of imperialism would spread to the American continents.

In the fifteenth century, colonizers from Spain, Portugal, France, Italy, England, Denmark, Amsterdam, Scotland, and Sweden traveled across oceans in search of goods and riches. The guise of religious missionary work was often used to justify violence and forced conversions to Christianity. Warfare, enslavement, rapes, plundering, and exposure to epidemic diseases were all used to belittle, disarm, and destruct Native populations. By the mid-sixteenth century, Native American populations had encountered notorious colonists such as Hernando de Soto (1539), Pánfilo de Narváez (1528), Juan Ponce de León (1513), and of course Christopher Columbus (1492).[14]

Over the next few centuries, major wars (such as the Beaver Wars of the sixteen hundreds, King Philip's War in the 1670s, and the French and Indian War between 1754 and 1763) led to alliances between different tribes, confederacies, and European countries. As colonies formed on the East Coast, each with their own economic, religious, and social pursuits, British tyranny soon became unbearable to white colonists. The American Revolution—the war that established the United States as an independent country—saw a series of battles, riots, alliances, taxation attempts, and treaties. It also signified the end of British colonization, the success of

14 Matthew Shea, "Exploration and Colonization of the North America," American Battlefield Trust, accessed May 29, 2020.

European mistreatment toward Native Americans, and the beginning of systematic oppression of minority groups that still lasts to this day.[15]

* * *

The struggle for independence and the shadow of colonization set the premise for part of this book. The forced removal of Native Americans from their lands is the original form of displacement now central to gentrification. In place of disease and germs decimating existing populations, it is capital and exorbitant costs of living. Instead of colonists and explorers in the Age of Discovery trying to expand trade routes, there are opportunistic and capitalistic real estate developers and buyers looking for a good return on investment. And instead of patting themselves of their backs for spreading their religion and "saving" the Native populations, residents move into neighborhoods and applaud themselves for raising property values and revitalizing decaying neighborhoods. These manifestations of colonialism are indeed vastly different from each other, but they have undeniable similarities. And perhaps even more undeniable is how these different manifestations shaped the cities we live, work, and play in today.

The distinction between ruler and subject as it relates to cities and government has been the guiding course for much of early American history. In fact, the debate between states' rights and how they fit into a broader federalist system is still

---

15 Alan Brinkley, *American History: A Survey* (New York: McGraw-Hill College, 1995).

ongoing today. The concentration of power in our governing structures is critically important, especially considering that cities are in a unique position to make positive changes at a global scale. Cities can utilize their concentration of people, economic activity, proprietary power, and innovation to shift global trends in a positive direction, as exemplified by the C40 coalition of cities working to address climate change.

The things we think about when we consider our cities say more about us than they do about the cities themselves—for our sense of belonging is characterized by the scents we pick up when we're in them. The places we live and interact in tell a lot about our history; the struggle for identity and power reveal themselves in the physical space, and the evolving virtue of cities allows us to be part of their journeys.

But it is now time to reevaluate, redesign, rework, and rethink ourselves *and* our cities to think about issues we know are important: racism, sexism, discrimination, oppression, equality, and accessibility.

2

CHESS, NOT CHECKERS

"Cities have the capability of providing something for every-body, only because, and only when, they are created by everyone."

JANE JACOBS

Jane Jacobs is one the most well-known figures in the realm of urban studies. She was a journalist, writer, and activist who advocated for community-based approaches to city building. Despite having no formal training in urban planning, she rejected things like suburban and auto-centric development in favor of localized economies, higher density mixed-use developments, and increased livability in cities. Personally, I think her lack of formal training is a key reason why Jacobs' voice and perspective are so valued: It is a fresh outlook from an actual city dweller and highlights the importance of residents being involved, engaged, and educated in how their neighborhoods develop.

The above quote was taken from her 1961 book *The Death and Life of Great American Cities*.[16] It speaks to the contingency of equitable offerings achieved through equitable input. In early American settlements, we see instances of residents having more say in how their areas and economies develop. This notion of representation is critical to fostering and maintaining a sense of belonging, both by current residents and incoming immigrants.

* * *

Even before America's independence, there were growing divisions and struggles for power. As industries popped up across the colonies, folks disagreed on what a new country should look and be like. The Transatlantic Slave Trade, which lasted into the eighteen hundreds, characterized the developing American economy and fueled the polarization between northern abolitionists and southern proponents of slavery (who relied on slave labor to produce and export cotton, tobacco, indigo, and other crops).

The time surrounding independence signified a desire to drive out Native Americans and Europeans, and planted seeds for the boisterous attitude that sprouts to this day. Perhaps more importantly, this period also represented ideological clashes between colonies: The North, which focused on an industrial economy and supported expansion of free states (new states without slavery) and the South, which supported an agricultural economy, the continued use of slavery, and the expansion of slavery into new states. American independence did little to

---

16 Jane Jacobs, *The Death and Life of Great American Cities* (New York: Vintage Books, 1992).

bridge this divide, and these attitudes would eventually snowball through the Civil War and beyond into Reconstruction.

In the country's early history, political action was like a game of chess, in that it required strategy, deception, aggression, courage, and foresight. And while politics back then may not have been a skillful art (considering that early politicians were mostly army generals and businessmen), it did require the five aforementioned skills in order to appease folks both North and South. In thinking about how to successfully drive out the French and defeat the British, George Washington—who we shall consider to be one of the first Grandmasters in this analogy—realized America had to expand beyond the Appalachian Mountains. This not only spurred economic development and connected the colonies, but helped speed the mobilization of troops.

In true Grandmaster fashion, Washington foresaw and urged his peers to look at infrastructure as key to a successful country. (As a private entrepreneur, Washington formed the Patowmack Company in 1785, one of the first privately funded internal improvements in the country, to construct dams and canals to make the Potomac River more navigable.)[17] After the American Revolution, he saw to it that lighthouses, dams, roads, and canals were built across the country. And soon enough, infrastructure was pushed to the forefront of American priorities; it would ease military access and mobility, facilitate the exploration and exploitation of the western frontier, and generate internal revenue via tolls. I

---

17 James P. Pinkerton, "A Vision of American Strength: How Transportation Infrastructure Built the United States," American Road & Transportation Builders Association, 2015.

spoke to Henry Petroski, professor of history and civil engineering at Duke University, about the role of early infrastructure. He notes, "If [roads, bridges, canals, and railroads] didn't exist, much more difficult raw materials and finished goods wouldn't have been able to been transported between states, between regions, and even between countries."

The construction of the Erie Canal in 1825 and the Granite Railway in 1826 were two key infrastructure projects that propelled the northern economy. Industries like lumber, textiles, ship-making, and fishing flourished in the North. As these industries grew, immigrants from Europe flocked to provide labor, and soon enough northern infrastructure and architecture evolved to play the part. Timber-framed, symmetrical, saltbox and colonial homes with central chimneys, casement windows, or shingles were common during this time.

In the South, access to fertile soil and a more suitable climate made states like Georgia and Mississippi optimal for farming and agricultural production. But the slow pace of industrialization and lack of road infrastructure increased reliance on rivers and tributaries for trade and transportation. Thus, many towns sprouted along waterways. Residential architecture typically consisted of brick and clay facades—materials that were local and abundant. Due to widespread use of wood and timber frames, as well as candles and kerosene lamps, dwellings in all colonies were often consumed by fire.[18]

---

18   Fiske Kimball, "Architecture in the History of the Colonies and of the Republic," *The American Historical Review* 27, no. 1 (1921): 47-57; Jackie Craven, "Guide to Colonial American House Styles From 1600 to 1800," ThoughtCo, last modified August 23, 2019.

After the American Revolution, the new republic began taking measures to build (or rebuild) its economy and landscapes. In the frenzy of war and early business ventures, most American cities started to develop their individual styles of architecture and planning. These early cities lacked the precision and foresight to plan roads and open market spaces, as once seen in ancient Rome and Mesoamerica. Instead, roads formed organically from horse and game trails—many of which were established by Indigenous groups, with their knowledge of watersheds and soils— that weaved through tough geography, around hills, and along rivers and waterways. This, along with challenging topography, is why some early cities, like Boston, lacked a grid system while other cities, like Philadelphia, were planned on rectilinear grid patterns from the jump (allowing families to easily settle by growing food on their own rectangular plots).

Newly settled immigrants in the North were able to survive off of subsistence farming, and occasional bartering and exchange with neighbors.[19] Individual families maintained their own farms and traveled to other towns via horse and river. In the South, which kept progressing into an agrarian landscape, churches (with gabled roofs, arched doors, and rounded windows) and taverns like those in England started popping up in town centers. As southerners grew wealthier, they started building bigger, as exemplified by plantation homes, and paid more attention to carpentry and finer details in paneling and furnishings.

---

19   Richard Lyman Bushman, "Markets and Composite Farms in Early America," *The William and Mary Quarterly* 55, no. 3 (1998): 351-74.

THE CIVIL WAR, RECONSTRUCTION, AND JIM CROW

The Civil War, by virtue of the fact that it was fought on American soil, was instrumental in destroying and reshaping the American landscape. While some cities experienced a population boom, other cities—like Charleston, Columbia, Vicksburg, Atlanta, Richmond, and Fredericksburg—were treated like pawns by both sides, who often sacrificed parts of the cities to sabotage opposing forces.[20] After the war, new protections and measures were put in place to ensure cooperation.

Despite conflicting plans, President Lincoln and his successor, Andrew Johnson, both agreed that the South should be allowed to rejoin the Union. During this **Reconstruction era**, which lasted from 1865 to 1877, northern investment and capital were directed into railroad development and economic opportunities in cities impacted by the war. This resulted in cities like Atlanta, Birmingham, and the Hampton Roads being centers of revitalization.

Reconstruction also witnessed the ratification of the Thirteenth, Fourteenth, and Fifteenth Amendments in 1865, 1868, and 1870, respectively. These amendments were passed to abolish slavery except as a punishment for crime (Thirteenth), grant citizenship and federal civil rights to those born or naturalized on US soil (Fourteenth), and extend voting rights regardless of race, color, or previous status

---

20 Sanso-Navarro, Marcos, Fernando Sanz, and María Vera-Cabello, "The Impact of the American Civil War on City Growth," *Urban Studies* 52, no. 16 (2015): 3070-085; Megan Kate Nelson, "Urban Destruction During the Civil War," *Oxford Research Encyclopedia, American History* (June 2016): 1-23.

(Fifteenth). Enforcement of these amendments was facilitated by the deployment of Northern troops, who also worked to prevent the continuation of segregation by white southerners and to maintain order.

Reconstruction was supposed to be a time to rebuild the South and facilitate the rejoining process. Instead, it turned out to be a grapple for political power resulting in the failure to enforce new amendments and reform the South's social fabric. Issues of land ownership and taxation became key principles of integration during the Reconstruction era. Formerly enslaved folks advocated for equal opportunities by demanding their own religious institutions, universal public education, financial independence, voting rights, and equal rights and protections under the Constitution.[21]

The Compromise of 1877 (an informal agreement that put Rutherford B. Hayes in the White House) effectively ended Reconstruction, and called for the withdrawal of Northern troops from the South. After Reconstruction came a series of laws and policies designed to disenfranchise and suppress the Black population in the South. These collectively became known as **Jim Crow laws** and enforced further segregation, disenfranchisement, and suppression of Black folks as well as some poor white folks living in the South.

In the 1896 landmark case *Plessy v. Ferguson*, the Supreme Court upheld the racial segregation of public facilities, so long as the facilities were equal in condition and offerings.

---

21 "Rebuilding the South After the War," PBS, accessed June 1, 2020.

This "separate but equal" doctrine would be applied to buses, trains, theaters, hotels, schools, and even housing blocks, through racially restrictive housing covenants—which were legally binding contracts between property owners and developers that prohibited residential transactions based on race, creed, and class.[22] These covenants often spanned entire neighborhoods and started as a way to shift the act of segregation from governments to private industries. The next few decades were rife with barriers like literacy tests, poll taxes, and strict eligibility requirements, all of which worked to further disenfranchise and suppress Black and poor people.

It wasn't until the mid-nineteen hundreds that the Supreme Court ruled segregation unconstitutional in a few ways. First, the 1948 ruling in *Shelley v. Kramer*, a dispute over a restrictive housing covenant in St. Louis, found that racial covenants were a violation of the Fourteenth Amendment's due process clause and thus were unenforceable by state and federal governments. Six years later, in the 1954 case *Brown v. Board of Education of Topeka*, the court declared racial segregation in public schools unconstitutional. Lastly, the 1967 case *Loving v. Virginia* struck down laws banning interracial marriages. In spite of these rulings and the Civil Rights Acts of 1964 and 1965, discrimination had already long been entrenched in housing, financial, and social institutions.[23]

---

22 Catherine Silva, "Racially Restrictive Covenants History," University of Washington, accessed June 5, 2020.

23 "Civil Rights and Equal Protection," Judicial Learning Center, accessed May 39, 2020.

* * *

Due to the extent of innovation, corruption, and greed following Reconstruction, the last two decades of the eighteen hundreds are commonly referred to as the Gilded Age. The institutionalized segregation and discrimination of Black and other minority folks that we see today—especially as it is conveyed spatially—is a result of intentional practices by those in positions of power. Black folks were granted more freedoms and rights directly following the Civil War, during Reconstruction, than later on in the Jim Crow South. Cities such as Charlotte and Atlanta had populations of Black people living more freely; during this era they could vote, own land, sue companies for discrimination, attend the same public facilities as whites and colored people (those of mixed ancestries), and even hold public office. In his book *Sorting the New South City*, historian Tom Hanchett notes that in 1877, Charlotte did not have class or race divides within neighborhoods: "More than a decade after the Civil War, Charlotte had no hard-edged Black neighborhoods.[...] Rather, African-Americans continued to live all over the city, usually side-by-side with whites."[24]

By 1896, some Southern state legislatures had Republican majorities—which, at the time, was the party for white populists, poor whites, and the formerly enslaved. Collectively, these legislatures worked to oppose white elitism by funding public education, capping interest rates, shifting taxes from corporations to individuals, and enfranchising illiterate

24 Thomas Hanchett, *Sorting Out the New South City: Race, Class, and Urban Development in Charlotte, 1875-1975* (Chapel Hill: The University of North Carolina Press, 1998), Chapter 3, Kindle.

voters. (Virginia and North Carolina both had their own parties to represent this group, known as the Readjuster Party and the Fusion Party, respectively.) Fearful of liberties and progressive reforms, the white elite and Democratic party employed paramilitary groups, such as the Red Shirts, to attack voter groups and launched campaigns to divide Republican voters, often in the name of racial superiority.[25]

Voter suppression induced by these white supremacy groups worked in their favor; Democrats regained control of the legislatures and unleashed a wrath of laws and policies to disenfranchise and discriminate against Black folks. One example of these policies involved reallocated resources from Black schools to white schools.[26] It was also around this time that the US was forcing Native Americans to culturally assimilate through Christianity and other Western principles, and tribes were limited to individual reservations. Furthermore, a slew of anti-Asian legislation sprouted across the western half of the country, as part of larger attitudes rooted in nationalism, racism, and imperialism.

* * *

Since the arrival of European colonizers—and subsequent massacre of Indigenous groups—Americans leisurely spread out and developed their economies, cities, and architectural identities. The heavy influences from European countries

---

25 Alana Semuels, "'Segregation Had to Be Invented,'" *The Atlantic,* February 17, 2017.

26 E.M Beck and Tolnay, Stewart, "Black Flight: Lethal Violence and the Great Migration, 1900–1930," *Social Science History* 14, no. 3 (Autumn 1990): 347–370.

were mixed and incorporated in America to facilitate colonial settlement. Americans' sense, or rather, *need* to feel like they belonged on this new continent was and is still manifested in the design of our cities today. One need look no further than the legacies of redlining, restrictive covenants, ghettos, urban sprawl, highways, policing, and now, gentrification.

Looking at just the original colonies, this is showcased through open city centers in New Orleans (French influence), Spanish colonial architecture in the southwestern United States, English characteristics in New England (casement windows, central chimneys, and window shutters, to name a few), and symmetrical facades in New York and Pennsylvania (courtesy of the Dutch and Germans). These architectural styles and design elements were vehicles used to distinguish the colonies from their empires, while certain elements—such as gabled roof structures, multi-purpose rooms, and exterior ornamentation (which itself was a reflection of inhabitants' religious beliefs)—remained similar enough to provide a sense of familiarity. On the other hand, some differences, especially in building materials and sourcing, gave colonists the freedom to deviate from the styles of their native countries. Nevertheless, the character of America is captured in our built environment.[27]

As in chess, where there are pawns and specialty pieces, politicians and those with power and money use their influence to silence the power of the pawns while protecting their own specialties. But even on a chess board itself, a piece's influence

---

27   Valerie Ann Polino, "The Architecture of New England and the Southern Colonies as it Reflects the Changes in Colonial Life," Yale-New Haven Teachers Institute, accessed June 3, 2020.

depends on its location. Similarly, the history of America is location-specific. That is to say, what was happening in one part of the country didn't automatically apply to other parts. Of course, there are general trends that impacted the entire nation, but those too were distributed unevenly. As different industries developed in different parts of country, the volatility of urban populations became more evident, the need for urban planning more urgent, and the bifurcated paths between privileged and oppressed more evident.

3

SHOW ME THE $$$

"The master's tools will never dismantle the master's house."

AUDRE LORDE

This quote was taken from a 1984 essay by Audre Lorde, who described herself as a "black, lesbian, mother, warrior, poet." In that essay, Lorde speaks to how systems of oppression cannot be resolved using the same tactics that were used to suppress. She goes on to say, "What does it mean when the tools of a racist patriarchy are used to examine the fruits of that same patriarchy? It means that only the most narrow perimeters of change are possible and allowable."[28]

In our current urban and political landscapes, we live in an environment created by those in positions of power. That is to say, there is intention behind pretty much everything we see in cities: streets, lights, vegetation, vehicles, advertisements, etc. There's a situational irony in using white and

---

28 "Audre Lorde," Poetry Foundation, accessed in April 29, 2020; Audre Lorde, *Sister Outsider: Essays and Speeches* (Berkeley, CA: Crossing Press 2007), 110-114.

patriarchal language and space to talk about experiences of the oppressed; this dichotomy sets a trap for some to feel like they must adapt to fit into or belong in a space. Much of this clash started after the Civil War, when laws and policies dictated the expression and use of space based on class and race, presenting us with a racial and spatial narrative and human experience.

* * *

As racial tensions sustained into the twentieth century, about 1.6 million Black Americans fled the South between 1916 and 1940—the first Great Migration. This migration featured rural migrants relocating into industrial cities of the Northeast and the Midwest to escape the racist South and search for better economic opportunities. The arrival of these southerners sparked conflicts in northern cities, as shortages of employment were exacerbated by economic depressions. Furthermore, immigration from European countries fueled ethnic tensions in cities, highlighting the limitations of urban systems at the time. Housing shortages, unsafe living conditions, and increasing poverty and crime rates all played a key role in the development of urban landscapes today. The rapid shift into cities during the early twentieth century required legislation and control of land use, which made way for zoning and financial lending from newly established banks.

In the Second Great Migration, from 1940 to 1970, another five million Black Americans left the South.[29] Continued

---

29   William H. Frey, "The New Great Migration: Black Americans' Return to the South, 1965-2000," The Brookings Institution, Center on Urban and Metropolitan Policy, May 2004.

agricultural industrialization brought an end to sharecropping (an agreement in which a farm owner grants a tenant to farm on their land in exchange for a share of their crops). This made it increasingly difficult for folks to support themselves financially, especially after the Great Depression decimated much of the South's economic livelihood. This migration featured more urban migrants, who filled both labor shortages brought by the war and inner-city neighborhoods that were being vacated by white families.

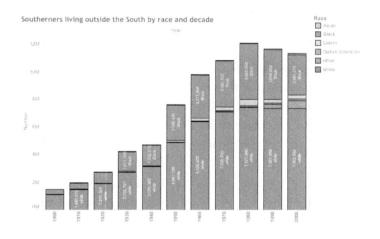

Figure 1: Breakdown of Southern migrants, 1900-2000.[30]

Both migrations were tied to two key phases of the twentieth century: the first being more institutional and infrastructure-based, with racialized zoning and financial institutions and housing covenants, which were almost all designed to

---

30 James Gregory, "Mapping the Southern Diaspora," The Great Depression in Washington State Project, accessed June 4, 2020.

segregate and disenfranchise Black folks; and the second being a spatial expansion of the first, with the growth of suburbs and sprawl fueled by cars and highways, and capped by resistance during the Civil Rights Movement. But what's almost always left out of conversations about the Great Migrations is how southern white migrants outnumbered southern Black migrants in every decade of the 1900s.[31] These migrations exist in a continuum that hosted the southern diaspora wherein reactions to the Great Migrations were intentional, malevolent, and etched into the built environment and social atmosphere for decades to come.

ROLE OF BANKS AND THE GREAT DEPRESSION

The role of banks and financial institutions in the American landscape is paramount. Banks were originally established in port cities as a way to lend money to merchants, and as economic activity grew across the country so too did the offerings and reliance on banks. Soon, state and regional banks assumed a key role in starting a business venture or purchasing land, but this was a privilege granted only to white folks.

In the 1860s, a wave of National Bank Acts led to stabilization of the banking system, including the establishment of the Freedman's Savings Bank in 1865. This bank was specifically made for Black Americans, and aimed to facilitate emancipated communities with economic development and financial wellbeing. The bank, headquartered in Washington, DC, was headed by white northerner John W. Alvord, who

---

31   Ibid.

had recruited Black Americans in the South to deposit their savings. Soon, there were thirty-four branches of the bank, holding over $65 million for Black folks, especially soldiers.

Three years before the bank closed in 1874, it was authorized to start providing business loans and mortgages—something that would've bridged the gap between Black and white families in terms of wealth and property ownership. However, economic panic in 1873 and a series of bad debts and speculative investments led to the bank's closure. Right before it closed Frederick Douglass was appointed head of the bank, but it was too late; almost $22 million in savings were lost and unreturned to depositors.[32] Though it only lasted ten years, the Freedman's Savings Bank represented a time of financial trust from the Black community, something that would soon become an estranged concept for decades to come.

Along with stable banking institutions came the birth of mortgages. A mortgage is a conditional sale in which the title of a property is held by a creditor (typically a bank) and the property is given to a debtor (typically the resident). Simply put, a mortgage is a loan secured by property. It's important to note that these mortgages were different than today's, in that they were short-term, required a 50 percent down payment, involved interest-only monthly payments, and required a balloon payment (a large payment at the end of term that consists of the loan's principal amount).[33] Today,

---

32   Marcus Anthony Hunter, "Black America's Distrust of Banks Rooted in Reconstruction," ChicagoReporter, February 22, 2018.

33   Carol M. Kopp. "Balloon Payment" Investopedia, last modified June 28, 2019; J.D. Roth, "A Brief History of U.S. Homeownership," Get Rich Slowly, last modified February 23, 2020.

mortgages are typically longer-term with a smaller down payment and higher value, and no balloon payment.

The development and expansion of the home mortgage system in the late-nineteenth century led to an increase in homeownership rate, which rose to 46.5 percent in 1900.[34] Soon enough, cities were naturally seeing more residential, commercial, and industrial areas—all of which called for a reform on land use zoning. Prior to this point, there weren't many restrictions on where and what people could build, which led to hasty urban planning that was unsafe and short-sighted. One of the chief instances that led to the creation of zoning was when mansions on Fifth Ave in Manhattan were displaced by high-fashion shops. In 1916, the city released a zoning code in reaction to the Equitable Building, which blocked windows and sunlight access of nearby buildings.

This first draft of zoning laws established height restrictions (relative to adjacent streets) and regulated land uses (limiting proximity of industrial land uses, such as factories and warehouses, to residential and commercial areas). In 1924, Herbert Hoover published a model of zoning laws for states to adopt called the Standard Zone Enabling Act (SZEA). As Secretary of Commerce, he also established the Advisory Council on Zoning, which handled the drafting and inspection of land use developments, laws, and ordinances.[35]

---

34 "Historical Census of Housing Tables: Homeownership," Department of Administration & Information, last modified March 1, 2013.

35 Salim Furth, "A Brief History of Zoning in America—and Why We Need a More Flexible Approach," Economics21, August 5, 2019.

As states implemented their own version of zoning, some were sure to uphold the legacy of Jim Crow. This led to Black communities being confined to certain neighborhoods with limited access to goods and services. One neighborhood in Tulsa, Oklahoma, however, managed to become one of the most successful and affluent Black communities in the history of America. Greenwood Tulsa was a bustling community built on the mining and oil industries, which provided an incentive for Black Americans all across the country to move there for a better life.

Part of the success of Black Wall Street, as it came to be known, was due to those strict Jim Crow laws that limited where folks could live and spend money. Thus, Black Wall Street was born and thrived in spite of segregation because the Black doctors, lawyers, businesses, and entrepreneurs lived and spent their money there—thereby creating a local economy and the services and businesses required to support it.

An accusation during Memorial Day Weekend in 1921 snowballed into one of the single worst racially-motivated massacres in American history. White rioters rampaged through Black Wall Street burning properties, looting stores, and killing Black folk. By the end of it, about 10,000 people were left homeless, up to 300 more killed, and more than $32 million in property damage was done. A Tulsa city commission found accounts that bodies of Black people were transported to different cemeteries in the area and that many residents couldn't return due to burned property deeds, lost financial records, and destroyed livelihoods.[36]

36　Alexis Clark, "Tulsa's Black Wall Street Flourished as a Self-Contained Hub in Early 1900s," History.com, last modified January 2, 2020.

Despite atrocities like this, the 1920s were mostly a time of economic prosperity and social change serviced by mass culture, jazz, women's suffrage, the start and end of prohibition, and the Harlem Renaissance (a famous literary movement that propelled Black culture onto the global stage). The "Roaring 20s" ended abruptly in 1929 with the Great Depression. Lasting until 1933, the Great Depression was a result of many things; a stock market crash, panic from banks, devaluing of gold, and international trade tensions were the biggest contributors.

Millions of Americans were affected by the Depression. Industrial production dropped by 45 percent, GDP dropped by 33 percent, unemployment topped 20 percent, and millions fell into a cycle of poverty. About 2 million Americans were left unsheltered, and many crowded into communities of tents and encampments.[37] As the depression lingered, more people lost their jobs, homes, and livelihoods. Homeowners were unable to pay mortgages, and renters were unable to make rent. Soon a package of legislation and programs employed by President Franklin D. Roosevelt (in what is known as the New Deal) helped bring the country out of the Depression, but some permanent damage remained, especially concerning racial and socioeconomic matters.

Those who were struggling before the Great Depression were often hit the worst and took the longest time to recover afterwards. It's also estimated that almost 2 million Mexicans and Mexican Americans were deported, often

---

37   "Great Depression History," History.com, last modified February 28, 2020.

forcefully, during what was known as the Mexican Repatriation.[38] Traces of abandonment plagued industrial cities like
Pittsburgh and Gary, Indiana. And if that wasn't enough, a
wave of severe dust storms in the 1930s comprised the Dust
Bowl—destroying crops, livestock, and the ecology of the
Great Plains, thus further displacing thousands of migrants
in search of better economic opportunities. Shifts seen as
result of these depressions and economic movements would
continue to contribute to the rise and fall of American cities,
as well as the increasing chasms between racial, social, and
economic classes.

NEW DEAL AND HOLC

By the time the New Deal rolled around, the federal government was pumping out legislation, policies, and programs to
stimulate the American economy. One of these programs was
the Home Owners' Loan Corporation (HOLC), established
in 1933. The HOLC was designed to help refinance home
mortgages, and more importantly introduced the disastrous
concept of **redlining**. Redlining was the intentional refusal
of public services, especially housing mortgages, to colored
and immigrant communities. To determine if an investment
was favorable or not, the HOLC created residential security
maps in 239 cities across America, which were eventually
used by banks, the Federal Housing Authority, and the Veterans Association. These maps color-coded neighborhoods into
four categories based on investment risk: green for the "best,"
blue for "still desirable," yellow for "definitely declining," and

---

38 Abraham Hoffman, *Unwanted Mexican Americans in the Great Depres-
    sion: Repatriation Pressures, 1929-1939* (Tucson, Arizona: The University
    of Arizona Press, 1974), 85-102.

red for "hazardous." Soon enough, banks were denying mortgages, loans, insurance, and healthcare, and access to retail businesses to communities of color—and they were getting away with it.

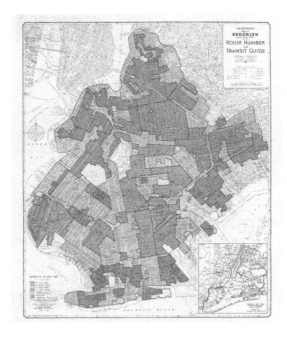

Figure 2: Redlined map of Brooklyn, New York City.

The Federal Housing Administration (FHA) was established in 1934 as part of the National Housing Act and increased the size of the housing market, protected lenders, and reduced the risk of lending from banks. It also cemented the concept behind redlining into American neighborhoods. Richard Rothstein, author of *The Color of Law*, spoke about redlining in a 2017 interview with NPR:

"The Federal Housing Administration's justification was that if African-Americans bought homes in these suburbs, or even if they bought homes near these suburbs, the property values of the homes they were insuring, the white homes they were insuring, would decline. [...] In fact, when African-Americans tried to buy homes in all-white neighborhoods or in mostly white neighborhoods, property values rose because African-Americans were more willing to pay more for properties than whites were, simply because their housing supply was so restricted and they had so many fewer choices. So the rationale that the Federal Housing Administration used was never based on any kind of study."[39]

The FHA also subsidized construction of residential subdivisions for white people and prohibited sales to Black folks. In fact, the whole concept of public housing was created to house only middle- and working-class white families who had lost their homes during the Great Depression. It soon became exceedingly evident that white projects were pretty vacant, while Black projects were overcrowded. Public housing authorities then decided to allow Black families to move into the white-only housing projects. As industries and white families moved out of these developments, projects became synonymous with poor people and slums. This association was deepened with the original Fannie Mae program of 1938 (which attempted to provide local banks with federal funds to aid in distribution of home loans and created a

---

39   Terry Gros, "A 'Forgotten History' Of How The U.S. Government Segregated America," NPR, May 3, 2017.

secondary mortgage market) and the GI Bill of Rights in 1944 (which granted extended rights and subsidized mortgages to returned war veterans).[40]

Of all the New Deal programs, the Public Works Administration (PWA) played the biggest role in the built environment; it funded and oversaw 34,000 projects completed between 1933 and 1939. Of all these projects, roughly one-third were devoted to the construction of streets and highways.[41] The PWA launched American infrastructure to the forefront of the American experience once again, as bridges, highways, hospitals, airports, and other landmarks that generated local and national pride were built. These infrastructure projects transformed cities into playgrounds for cars, which became the default for many American families.

1950S & ONWARD

Starting with the invention of the Model T by Henry Ford in 1908, personal vehicles became affordable enough that families across the country started indulging. By 1930, about half of all American families owned a car, and about a one-third of registered vehicles were owned by farmers.[42]

---

40   Johnson Hur, "History of the 30 Year Mortgage—From Historic Rates to Present Time," BeBusinessEd.com, accessed June 3, 2020.

41   Public Works Administration, *America Builds: The Record of PWA. Public Works Administration* (Washington D.C: U.S. Government Printing Office, 1939), 284-290; Louis Hyman, "The New Deal Wasn't What You Think," The Atlantic, March 6, 2019; "Public Works Administration (PWA), 1933-1943," The Living New Deal, accessed June 11, 2020.

42   "STATE MOTOR VEHICLE REGISTRATIONS, BY YEARS, 1900 - 1995," U.S. Federal Highway Administration, April 1997.

Upon the return of soldiers following World War II in 1945, the shift toward a more independent and isolated lifestyle became evident. The postwar rise of consumerism that started around the mid-1940s continued well into the 50s and 60s, fueled by relocation to the suburbs and reliance on automobiles to get around. Families, and the businesses that supported them, started filling up the suburban landscapes. A big part of the draw of suburbs is the promise for more space, both inside and outside the house, something not as common in city centers.

Sonia Hirt, a professor of landscape architecture and planning at the University of Georgia and author of *Zoned in the USA*, highlighted the American desire for more space: "American culture, to begin with, is unusually spacious, in the sense that people think of space as part of American culture […] it isn't part of the French or British cultural experience.[…] This is partially part of the American promise—that you can have more room."[43] To connect them from the cities they left, the automobile provided an easy link for families to the familiarity of an urban core. As Americans started incorporating travel into their lives, the need and desire for interstate travel arose.

In 1956, President Dwight Eisenhower signed the Federal Aid Highway Act into law. The bill, also known as the Interstate and Defense Highway Act, called for over 40,000 miles of infrastructure to further allow for safe transcontinental travel. This decision was largely made as a response to the

---

43   Joe Pinkser, "Why Are American Homes So Big?" *The Atlantic*, September 12, 2019.

threat of atomic warfare striking the US; the interstates would allow for quick mobilization out of dense urban cores. Poor infrastructure and lack of organization was also stunting economic growth and transportation of goods. At the time, more that 36,000 motorists were being killed every year from insufficient road infrastructure, and civil suits related to accidents and traffic were placing a burden on the country's court system.[44] The Interstate Highway System would eventually cost $128.9 billion, and take over forty-five years to build. Unfortunately for us, highways have disrupted more than just our time and our money.

Part of the ease of building such vast networks of roads in America was due to lack of development in much of the country. Unlike places in Europe (and even the first American settlements) which had been developed and established for far longer, cities that sprung up as a result of the highway system and automobile bypassed the traditional city planning processes. For example, roads and street networks were designed for cars and driving, instead of pedestrians and walking.

Another example is the intentional zoning and differential planning of residential, commercial, and industrial areas (instead of a radial and organic expansion of urban areas). Outside of the coastal and trading cities of America, settlement into the western half of the continental US was limited before the 1920s (due to cost and lack of infrastructure/options), and any transportation networks that did exist were

---

44   Richard F. Weingroff, "Original Intent: Purpose of the Interstate System 1954 - 1956)," Federal Highway Administration, last modified June 27, 2017.

owned and operated by private companies.[45] Slowly, a cooperative effort between public and private entities led to more roads being built, which allowed for both more personal and business travel.

The unhealthy, herd-like adoption of the automobile by older generations is a key reason our cities look the way they do. Born between the mid-1940s and the mid-1960s, baby boomers were the first real audience and supporters of personal cars in America. The onslaught of WWII, the prevailing Cold War, and the coexistence of numerous social movements were instrumental in laying the foundation of American struggles that shaped the baby boomer generation.

Automobiles allowed for a personal break from everyday life. For those who could afford one, cars were private sanctuaries that enabled short travel, independence, autonomy, and escapism. In 2016, an estimated 76 percent of Americans drive alone to work, which demonstrates the heavy dependence on the automobile that still exists today.[46] (Luckily, the trend of obsessive car ownership is changing, evident in data released by the Brookings Institute: Twenty-one of the fifty most populated cities experienced a significant decrease in driving.)

Interstate highway systems provided the tracks for suburbanization and, around the same time, the rise of shopping malls. Demand for shopping centers outside of the city increased, and development of shopping malls on greenfields (land

---

45 Jeff Desjardins, "Visualizing 200 Years of U.S. Population Density," Visual Capitalist, February 28, 2019.

46 Adie Tomer, "America's Commuting Choices: 5 major Takeaways from 2016 Census Data," The Brookings Institute, October 3, 2017.

that hasn't been developed before) began to be incentivized in the 1950s. New legislation, changes to corporate tax laws, depreciation, and the introduction of Real Estate Investment Trusts (REIT) in 1960 allowed income taxes to be avoided for investors who worked together.[47] Out of these changes came more shopping malls, suburban developments and, of course, consumer spending. Over time, strip malls and shopping centers appeared in suburbs to cater to residents, and for the past five decades or so suburbs and shopping malls have sustained a symbiotic relationship with each other. The popularity of shopping malls ushered in and signified the reality of a trend that still persists: American consumerism. This consumerism can be applied and understood by looking at the rapid adoption of personal vehicles, homeownership, household appliances and, of course, television and media.[48]

Indeed, the role of media and television played an important role in portraying suburbs and the notions of normalcy that are encouraged by them. In a review of Lynn Spigel's *Welcome to the Dreamhouse: Popular Media and Postwar Suburbs*, Erin A. Smith draws attention to Spigel's commentary on suburbs and the entertainment industry at the time:

> "*Spigel attends to the redlining of older people, single people, gays and lesbians, and people of color from suburban housing, and the elevation of young, white, middle-class nuclear families as the 'norm' for us all. [...] Spigel argues that not only did television and the suburbs largely represent white, middle-class*

47 Robbie Moore, "The Death of the American Mall and the Rebirth of Public Space," *The International,* February 26, 2013.

48 "The Rise of American Consumerism," PBS.org, accessed June 10, 2020.

nuclear families, but also middle-class ideas about families (and the public/private distinction underwriting them) invisibly structured (and continue to structure) our ways of telling stories, our visual field, and our ways of being in the world."[49]

Susan Edmunds, in a journal essay titled "Accelerated Immobilities: American Suburbia and the Classless Middle Class" comments on the pseudo-entrapment of American suburbs, and refers to a 2001 novel that explores the same topics: "In *White Diaspora: The Suburb and the Twentieth-Century American Novel* Catherine Jurca examines best-selling novels from roughly the same period to understand why suburbanites feel homeless at home, trapped in lives which provide material comfort at the cost of 'spiritual, cultural and political problems of displacement' so intense as to redefine the nation's most privileged citizens as 'transients who will never get to move.'"[50]

These findings may have more to do with the sprawling development, lack of stimulating design, cookie-cutter formats, and standardized room arrangements in suburban residential homes than we like to believe. These sentiments and observations about the impact of suburbia on American life and the idea of belonging show themselves in a myriad of ways—from racially restrictive housing covenants, migration patterns of socioeconomic classes, and even in socially patterned rhetoric surrounding diversity, inclusion, and representation.

---

49 Erin A. Smith, "The Media, the Suburbs, and the Politics of Space," *American Quarterly* 54, no. 2 (2002): 359-67.

50 Susan Edmunds, "Accelerated Immobilities: American Suburbia and the Classless Middle Class," *American Literary History* 15, no. 2 (2003): 409-21.

* * *

Discriminatory lending programs, restrictive covenants, and spatial segregation fused together to deny minorities their own freedom and space not just in the suburbs, but also in urban cores. As mentioned in Chapter 2, a wave of Supreme Court cases in the 50s and 60s capped the Civil Rights Movement with *some* equal protections and rights (most notably the end of racially restrictive covenants). On the heels of these cases, the US Department of Housing and Urban Development (HUD) was established in 1965 to address America's housing needs and enforce fair housing laws.[51]

One of the first and biggest milestones of the HUD was passing Title VIII of the Civil Rights Act, more commonly known as the Fair Housing Act of 1968. This piece of legislation extended a commitment to equal access to housing regardless of race, religion, color, national origin, sex, disability, or familial status.[52] For the first time, refusal to sell or rent based on someone's appearance and background was illegal. (It's important to note that a 1988 Amendment expanded coverage to families with children, and that coverage for the LGBTQIA+ community is not uniform across the country, despite the HUD's Equal Access Rule.)[53]

Despite new legislation and rulings, there was and still is a great deal of discrimination against protected classes in

---

51 "Questions and Answers About HUD," U.S. Department of Housing and Urban Development, accessed May 6, 2020.

52 "Housing Discrimination Under the Fair Housing Act," U.S. Department of Housing and Urban Development, accessed May 6, 2020.

53 "Equal Access for LGBT Individuals," National Housing Law Project, accessed May 6, 2020.

the housing and rental markets. A study done by the HUD with 8,000 test subjects in twenty-eight metropolitan areas featured a pair of potential clients, one of them white and the other Black, Hispanic, or Asian. These pairs presented the same gender, age, and economic background to their respective housing providers, but the clients who belonged to non-white test groups were subject to more discrimination, despite equal qualifications. The study also found that white clients were shown more homes and apartments than minority clients, an injustice that has existed since at least the 1900s.[54] Prejudice experienced by minority communities all across America has shaped the market and landscape of American neighborhoods that we see today. Lastly, despite coverage of equal access to housing under the law, the FHA has consistently discriminated against Black and minority families when it comes to home insurance.

* * *

The intent of suburbs and new equal rights didn't necessarily fail, it simply worked *too* well. Rapid increases in affordability and popularity diminished the exclusivity of suburbs, and systemic discrimination was already long-ingrained into cityscapes. Withdrawal from cities and their offerings crippled city budgets, social capital spending, and urban vibrancies, therefore reducing the extent and draw of those same areas. But despite new trends, we're now actually seeing more ethnically diverse families and immigrants move to suburbs directly, skipping cities altogether.

---

54 "Housing Discrimination Against Racial and Ethnic Minorities 2012," U.S. Department of Housing and Urban Development Office of Policy Development and Research, June 2013.

Many experts think the peak of urban sprawl has passed and, because Americans are marrying later and having fewer children, the need and desire for big homes and lawns is being questioned. Malls are closing (in favor of online shopping), and car ownership (per person and per family) is decreasing as younger people are using alternative methods of transportation.[55] These are just a few of the problems suburbs face in retaining their typical populations, as residents crave a more varied lifestyle.

To think that suburbs—places that have always seemed so "normal" and customary—could gain a new reputation speaks to the nature of cities. The last thirty years of the twentieth century saw the War on Drugs and broken windows policing, more population mobility and economic booms, and early forms of gentrification in cities like Portland, Oregon and New York City. If the eighteen hundreds cemented the role of cities in our lives, the nineteen hundreds saw the struggle created by a sense of entrapment. The twentieth century started amid Jim Crow laws and public, acceptable discrimination and segregation. It ended with a glass ceiling for equality, and numerous patterns of the same underlying discrimination and segregation.

This abridged history serves as a backdrop for Part 2 of the book. While these were changes made and felt across the country, different cities dealt with each in their own unique ways. How they did says a lot about themselves, and the impacts of events in the 1930s are still decimating parts of

---

55   Elisabeth Rosenthal, "The End of Car Culture," *New York Times*, June 29, 2013.

cities today: An estimated 74 percent of neighborhoods that were redlined are still economically depressed.[56] In 2020, we still face issues of discrimination, disenfranchisement, inequality, and urban belonging. To fix this, we must first understand the problem with both the master's tool and the master's house. Unfortunately, the problems are complex, entrenched, and institutionalized—but that doesn't mean the solution has to be as well.

---

56 Bruce Mitchell, "HOLC 'Redlining' Maps: The Persistent Structure of Segregation and Economic Inequality," National Community Reinvestment Coalition, March 20, 2018.

PART II

REGIONAL DIFFERENCES

4

THE NORFEAST

"In Boston they ask, how much does he know? In New York, how much is he worth? In Philadelphia, who were his parents?"

MARK TWAIN

I used to wake up feeling like a champion. As a teenager, much of my identity was like a marionette, in that I tried to mold myself in the shadow of the "typical" American boy. I so desperately wanted to fit into a prescribed image, not knowing there were other options. And so, I grew up trying to convince myself that I was a dedicated sports fan.

Of course, it didn't help that for almost my entire life, Boston was known as the "city of champions," thus planting a seed of hometown pride in me. But as I grew older, I realized that my claim to championship status was all by chance, that I didn't know anything about Boston's real history, and that the bravado that runs through the blood of Bostonians is unlike anything else. Here, fans would hurl racial slurs at visiting teams. Here, Red Sox fans would try to fight Yankees fans. And here, fans would go all out to support their team—all to uphold a championship legacy.

It wasn't until I started working at the West End Community Center that I really learned about the city's history. Before it was demolished in the 1950s the West End was home to a vibrant, working-class neighborhood, one of first Black public schools in America, and was a place that served as a refuge for many immigrant and minority groups—many of whom now form the ranks of Boston sports fans. Knowing this history helped me understand that pride was an essential source of happiness and belonging, and a power that only touches select cities. But unlike history, I think pride in being a sports fan stems from the desire to belong, to cement yourself in historic moments, and to be able to say, "I was there."

* * *

The Northeast has always been calling the shots. It was the site of the first few colonial settlements, it fueled the colonial era, it was instrumental in the American Revolution, it oversaw the Civil War, and it developed like no other part of America. Aside from its critical role in the formation of America, the Northeast remains a key part of the country. It consists of the six states of New England as well as Pennsylvania, New York, and New Jersey, and is home to almost 56 million people.[57] The Northeast is the most culturally diverse, economically developed, and densely populated region in the country, featuring the cities of Boston, Philadelphia,

---

57 "2019 U.S. Population Estimates Continue to Show the Nation's Growth Is Slowing," U.S. Census Bureau, December 30, 2019.

New York City, Washington DC, Baltimore, and Pittsburgh. But three of these cities in particular—Boston, New York City, and Washington, DC—provide us a lens to explore gentrification and the history of change in cities.

* * *

BOSTON, MASSACHUSETTS

Since its founding in 1630, Boston has played a central role in early wars, religion, politics, transportation, commerce, finance, and education. It was instrumental in the American Revolution, the anti-slavery movement, and waves of immigration. After the Civil War, the city's Brahmin Elite—a community of upper-class aristocrats, writers, philosophers, historians, and more—flourished and were seen as community leaders and philanthropists. Transportation, new developments, and racial tensions defined Boston up until WWII, after which Boston expanded to focus on higher education, medicine, and technology.

NEW YORK CITY, NEW YORK

After serving as a major seaport up until the American Revolution, and then as the nation's first capital, New York City became a haven for immigrants in the nineteenth century. After the Commissioners Plan of 1811 (which brought the grid pattern to Manhattan) and the opening of the Erie Canal in 1825, New York was able to connect with Midwestern markets and establish itself as an economic and commercial center. After the war, it continued to be the first-stop shop for new immigrants. Tourism, education, and industrialization flourished during the Gilded Age. The consolidation and creation of its five boroughs took place in the early nineteen hundreds, when New York became the center for commerce, communications, finance, popular culture, and high culture. After World War II, New York became and remains one of the world's top cities for finance, culture, and tourism.

WASHINGTON, DC

In 1791, following the American Revolution, President George Washington declared Washington, DC the country's permanent capital. Shortly after, French architect Pierre L'Enfant drafted a city plan designed to connect the city and its riverfronts via a grid pattern with grand avenues, open circles, and plazas. The city plan was revised in the McMillan Plan, released in 1901, which served to update the city based on new developments. The years surrounding the Civil War saw a huge increase in the city's Black population, with racial tensions in flux for decades thereafter, positioning the city as the center of the Civil Rights Movement in the 1960s. Since then, DC has been supported by the education, tech, and tourism industries and, of course, government and bureaucratic work.

* * *

INDUSTRIALIZATION

At the start of the twentieth century, each of these cities experienced an increase in population, economic activity, and racial tensions. As the American economy pivoted from an agricultural focus toward a more industrial one, concentration of jobs and people shifted from rural countrysides into rapidly-growing city settings. The Industrial Revolution required lots of labor which, considering large groups of European immigrants coming to these cities, was not an issue. The Civil War accelerated not only the rate of industrialization, but also the rate of urbanization: 11 million people moved from rural countrysides to urban areas between 1870 and 1920, plus an additional 25 million immigrants from abroad.[58]

At the time, cities in the Northeast specialized in areas like manufacturing, politics, and education, and religious and other social clubs were quite common. This expansion warranted development of bedroom communities (or commuter towns) outside of city limits and mass transit systems (such as trolleys, omnibuses, subways, etc.) to transport residents. With wealthier folks settling outside of city centers and using transit to get to work, real estate development and speculation was neatly positioned to continue growing, creating different parts of every city.

This started a trend that would continue up into the twenty-first century and gave rise to the notion of inner-city neighborhoods being reserved for the lower-income and immigrant communities. As these trends continued, crime and disease—such as cholera, dysentery, and typhoid fever—grew rapidly in urban settings. Eventually, cities started developing sewage systems, paving roads, and passing legislation to improve housing conditions. Prior to this, cities

---

58 David Kennedy and Lizabeth Cohen, *The American Pageant: A History of the American People, 15th Edition* (Stamford, CT: Cengage Learning, 2013), 539-540.

lacked systems of trash collection, waste treatment, or water purification.[59] By 1900, almost 40 percent of Americans were living in cities; that number would surpass 50 percent just twenty years later.[60]

THE RISE OF SLUMS

Rapid increases in both people and economic activity during the eighteen hundreds led to a new type of reality: the urban slum. Combined with the lack of building regulations and unsafe living conditions, these slums popped up in cities across America and posed major public health concerns for residents.[61] Oftentimes, working class and immigrant populations huddled into tenement housing— small, often attached apartments that were up to six stories high and had poor maintenance and sanitation. These tenements were sometimes called "rookeries" or "railroad flats" because of cramped and windowless internal rooms. In 1865, an estimated 500,000 people lived in tenements in New York City alone.[62] This type of building and housing was so common due to the feasibility of building on 25-by-100-foot lots to maximize land coverage, especially in grid system areas. The middle- and upper-classes that

---

59 "38b. The Underside of Urban Life," U.S. History, accessed April 8, 2020; "Cities During the Progressive Era," Library of Congress, accessed April 8, 2020.

60 "Urban and Rural Populations in the United States," Our World in Data, accessed June 3, 2020.

61 Alexander von Hoffman, "The Origins of American Housing Reform," Harvard University Joint Center for Housing Studies, August 1998.

62 "The Rise of the City," Lumen Learning, accessed April 16, 2020; Zachary J. Violette, "Nineteenth-Century Working-Class Housing in Boston and New York," Society of Architectural Historians, accessed May 24, 2020.

did remain in cities stayed in apartments or urban mansions, and it wasn't until the 1890 publication of *How the Other Half Lives* by photographer Jacob Riis that people started caring about urban slums.

Figures 1 and 2: Tenement housing in New York City.

Starting in the mid-1920s, a man by the name of Robert Moses embarked on a pursuit to change New York City's landscape. Moses became known as a "master builder," as he was responsible for overseeing the construction of thirteen bridges, over 650 playgrounds, over 400 miles of parkways, and 150,000 housing units—spending over $150 billion in the process. His projects include the Triborough Bridge, Brooklyn Heights, Washington State Park, Throg's Neck Bridge, Brooklyn Battery Bridge and Tunnel, the UN Headquarters, and the Belt Parkway.[63]

But despite his achievements and influence on New York, Moses had a reputation for favoring cars over people, being racist, and disliking poor folks. As Robert Caro writes in his 1974 biography on Moses, "To build his highways, Moses threw out of their homes 250,000 persons—more people than lived

---

63   Sydney Sarachan, "The Legacy of Robert Moses," PBS.org, January 17, 2013.

in Albany or Chattanooga, or in Spokane, Tacoma, Duluth, Akron, Baton Rouge, Mobile, Nashville or Sacramento. He tore out the hearts of a score of neighborhoods."[64] Due to his desire to build megastructures, Moses became an early proponent of slum clearing (also known as **urban renewal**).

URBAN RENEWAL

By the early nineteen hundreds, and again in the 1950s, city officials across the country started releasing plans for urban renewal. At its core, urban renewal is the process of redeveloping run-down areas in cities as a means to promote economic activity. Typically, this involves government seizure of privately held properties (via eminent domain) and transfer of the land to private developers.

The terms "urban decay" or "urban blight" are often used in conversations around urban renewal. These terms refer to areas that have been subject to disinvestment (sometimes through depopulation or deindustrialization), neglect, poverty, or crime. Nevertheless, urban renewal typically plays out in three ways:

1. Redevelopment, which involves clearing of existing buildings and structures and constructing new ones in their place,
2. Rehabilitation, which involves repairing existing buildings and structures and restoring them to their original purposes, or
3. Preservation, which involves restoration of existing building stock and neighborhood design elements.

---

64   Alexander von Hoffman, "A Study in Contradictions: The Origins and Legacy of the Housing Act of 1949," *Housing Policy Debate* 11, no. 2 (2000): 299.

Soon enough, the topic of housing in cities became a central issue in American life and politics. The passing of the National Housing Act of 1949 created a contradictory approach to urban housing in that it granted federal funds to clear blighted and affordable areas, yet fell extremely short of its intent to build better affordable housing. Its original goal of building 810,000 units in six years (which, by the way, only addressed 10 percent of national need) ended up taking twenty years and destroyed hundreds of thousands of affordable housing units in the process.[65]

In the Northeast, urban renewal provided a path to redevelopment of decaying areas, such as the Lower East Side in Manhattan, in Southwest DC, and the West End in Boston, among many other neighborhoods. The West End, a neighborhood home to prominent Black, Irish, and Jewish communities, was demolished in the late 50s, with over half of the entire neighborhood (forty-six acres) leveled and some 2,700 families displaced. As in most parts of the country, renewal this time around made way for large interstate highways, public works, and more expensive housing alternatives, which attracted wealthier residents and businesses at the expense of low-income communities.

WHITE FLIGHT & BLOCKBUSTING

After the Supreme Court rulings in *Shelley v. Kramer* (1948) and *Brown v. Board* (1954), Black families were able to move more freely than before. This start to residential integration

---

65   Alan Pyke, "Top Infrastructure Official Explains How America Used Highways to Destroy Black Neighborhoods," Think Progress, March 21, 2016.

coincided with a phenomenon known as **white flight**, a term used to describe the fleeing of white families to suburbs upon arrival of Black and other minorities in cities. If gentrification could be likened to tides of the ocean, where inner-city neighborhoods represent the shore, white flight would represent the low tide, which is to say it is encapsulates the "retreating" of the water away from the coast.

* * *

Moving to the suburbs gave city dwellers access to land and businesses outside their immediate urban settings. But the extension of economic activity and draw of the suburbs generally enticed wealthier—and whiter—families. After all, they could use highways to drive easily and directly to their city workplaces, and still live in a bigger house with more land. As they left the city, so too did their taxes and social capital, which crippled city budgets and tax bases. Voluntary out-migration of white families was facilitated by the new interstate highway system, the rise of the personal automobile, racial integration within neighborhoods and schools, and a practice known as **blockbusting**.

Blockbusting was the intentional positioning of Black folks in white neighborhoods to "scare" white residents into underselling their homes and fleeing the neighborhood. Black people were hired to push baby carriages, play loud music, and stage fights in white neighborhoods. Such manipulation was choreographed by realtors, who then spread rumors of a declining neighborhood and impending depreciation, which worked to perpetuate white flight and, in some cases, ended up actually decreasing property home values.

Companies then generated even more business by selling homes to white families in new suburbs and neighborhoods. And if that wasn't bad enough, agents would increase the prices of existing city properties, through something called a "Black Tax," and upsell to Black families, which worked because there were already few options for Black families.[66] The modern-day equivalent to this exploitation would be landlords taking advantage of a captive market by charging higher rents in poorer areas (because they know residents would struggle to find other housing due to a history of evictions or other issues).[67] This overreaching abuse of power was done by brokers and agents in order to flip higher profits, promote suburbanization, and exacerbate residential segregation.

In New York, blockbusting was common in the neighborhoods of East Flatbush, Bed-Stuy, Crown Heights, Laurelton, and Cambria Heights, among others. By funneling white families into suburbs, inner-city neighborhoods became devoid of the existing tax bases, and soon, these neighborhoods suffered from reduced public services and dwindling public school quality, compounding an additional layer of economic segregation.

Panic caused by speculators was just one of many components in racial segregation incurred at the hands of real estate companies. Blockbusting speaks to the troubled history of belonging for Black communities. At first, Blacks folks were redlined in already-deteriorated neighborhoods, without equal access

---

66   Brent Gaspaire, "Blockbusting," Blackpast, January 7, 2013.
67   Violet Ikonomova, "Report: Gentrification Not a Problem in Detroit," *Deadline Detroit*, April 24, 2019.

to housing mortgages and loans. Next, they were used as props to aid in white flight and as fuel for suburbanization. Shortly after, they were exploited and left with minimal choice, paying inflated prices for inner-city homes. Instability of Black neighborhoods at the hands of racist policies and institutions has been decades in the making; gentrification and displacement are just the newest iterations.

Up until the early nineteen hundreds the Fourth Ward in the northern part of Washington, DC was mainly rural and unsettled. As developers started constructing more homes and neighborhoods in the 40s and 50s, they added racial restrictions—exclusively allowing only white, non-Jewish families. But starting in the 50s, Black families began moving into the southern parts of the Fourth Ward. At the same time, realtors realized that Black families were willing to pay more for these homes (as they had fewer options), and again spread fear of racial integration among white residents. The white flight and blockbusting that followed were so strong that within just twenty years, the Fourth Ward went from exclusively white to overwhelmingly Black.[68]

It's important to mention that white flight is still happening today. Indiana University sociologist Samuel Kye examined 27,891 census tracts from the 150 largest metropolitan areas between 2000 to 2010 and found that almost 12 percent of these tracts witnessed white flight, with an average magnitude loss of 40 percent of their white populations. Kye writes, "White flight eventually becomes more likely in middle-class

---

68   Sarah Jane Shoenfeld, "How Segregation Shaped DC's Northernmost Ward," Greater Greater Washington, September 14, 2017.

neighborhoods when the presence of Hispanics and Asians exceeds 25 percent and 21 percent, respectively."[69]

Another study that looked into spatial dynamics of white flight found the same out-migration by white families: "Growing concentrations of non-white minority residents in nearby tracts significantly increase the likelihood that whites will leave their neighborhood of residence."[70] White flight phenomena are related to the group threat theory, which states that majority groups feel threatened when minority groups grow in size or power. One poll from the Public Religion Research Institute found that almost a third of Americans surveyed think having a non-white majority would be a negative thing for the country.[71] Keeping with the ocean metaphor from earlier, this desired self-segregation signifies a high tide of white families moving back into cities, threatening a wave of gentrification in inner-city neighborhoods.

HIGHWAYS

The demographic split between whites and nonwhites created by white flight and blockbusting is engrained in built environments via the interstate highway system. According to Anthony Foxx, Secretary for the US Department of Transportation, the first twenty years of highway development

---

69 Samuel H. Kye, "The Persistence of White Flight in Middle-Class Suburbia," *Social Science Research*, vol. 72 (May 2018): 38-52.

70 Kyle Crowder and Scott J. South, "Spatial Dynamics of White Flight: The Effects of Local and Extralocal Racial Conditions on Neighborhood Out-Migration," *American Sociological Review* 73, no. 5 (2008): 792-812.

71 Jones, Robert P., Daniel Cox, Rob Griffin, Molly Fisch-Friedman and Alex Vandermaas-Peeler, "American Democracy in Crisis: The Challenges of Voter Knowledge, Participation, and Polarization," *PRRI*, 2018.

resulted in the displacement of some 475,000 families and over a million Americans. Foxx notes, "Nothing in our built environment is accidental. [...] To understand this point, we need to step back and understand how most things in our built environment are the product of intentional design." [72]

As engineers and developers designed interstate highway systems, they looked to plan highway routes through neighborhoods with poor or minority communities—giving them excuses to disrupt, dissolve, and destroy these neighborhoods. Together with housing bills and incentives for developers, some highways divided or completely isolated certain neighborhoods as a means of cutting them off from other parts of the city, thus removing walkability or accessibility to businesses. This containment, enabled by the new highways and commercial corridors, removed vibrancy and connections that once existed. Furthermore, increased levels of noise and air pollution flooded these neighborhoods, making life between highways even more undesirable.

In their book *Changing Lanes*, Joseph DiMento and Cliff Ellis shed light on the evolution of urban freeways. DiMento talks about the role of highway and construction engineers on the highway network: "They were trained to design without much consideration for how a highway might impact urban fabric. [...] They were worried about the most efficient way of moving people from A to B." The failure of highway engineers to understand the impacts of their designs gave rise to urban planning as a profession, and demonstrates why we now value interdisciplinary approaches to building

---

72 Alan Pyke, "Top Infrastructure Official Explains How America Used Highways to Destroy Black Neighborhoods."

and designing spaces. DiMento continues: "There was also a racially motivated desire to eliminate what people called 'urban blight.'[…] The funds were seen as a way to fix the urban core by replacing blight with freeways."[73]

Eventually, highway development evolved to include ring roads, or beltways (a series of connected roads that looped around an urban core). The logic behind beltways is to reduce congestion within the ring, allowing drivers who don't need to actually go to the city to circumnavigate it altogether. But this type of traffic alleviation doesn't come at no cost. Ring roads often encase and enclose the communities within them, shutting them off from outside areas. They also physically separate the communities on either side of them and can sometimes turn a blind eye to urban sprawl—the uncontrolled, unplanned, or unrestricted outward growth of an urban area.

The Capital Beltway (I-495) in Washington, DC, is a great example. The sixty-four mile highway that connects suburbs in Maryland and Virginia was completed in 1964; by the end of the twentieth century, the communities and suburbs that existed beyond the Beltway became home to the wealthiest parts of the cities, such as Fairfax, Montgomery, and Loudoun counties. The DC area as a whole became less dense and more spread out. In fact, there was a 12 percent decrease in density from 1982 to 1997. But by 2000, the draw for life beyond the beltway drained the city's job pool, leaving only 24 percent of jobs in the DC metro area within the city itself.[74]

---

73 Charlie Surrel, "Why Did The U.S. Let Highways Ruin Its Cities, And How Can We Fix It?" FastCompany, May 31, 2016.

74 "A Region Divided: The State of Growth in Greater Washington, D.C.," The Brookings Institute, 1999.

The Capital Beltway became an informal marker of where the city put its focus: 80 percent of public funds went to improving roads beyond the beltway, compared to just 10 percent for within. Data from the Brookings Institute found that by 2010, almost half of jobs in the DC area were more than ten miles from the city's core. Education, race, income, wealth, and jobs were all divided, and the beltway was, in many ways, the divider. Despite composing 32 percent of the entire region's population, the district and Prince George's county hold 70 percent of the region's Black population, and by 1996, almost half of the area's low-income residents lived in the District alone.

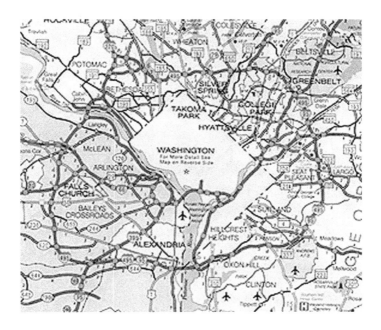

Figure 3: The Capital Beltway in Washington, DC.

* * *

TRADEMARKS OF GENTRIFICATION

Gentrification often has a few trademarks shared by cities across the country. Of course, these are not all requirements of gentrification, but rather an assortment of outcomes that can help quantify or contextualize what gentrification actually is.

INFLUX OF WEALTHIER & MORE-EDUCATED RESIDENTS

An influx of wealthier residents alone is not gentrification. It can cause, enforce, or coincide with other trademarks, however, such as increased police calls/presence, increased (and recognized) demand for public services, or increased demand and cost of living. Similarly, a rapid influx of college-educated folks into an area can very well trigger gentrification, as they often demand certain services (dining establishments and hang-out spots) that can bring an additional layer of change to the local economy and landscape.

A study out of Harvard University found that changes in a neighborhood's business landscape was shaped more by the presence of college-educated residents and less so the age or race of residents.[75] Spikes in food establishments and grocery stores proved to be indicators of upticks in college-educated residents. Likewise, neighborhoods with fewer dining establishments typically have higher populations of less-educated

---

75   Glaeser, Edward L., Hyunjin Kim and Michael Luca, "Nowcasting Gentrification: Using Yelp Data to Quantify Neighborhood Change," NBER Working Paper No. w24010, 2017, quoted in Dina Gerdeman, "How to Know If Your Neighborhoods Is Being Gentrified," Harvard Business Review, May 23, 2018.

residents. An influx of wealthier and college-educated residents can sometimes warrant for conversion of family-size rental housing to smaller units, further deceasing housing supply and affordability.

In Brooklyn, the rapid in-migration by whiter, wealthier, and more fiscally conservative residents reveals itself in the courtroom. This, now known as the "Williamsburg Effect," sees further criminalization of plaintiffs and defendants in cases. Juries who don't know the history and optics of crime in the area are less likely to understand and resonate with defendants, and award plaintiffs with lower amounts of money in settlement cases.[76]

REALLOCATION OF PUBLIC SERVICES

The influx of the wealthy into gentrifying neighborhoods influences public offerings and services. These services can include trash collection, street cleaning, public school education, and sometimes even transit options. This reallocation/increase of public services could stem from two places: either the increase of social capital and taxes being brought by the wealthier residents, or the newfound recognition of these areas as determined by factors of new residents, such as race or class.

An unseen outcome brought by wealthier folks into gentrifying neighborhoods is the increased amount of police stops, nuisance calls, and 911 calls. These arise because new

---

76   John Saul, "When Brooklyn Juries Gentrify, Defendants Lose," NY Post, June 16, 2014; Nicole Akoukou Thompson, "The Williamsburg Effect: The Gentrification of Brooklyn Is Being Reflected in the Court System," Latin Post, June 17, 2014.

residents are more likely to report any ethnically diverse neighbors for things like loitering, playing music, completing murals, and other low-level disturbances.[77]

DISPLACEMENT

It's almost impossible to say that gentrification directly causes displacement. While displacement is central to gentrification, this represents a misunderstanding of factors that can influence both phenomena: changing economies, unjust legislation and policies, waves of entrepreneurship, and residual disadvantages from decades of mistreatment. At best, there's a correlation between the two, but whether or not it is a positive correlation depends on the neighborhood. This is because there's many, many ways to measure displacement (things like outmigration and demographic of residents, education levels, average incomes, home values, and patterns of settlement and investment). Sometimes, displaced residents can accrue additional burdens that arise from a spatial mismatch between where folks live and where suitable jobs exist.[78]

INCREASED COST OF LIVING

One of the biggest talking points surrounding gentrification is increased cost of living in a neighborhood. This has been notoriously linked to rates of displacement and remains

77 Abdallah Fayyad, "The Criminalization of Gentrifying Neighborhoods," *The Atlantic*, December 20, 2017; Ayobami Laniyonu, "Coffee Shops and Street Stops: Policing Practices in Gentrifying Neighborhoods," *Urban Affairs Review* 54, no. 5 (January 23, 2017): 898-930; Tanvi Misra, "Yes, 311 Calls Nuisance Calls Are Climbing in Gentrifying Neighborhoods," Bloomberg CityLab, October 18, 2018.

78 DeAndrea Salvador, "Can Curbing Gentrification Help Stop the Climate Crisis?" The Week, February 18, 2017.

instrumental in the affordability and housing crisis. One example is Washington, DC, a city hit especially hard by gentrification. A study published by the Coalition for Nonprofit Housing and Economic Development found that between 2002 to 2007, the cost of buying a house doubled, and the average rent increased by 33 percent, followed by another 16 percent increase in the subsequent three years.[79]

Such dramatic increases spell trouble for residents in gentrifying neighborhoods and remain a key reason many are turned off by the process of gentrification.[80] Increasing costs of living have been used to justify gentrification, as it increases home values and public services, but it has also been used to disavow gentrification, as it drives out long-standing residents, businesses, community markers.

PUBLIC INVESTMENTS

Neighborhoods and cities are constantly changing. When the rate of change is slow, our understanding of change is blurred and assimilated in our minds. When the rate of change is fast, however, we can more easily identify impacts in our communities and ecosystems. Therefore, when areas marked by a history of disinvestment are exposed to waves of high investments in a short amount of time, the holes in our social and housing systems become glaringly evident. Public investments—such as parks, open spaces, and schools—can increase cost of living and home values, as they make places more favorable. But if we know what residents find desirable,

---

79 "An Affordable Continuum of Housing... Key to a Better City," Coalition for Nonprofit Housing & Economic Development, 2010.

80 "Washington Post-Kaiser Family Foundation Poll," *Washington Post*, accessed May 16, 2020.

why aren't we taking steps to more equitably make these things accessible to all communities?

Jason Richardson, a director at the National Community Reinvestment Coalition, notes that "the emergency is that there is widespread disinvestment in low-to-moderate income communities to start with. It's all related to the same core issues, which are disinvestment in communities that periodically are seeing shifts into these periods of hyper-investment, and that's what becomes gentrification."[81]

*   *   *

These trademarks are reflected not only in the real world, but in the digital realm as well, via platforms like Yelp and Street-Score. (Yelp is an online repository that allows the general public to review businesses and services. StreetScore uses Google Street View and machine learning to analyze indicators, such as paint and color schemes of buildings, landscaping, and number of dining establishments, to determine the perceived safety of a street). Both platforms crowdsource surface-level information to rate neighborhood markers, which can be dangerous if users and designers of these platforms aren't aware of how such data is used and perceived.

A study out of Harvard found a correlation between the presence of certain establishments (and ratings left by new residents) and changes in neighborhood demographics. For example, "the entry of a new coffee shop into a zip code

---

81   Richardson, Jason, Bruce Mitchell, and Jad Edlebi, "Gentrification and Disinvestment 2020," National Community Reinvestment Coalition, June 2020.

in a given year is associated with a 0.5 percent increase in housing prices." Likewise, perceived neighborhood safety is "most positively associated with increases in the number of vegetarian restaurants, Starbucks and cafes, and wine bars." [82]

These observations perhaps say more about us as humans than the neighborhoods themselves. Do we desire safe neighborhoods, or do we desire businesses with unsuspecting clientele? Are we just chasing safety because of the economic benefits or because we actually wish to improve a place? What's more important to us: actual safety or perceived safety?

PUBLIC WORKS

The role of public works—big, governmental infrastructure projects—in the twentieth century creates a more concrete visualization of the various trademarks and indicators of change in a city. The advent of interstate highways tackled the issue of at-grade (level) crossings, allowing for increased capabilities for concurrent travel routes. As new highway construction picked up, however, people began to notice the downsides of ubiquitous streaks of concrete circling their cities and neighborhoods. Moreover, residents who were in jeopardy or were directly displaced by highways immediately understood the ramifications, as seen by anti-road and highway protests that erupted across the country in late 1950s and 60s.

In Boston, the proposed expansion of Interstate 95 by state officials involved building a series of highways that would

---

82   Glaeser, Edward L., Hyunjin Kim and Michael Luca, "Nowcasting Gentrification: Using Yelp Data to Quantify Neighborhood Change."

intersect and dissect many low-income neighborhoods. This plan was seen as another attempt to appease the wealthy who had moved to the suburbs and wanted more direct routes to workplaces. Thousands of residents from surrounding cities gathered to protest the expansion, ultimately pressuring Massachusetts Governor Francis Sargent to secure federal funding to expand the mass transit system and build a new city park in place of the highway.[83] The "People Before Highways" movement ran in tandem with other movements at the time: chiefly those for Civil Rights, women's rights, and anti-war sentiment, highlighting the intersectionality between cities and the built environment.

Highways weren't the only type of public works project that ravaged communities. The expansion of Boston Logan Airport in the 1960s and 70s was made possible by seizure and bulldozing of the beloved Wood Island Park (designed by Frederick Law Olmsted) and Neptune Road in East Boston. The area had long been home to immigrant communities and, when it fell into despair and neglect in the early nineteen hundreds, many saw it as excuse for airport developers to bulldoze and claim the land to expand the airport. East Boston was able to bounce back after the expansion, but for decades the airport was the source of substantial air and noise pollution for nearby residents.[84]

Perhaps the most notable infrastructure project in Boston would be the central artery/tunnel project that started in

---

83 Carly Berke, "People Before Highways: A Discussion with Dr. Karilyn Crockett," Boston University Initiative on Cities, accessed June 13, 2020.

84 Mark Byrnes, "40-Year-Old Images Show East Boston Grappling With an Expanding Logan Airport," Bloomberg CityLab, May 6, 2013.

1982 and took thirty-five years to complete. Also known as the Big Dig, it was the most expensive construction project in the history of the country—largely due to cost overruns and logistical issues (such as saltwater intrusion and design flaws). The project was originally designed to alleviate and reroute city traffic, which it ultimately did. Ultimately burying of the I-93 central artery allowed for more access to the Seaport district and the airport, and made space for future development, public transportation, and the seventeen-acre Kennedy Greenway (which provided some green space in the city).[85] Today, it's almost impossible to move throughout the city without interacting with the Big Dig.

TRANSIT-INDUCED GENTRIFICATION

The key to any good city in the world is public transportation. It leads to better mobility, jobs, cleaner and safer travel, healthier residents, and time and cost savings. For this reason, many urban designers and planners advocate for something called transit-oriented development (TOD): the philosophy that people and activities should be centered around public transit. This is the principle behind livable, walkable, and connected neighborhoods. But recently, the term transit-induced gentrification (TIG) entered the lexicon surrounding urban mobility and can be defined as "the relationship between transit investments and the demographic shifts common in gentrifying neighborhoods."[86]

---

85 "The Big Dig: Project Background," Mass.gov, accessed May 29, 2020.

86 Zuk, Miriam, Ariel H. Bierbaum, Karen Chapple, Karolina Gorska, Anastasia Loukaitou-Sideris, Paul Ong, and Trevor Thomas, "Gentrification, Displacement and the Role of Public Investment: A Literature Review,"

TIG becomes an issue when it's linked to displacement, especially when transit development counters existing patterns of disinvestment. Given the benefits of transit access and increased foot traffic, many businesses and developers often look to situate themselves by train stations and, oftentimes, this proximity is actualized into surrounding developments, which ends up increasing the costs of housing and living. In turn, this can result in lower-income residents—who benefit the most from public transit—being priced out of those areas.

Current development of the Purple Line, a light rail development in Washington, DC's suburbs, has received stark opposition from housing advocates who worry the $2 billion project will price out and displace current low- and middle-class residents. Already, new apartments and luxury housing are using adjacent land to price their units at rates higher than what the average resident can afford. Luckily, the Purple Line Corridor Coalition has been proactive in putting together a plan to increase affordable housing, deploy low-cost loans, strengthen tenant protection laws, and mitigate any potential threats of gentrification and displacement.[87]

But such foresight hasn't always been the norm. A study on TIG out of the National Center for Smart Growth at the

---

Community Development Investment Center and Federal Reserve Bank of San Francisco, Working Paper 2015-05 (August 2015): 20.

87   Katherine Shaver, "Suburbs Seeking Transit Look for Ways to Keep Residents from Being Priced Out," *Washington Post*, November 28, 2016; Ally Schweitzer, "How To Limit Gentrification Along The Purple Line, According To Housing Advocates," NPR, December 12, 2019; Jeff Turrentine, "When Public Transportation Leads to Gentrification," National Resources Defense Council, June 1, 2018.

University of Maryland discusses concerns related to TOD and its impacts on surrounding neighborhoods, and found increases in home values and incomes in census tracts near newly-opened transit stations.[88] Similar stories of TIG can be found in Chicago, Portland, and San Diego. The role of transit in gentrification and displacement fits into a larger discussion about the role and impact of public infrastructure and mobility. For cities of all sizes, it's important to continue pursing TOD—but it's critically important to pair development with affordable housing measures and protections for low- and mixed-income residents.

* * *

RESOLUTIONS

As the densest population corridor in the country, the pressure to support resident well-being in the Northeast is a situation with high-stakes and high-rewards. In the above three cities alone, there are a few promising strategies to combat histories of discrimination and spatial segregation. Some general strategies against gentrification and rising living costs is to alleviate car dependency and thoughtfully develop and expand transit options, build and allocate more affordable-housing, and invest in and empower marginalized communities. Above all, it is critically important to focus and utilize local assets and resources to combat these issues and preserve the place for all communities.

---

88   Caset Dawkings and Rolf Moeckel. "Transit-Induced Gentrification: Who Will Stay, and Who Will Go?" University of Maryland, October 18, 2014.

For Boston, this might be the presence of some of the world's top institutions—Harvard, MIT, Tufts, and Northeastern, to name a few—and organizations such as City Life/Vida Urbana, ReclaimBoston, Alternatives for the Community & Environment, and MASS Design Studio.

For New York, this might be the diversity, knowledge, and talent across all five boroughs. A few organizations and firms dedicated to bringing equity and justice to New Yorkers are the Brooklyn Anti-Gentrification Network, Black Alliance for Just Immigration, the Association for Neighborhood and Housing Development, and Designing the WE.

For DC, this might include reigniting the "Chocolate City" sentiment by building up Black business and communities, or utilizing its many think tanks to demand and ensure more equitable treatment for all residents. Organizations such as ONE DC, the Coalition for Nonprofit Housing & Economic Development, Building Bridges Across the River, and Empower DC are leading the charge against urban inequalities.

* * *

Through all of these facets, the Northeast has evolved tremendously since the days of colonialization. Now, it must continue evolving into the smart, urban corridor it was destined to be, and start implementing measures to promote equity, justice, and inclusion. But in the South, the evolution of urban settings took a different path, thus requires a different set of solutions.

5

THE SOUTH

———

When people talk about southern culture, they almost always seem to mention something about tradition, freedom, or history. But when I think about the South, I almost always think about slavery, the Confederacy, and ignorance. I was disappointed—but not surprised—when I learned that there are still around 700 statues of Confederate veterans in the South. These statues were mostly built throughout the Jim Crow era, from the late-eighteen hundreds to mid-nineteen hundreds, and seem to glorify southern rebellion and the Confederacy—serving as constant reminders of the ugly and scorched history of the South.[89] The case for the statues is exactly what, to me, southern tradition, freedom, and history is built on. Personally, I don't think these statues should have a place in public spaces, as they perpetuate antebellum sentiments and misconstrue the actual history of America.

There are also the antiquated expectations of gender roles and language in South. Part of this stems from ties to southern

---

89 Becky Little, "How the US Got So Many Confederate Statues," History. com, last modified June 12, 2020; "Whose Heritage? Public Symbols of the Confederacy," Southern Poverty Law Center, February 1, 2019.

English colonists, mixed with socially conservative Protestantism and strong, traditional family loyalty. The First and Second Great Awakening reignited southerners' religious beliefs, giving the South the title "Bible Belt." And for a long time, the South has generally had lower percentages of high school graduates, incomes, housing values, and costs of living.[90]

Another facet of southern history and tradition is the ubiquity of southern hospitality. Yet as a product of the Northeast, I find it slightly condescending and ingenuine, partly because it is expected of southerners. Where the Northeast is friendly without being nice, the South is nice without being friendly. But through it all, southern culture is built on two key foundations, among others: music and food.

In early settlements, music was an outlet and unifying practice for southerners. Traveling evangelical preachers used music to recruit new followers, enslaved folks incorporated folklore and spirituality into blues, and working class southerners played country music in bands and at barn dances. Compared to music, food provides a more a palpable window into the history of the South. From influences ranging from Cajun, the Gullah-Geechee people, the Caribbean, and West Africa, southern food is rich with cultural significance and comfort. With thousands of fans across the country, southern food adopted ingredients and techniques from those who have owned and shared parts of the South: barbecuing, squash, and corn from Native American tribes

---

90 Christopher A. Cooper, and H. Gibbs Knotts, "Defining Dixie: A State-Level Measure of the Modern Political South," *American Review of Politics* 25 (2004): 25–39.

as well as baking and dairy products from Europeans colonists, and beans, spices, and rice from West African and Caribbean countries.

One particular novelty of southern food is "soul food." As Adrian Miller, author of award-winning book *Soul Food*, notes: "Southern food is the mother cuisine that soul food claims heritage to, but soul food is distinct unto itself."[91] Historically the food of the Deep South, soul food typically consists of a combination of chicken/pork/fish, greens, candied yams, black eyed peas, mac and cheese, and cornbread.

And as Black folks left the South during the Great Migrations, they took their cuisine with them. Because availability of key ingredients varied across the country, substitutes were used to re-create and translate a sense of home and familiarity. The title of "soul" followed the food and came in the 1940s as a way to keep the brand of Blackness in line with music and culture. In any case, the abridged history of these two cultural staples provides a fitting backdrop for understanding the southern way of life.

* * *

NEW ORLEANS, LOUISIANA (NOLA)

New Orleans is a city unlike any other in America. Its position along the Mississippi River and Gulf of Mexico helped establish it as a trading port in the seventeen hundreds.

91   Sam Worley, "Where Soul Food Really Comes From," EpiCurious, June 29, 2018; Justin Bolois, "8 Common Soul-Food Myths, Debunked," First We Feast, April 23, 2015.

Control of the city shifted back and forth between the French and Spanish, and these colonial influences can be seen in cuisines, building styles, public infrastructure, music, and local culture. The city was prized during the Civil War because of its port access and has since retained that significance. Since the beginning of the twentieth century, New Orleans developed and capitalized on its culture of jazz, food, and entertainment. Today, New Orleans remains a resilient and prideful city. It thrives off of tourism, oil and gas, and healthcare. Despite a slew of deadly hurricanes—like Katrina, Gustav, and Laura—the city's motto embodies its jubilant nature: *"Laissez les bon temps rouler"*—French for "let the good times roll."

ATLANTA, GEORGIA (ATL)

In the mid-eighteen hundreds, Atlanta got its jump from a convenient location along railroad routes. By the Civil War, it became a railroad hub for the southern half of the country and was soon a distribution hub for military supplies and products. After the war, Atlanta retained its reputation as a transportation hub and expanded its economy to include manufacturing, business, and finance. In 1936, Atlanta became the first city in the country to construct a public housing project.[92] Throughout the twentieth century, a group of elite colleges and new businesses enabled growth of a Black middle and upper class, helping to establish Atlanta as a major center of the Civil Rights Movement. Despite championing themselves as "the city too busy to hate," sub-

---

92   Irene V. Holliman, "Techwood Homes," Georgia Encyclopedia, last modified August 26, 2020.

urbanization fueled segregation in the city and, along with the now-removed Atlanta Wall, marked a spatial segregation along the urban fringe. Today, Atlanta is home to the world's busiest airport, thirty of the Fortune 500 companies, and remains a feature city of the South.

NASHVILLE, TENNESSEE

Founded in 1779 during the American Revolution, Nashville grew due to its access to the Cumberland and Ohio Rivers, and later, important rail routes. Prior to the Civil War, in which Nashville turned into a center for iron production, the city government owned slaves to build and maintain infrastructure—even designating entire slave auction blocks in the heart of the city.[93] Following the war, a wave of lynchings and segregation took place as Nashville became the anchor of the Lost Cause of the Confederacy, a movement that idealizes the principles of the antebellum South. In the early nineteen hundreds, the Jefferson Street area became a booming center for the Black community; the rise of jazz, blues, and country music updated the city's reputation. By the 1960s, suburbanization and the manufacturing industry had transformed the city. Today, Nashville holds the title "Music City," and is sometime referred to as the "Athens of the South" for its concentration of higher education institutions and Greek and Renaissance Revival architectural styles.

* * *

93 George Zepp. "Slave Market Included Auction Blocks, Brokers Offices in Downtown Nashville," *The Tennessean*, April 30, 2003, 16.

THE FALLOUT OF THE CIVIL WAR

Each of these cities was instrumental in the Civil War and were forerunners of change after Southern defeat. Reconstruction, as mentioned in Chapter 2, was essentially a plan to rebuild the South and protect formerly enslaved populations before the readmission of Southern states. During this period, southern cities saw the arrival of "carpetbaggers," a derogatory term used to describe northern teachers, businessmen, politicians, and missionaries who were believed to intend exploitation of the South. The Freedman's Bureau, established in 1865, facilitated the relationship between formerly enslaved folks and former slaveholders. The Bureau was created by northern politicians and provided food, shelter, clothing, and counsel on legal and labor matters.

As Reconstruction ended, the Jim Crow era ushered in a new, institutionalized version of segregation and racism. These laws rendered it illegal for folks of different skin color to dine at the same restaurant, use the same bathrooms, play at the same parks, learn at the same schools, and even attend the same hospitals. Even before the Civil War, the establishment of Black Codes suppressed Black people's rights and liberties—prohibiting and restricting things like voting, independent farming, bearing arms, and requiring special taxes and licenses to conduct business or get married. Black Codes were also present in states outside the South (like Ohio, Indiana, Michigan, and Connecticut).[94] To enforce these harsh and cruel laws, vigilante and paramilitary groups such the Ku Klux

---

94 Stephen Middleton, "The Black Laws: Race and the Legal Process in Early Ohio," (Athens, Ohio: Ohio University Press, 2005): 74-115; Roger D. Bridges, "Codes," Northern Illinois University Libraries, accessed June 7, 2020; "The Black Law of Connecticut (1833)," Yale University

Klan, the White Leagues, and the Red Shirts were formed in the 1870s.

These laws essentially prevented and prohibited the coexistence of people within a space. As part of the "separate but equal" doctrine, almost every public space was divided, a constant reminder to Black and colored folks that they were not welcome. Despite advances brought by the Civil Rights Movement, many white southerners refused to accept the newfound statuses of people who didn't look like them—as exemplified by the mob of a thousand white southerners who denounced the Little Rock Nine, a group of nine Black schoolchildren, from attending the Central High School in Arkansas in 1957.

Parallel to ongoing racism and bigotry, the oil and mining industries created an economic boom in the early twentieth century. These industries renewed the exploitative attitudes already present in the South and were critical in establishing patterns of environmental racism. Since capital was inextricably tied to politics, the path for continued exploitation and suppression was clear. These disparities were so deep-rooted and normalized in institutions and the built environment that even after the formal end of segregation the spatial, social, and economic fallout still exist to this day.

GERRYMANDERING

Given the many migration patterns and economic shifts that have shaped and continue to shape the country, the idea of

Gilder Lehrman Center for the Study of Slavery, Resistance, & Abolition, accessed June 7, 2020.

representation remains a sensitive issue. As a result, the process of redistricting is completed every ten years as a way to keep congressional districts accurately represented. In most states, district lines are drawn by state legislatures or political commissions. During this process, some legislators take advantage of their power to engage in **gerrymandering**, a process of manipulating district boundaries to limit representation for certain populations. This is something done on both sides of the aisle (and around the world), and works by using two main strategies: cracking, which involves dividing and dispersing voters into surrounding districts, and packing, which involves consolidating and concentrating voters into fewer districts.[95]

Figure 1: How cracking and packing work to distort representation.[96]

Gerrymandering plays into a larger discussion of voter suppression and public resource allocation, and is done in order to suppress voters in certain areas (racially motivated) and to protect incumbent office holders (partisanship). The incentive for gerrymandering is to increase the effect of one voting bloc while decreasing the effect of another. This includes

---

95 "Messages from Mission 2: Partisan Gerrymander," USC Annenberg, accessed May 15, 2020; "7 Things to Know About Redistricting," Brennan Center, last modified July 3, 2017.

96 Jeanette Petti, "Rigging Elections: A Spatial Statistics Analysis of Political and Unintentional Gerrymandering," Cornell Policy Review, October 18, 2017.

keeping incumbent politicians and parties in office, diluting opposition party votes, and increasing congressional representation for certain demographics, thus dictating where funds and resources are directed.

Take Louisiana, for example. The 2010 drawing of districts resulted in six congressional seats: five for Republicans and one for Democrats. District 2 (the strip of land that connects Baton Rouge and New Orleans), the only part of the state that is Democratic and has a non-white majority, is an example of packing. A proportionate congressional representation, which is done by analyzing raw overall votes in the state, would allocate two districts, and thus congressional seats, to be Democratic. But because of the 2010 drawing, District 2 packed most Democratic voters into a single district.

This is just one, tiny example. Across Louisiana, there are about twenty-five instances of parishes being divided by district lines, many of which were done to isolate predominantly Black or Democratic communities.[97] Across the country, gerrymandering is even more common and can be responsible for flipping entire election outcomes. And as a result, many federal funds and resources are unevenly distributed, leading to further distortions when it comes to representation in a spatial context.

This has serious ramifications when it comes to education, especially when you consider that schools in the South are as segregated now as they were following the 1954 ruling in *Brown*

---

97 Steven Wagner, "Evidence and Implications of Gerrymandering in Louisiana," University of Notre Dame, accessed June 8, 2020; Joseph R. Thysell, "Race Gerrymandering in Louisiana," *International Social Science Review* 77, no. 3/4 (2002): 171-84.

v. Board. But just like how gerrymandering can be used to segregate voters, it can also be used to integrate schools.[98] That is, if students attended schools closest to them, it would end up perpetuating levels of segregation that already exist in their neighborhoods. For this reason, like the controversial desegregation busing programs in the 60s and 70s, attendance zones are often drawn to minimize this effect, aiming to make classrooms less segregated. Sometimes, however, wealthier families choose to enroll their children in private or charter schools or move out of diverse neighborhoods altogether, which ends up depleting tax bases and changing the makeup of classrooms.

There's something to be said of the similarities between redlining and gerrymandering. In the 1930s, the Home Owners' Land Corporation used data from real estate professionals to create maps based largely on race and lending risk. Banks and lenders then used these maps to justify the denial of homes, loans, public services, and other resources to non-white populations. This created a cycle of underinvestment and divestment in "hazardous" and "definitely declining" neighborhoods—those with large concentrations of Black, Jewish, Italian, and other minorities—in favor of more traditional and affluent neighborhoods. In gerrymandering, politicians use data to literally divide districts, which results in some neighborhoods receiving more representation and resources than neighborhoods that deviate from incumbent legislatures, political views, and resident demographics.

---

98   Alvin Chang, "We Can Draw School Zones to Make Classrooms Less Segregated. This is How Well Your District Does," Vox.com, last modified August 27, 2018; Gary Orfield, and Erica Frankenberg, "Brown at 60: Great Progress, a Long Retreat and an Uncertain Future," The Civil Rights Project, May 15, 2014.

COLONIAL INFLUENCES

Visually, some American cities look different than others, but New Orleans is a city in its own league. It has been sequestered under French and Spanish rule, lathered with Creole culture, and built by descendants of great Western African civilizations. The French Quarter and the Central Business District contain some of the most distinctive architectural and design elements that exist in the city: flat-tiled roofs, pastel-colored stucco on building exteriors, and ornate cast-iron galleries and balconies, embellished with flowers, letters, and Adinkra symbolism. In fact, much of the calligraphy and iron work found in New Orleans can be traced to enslaved West Africans working with French and Spanish blacksmiths and colonizers. These symbolisms can be likened to the decorative carvings and hieroglyphs found in ancient Greece, Rome, and Egypt, and show that our environment has long been a canvas for life, stories, and values.[99]

In terms of architecture itself, Creole influence can be seen across the city, especially in residential neighborhoods. This style contains timber frames with brick or mud infill, steep rooflines, large galleries, dormers, and French doors. The prevalence of French-styled cottages, American cottages, Spanish-influenced townhouses, and double-gallery homes all prove the extent to which culture is engrossed in the built environment. New Orleans also has tons of shotgun homes, which are narrow (less than fifteen feet wide), single-story homes with shuttered

---

99 Morgan Randall, "The Storytelling Ironwork of New Orleans," *Atlas Obscura*, August 24, 2017.

windows, front porches, double-pitched roofs, stucco walls, gingerbread trimmings, and simple floor plans to allow for cross-ventilation.[100]

Some Spanish influences reveal themselves in things such as arches, courtyards, "in-between" floors, and Baroque-style government buildings. In addition to dwellings, New Orleans has a lot of cemeteries, designed landscapes, and public city plazas or centers, which all play a role in the history of the city. Congo Square was one of the only public spaces where enslaved populations could play, perform, and listen to music, which was polyrhythmic and memorialized their histories.[101]

Even the cemeteries reflect architectural styles of the city and feature above-ground caskets, tombs, and wall vaults (due to high water tables). Some are even home to jazz funerals, a celebratory tradition linked to formerly enslaved and West African populations. Jackson Square, located in the French Quarter, is one of the most well-known public spaces in the country; it was the sight of public executions, lynchings, the signing of the Louisiana Purchase, and the famous Moonwalk Boardwalk, serving as an arsenal during Reconstruction.

FOOD AND SCARCITY

Each of these cities is renowned for its food specialties: New Orleans has an eclectic mix of seafood, Cajun spice, and soul food, Nashville has its hot chicken and biscuits, and Atlanta

---

100 Richard Campanella, "What Makes Architecture 'Creole'?" Nola.com, last modified July 19, 2019.

101 Lawrence N. Powell, "Unhappy Trails in the Big Easy," Southern Spaces, January 17, 2012.

has its chicken and waffles as well as fusion cuisines. Food anywhere can tell us a lot about a place. This includes dining establishments, the culinary influences and ingredients, the variety in grocery stores and markets, and so on.

Longstanding southern culinary traditions (fried foods, heavy gravies, biscuits, sugary desserts, lard for shortening, etc.) and their connection to unhealthy lifestyles have been a subject of interest for many experts. The prevalence of obesity and Type 2 diabetes in states like Mississippi, Alabama, and Louisiana are among the highest in the country. Southerners also suffer from lower average life expectancies, have more relaxed smoking bans, less access to healthcare, and less physical activity.[102]

But our food systems nationwide, like many aspects of our urban settings, are deeply flawed. Some of the larger systematic issues shaping much of our functional landscapes—capitalism, colonialism, and unsustainability, to name a few—have also ruptured our food system. One of the most visible markings of this is something called "food apartheid."

More commonly known as food deserts, the term food apartheid is more intentional. Karen Washington, a food justice advocate, highlights the distinction: "[Food desert] makes us think of an empty, absolutely desolate place. But when we're talking about these places, there is so much life and vibrancy and potential. Using that word runs the risk

---

102 Jay Maddock, "These Five Charts Help Explain Why the South Is So Unhealthy," Vice, February 8, 2018.

of preventing us from seeing all of those things."[103] As such, researchers at John Hopkins prefer the term "healthy food priority areas."[104]

Regardless, these areas can be defined as ones that lack sufficient access to affordable and nutritious food. In 2019, the Department of Agriculture found that 13.7 million households were food unsure—that comes out to almost 11 percent of the population.[105] This was measured by the number of households unable to acquire or buy enough food to satisfy their members' needs. But for urban areas in particular, high population density, increasing rates of urbanization, and decreasing availability of supermarkets all pose great threats to city residents.

Washington goes on to point out the interconnectedness between food systems and healthcare: "The healthcare industry is part of this conversation. [...] In my neighborhood, there is a fast-food restaurant on every block, from Wendy's to Kentucky Fried Chicken to Popeye's to Little Caesar's Pizza. Now drugstores are popping up on every corner, too. So you have the fast-food restaurants that of course cause the diet-related diseases, and you have the pharmaceutical companies there to fix it. They go hand in hand."[106]

---

103 Anna Brones, "Food Apartheid: The Root of the Problem with America's Groceries," *The Guardian*, May 15, 2018.

104 "Report: 'Food Desert' Gets a Name Change in Response to Baltimore Community Feedback," John Hopkins Center for A Livable Future, January 17, 2018.

105 "Key Statistics & Graphics," USDA Economic Research Service, last modified September 9, 2020.

106 Anna Brones, "Food Apartheid: The Root of the Problem with America's Groceries."

There are numerous studies across the country that link a higher density of unhealthy convenience stores and fast-food restaurants to lower-income, Black, and Latinx neighborhoods than in whiter and more affluent neighborhoods.[107] Likewise, lack of proximity to grocery stores has a negative impact on the health of residents of these neighborhoods. Understanding the implications of food insecurity is critical for cities and communities to address. The probability of more public health issues (such as obesity or hypertension)—as enabled by unequal distribution of healthy dietary choices—poses a serious threat for the country as whole. To combat that, cities should promote healthy lifestyles by striving to help and educate their residents about nutrition, and work to bring healthier food choices into their neighborhoods.

SUBURBIA, CAR DEPENDENCY, AND SPRAWL

The context of food patterns and history helps to explain the higher concentration of health issues in the South, but we can't ignore the spatial settings that perpetuate these issues. With the rise of the personal vehicles came the rise of gas stations, automobile repair shops, and huge dealerships. At the time, existing infrastructure for streetcars, elevated railroads, and omnibuses in the North were owned, operated, and constructed by private corporations and local organizations. In the South, commercial railroads were still being utilized to send and receive goods, but public transit never reached the level it did in other parts of the country, mostly because it

---

107 Hilmers, Angela, David C. Hillmers, and Jayna Davis, "Neighborhood Disparities in Access to Healthy Foods and Their Effects on Environmental Justice," *Am J Public Health* 109, no. 9 (2012):1644-1654.

didn't need to. The already-spaced out development, slow rate of urbanization, blistering summer heat, and widespread adoption of cars by southerners had already given rise to auto-centric culture.

Car ownership rates among southerners is considerably higher than coastal and more urban areas. In Nashville, over 94 percent of households own a car. In Atlanta and New Orleans, that value is 84 percent and 80 percent, respectively—and these are just in three major cities, where some form of alternative transportation exists.[108] But advancements in energy consumption and car safety—like catalytic converters, air bags, seat belts, and reconfigured energy transmission—have prevented any strides away from southern car dependency. In the words of Hester Serebrin, policy director of the Transportation Choices Coalition: "We've gone so far down the car road, so to speak, that investments in other things often are perceived as *taking away* something that car owners have."[109]

Car dependency in the South has kept suburbs alive. This dependency has played a major role in the process known as **urban sprawl**. The term is used interchangeably with suburban sprawl, and aside from the auto-centric nature and single-family homes of the latter, the two are pretty indistinguishable; suburban sprawl is simply the outer fringes of urban sprawl.

---

108 Mike Maciag, "Vehicle Ownership in U.S. Cities Data and Map," Governing, November 28, 2017.

109 Eve Andrews, "Why Do Cities Keep Building All this New Stuff for Cars?" Grist, April 17, 2019.

The draw of single-family homes is a key factor in attracting folks into the suburbs, especially because it is inseparable from the idea of the American dream. Built upon principles of conformity, uniformity, and cheapness, some cities have embraced this vision—resulting in monoculture not only in housing type, but in vehicle type, neighborhood development, and even fast food offerings.

Urban sprawl is associated with an array of adverse environmental effects and increased car dependency. Moreover, it can be seen in strip development or leap-frog development (scattered development that requires an extension of public utilities), both of which further the argument that suburbs and the expansion associated with suburban sprawl remain a roadblock to sustainable development.[110]

Atlanta and Nashville were found to have the two worst cases of urban sprawl in metropolitan areas with over 1 million residents. A 2014 report released by Smart Growth America used four primary factors (residential and commercial density; variety of homes, jobs, and services in a neighborhood; strength of downtown and activity centers; and street network accessibility) to assign a sprawl index score to over 200 cities. The report found a few interesting connections between quality of life and index scores: "Individuals in compact, connected metro areas have greater economic mobility. Individuals in these areas spend less on the combined cost of housing and transportation, and have greater options for the type of transportation to take.

110 Bernadette Hanlon, "Beyond Sprawl: Social Sustainability and Reinvestment in the Baltimore Suburbs," in *The New American Suburb*, ed. Katrin B. Anacker (New York: Routledge, 2018): 133-153.

In addition, individuals in compact, connected metro areas tend to live longer, safer, healthier lives than their peers in metro areas with sprawl."[111]

An earlier volume of the report released in 2002 found links between sprawl and physical inactivity, obesity, poor air quality, traffic fatalities, teenage driving, reduced social capital, and increase in emergency response and commuting times. Other reports have found that suburbanites are less healthy compared to their urban counterparts, as they walk less, eat more, and exercise less.[112] According to the sprawl index, seven of the bottom ten cities (with over 1 million residents) were located in the South. For medium-sized areas (between 500,000 and a million residents), all of the bottom ten were in the South. And for small metro areas, the South claimed six out of the bottom ten.

This should not come as a surprise, considering the South's spatial development. Still, this goes to show that urban sprawl rampant through the South brings with it tons of adverse effects on community health and well-being. In Nashville, this urban sprawl is correlated to wealth and income segregation, of which the city ranks seventh and tenth worst in the country, respectively.[113] As it happens, wealthier folks tend to live amongst themselves and poverty is concentrated in a few areas, which means things like public schools,

---

111 "Measuring Sprawl 2014," Smart Growth America, April 2014.

112 Richard J. Jackson, and Chris Kochtitzky, "Creating A Healthy Environment: The Impact of the Built Environment on Public Health," Centers for Disease Control and Prevention, accessed July 1, 2020.

113 David Plazas, "Is Nashville in an Urban Crisis?" *The Tennessean*, last modified January 10, 2019.

healthcare, and access to jobs are unevenly distributed. If gone unchecked, this gap will only get wider and wider, eventually eating into the middle class.

In Atlanta, upward of 5.5 million people live outside the perimeter of the eight-lane Interstate 285.[114] As neighborhoods in the city's urban core increase in cost of living, younger and less affluent folks become priced out. As they move, many demand services and establishments that exist in the city. For example, suburbs like Avalon and Kennesaw are creating developments with select establishments, like Whole Foods, to cater to younger folks. Other suburbs beyond the perimeter lack decent sidewalk and transit infrastructure, which in turn promote car dependency and sprawl.

In the 1990s, Atlanta was described as the poster child for urban sprawl, growing from fifty miles from north to south in 1970 to over 120 miles today.[115] Part of this lies in the fact that Atlanta has no geographic limitations—there are no mountains or bodies of water to provide a natural border. Luckily, however, Atlanta has seen its peak of sprawl and is taking steps to reverse the damage; despite composing less than 1 percent of the city's development, 60 percent of real estate growth is now found in areas around transit centers and walkable neighborhoods.[116]

---

114 Nick Van Mead, "A City Cursed by Sprawl: Can the BeltLine Save Atlanta?" *The Guardian*, October 25, 2018.

115 Nina Ignaczak, "Metro Detroit Gets Ready to Grow with Transit-Oriented Development," Metromade Detroit, January 16, 2014.

116 Christopher B. Leinberger, "The WalkUP Wake-Up Call: Atlanta," The George Washington University School of Business, 2013: 4.

NOLA: CLIMATE GENTRIFICATION

When Hurricane Katrina struck the Gulf Coast in 2005, the city of New Orleans was hit particularly hard—largely due to faulty engineering of the city's levee system and missed warnings signs for the "potential for large loss of life."[117] According to the American Society of Civil Engineers, there were over 1,200 fatalities, with an estimated 80 percent of the city submerged under water. Of all the neighborhoods flooded, 80 percent were neighborhoods of color. Luckily, New Orleans was able to rebound, but the city that returned was different.

On top of the thousands of homes destroyed, the city further demolished public and affordable housing units. Plans to rebuild newer and safer public housing in their place has taken too long and failed to go far enough. A 2009 report out of the Greater New Orleans Data Center found that four years after Katrina, almost 20,000 residents were still unable to find affordable housing.[118] Many residents who lost their homes were relocated to cities like Atlanta, Houston, and Phoenix, and the vast displacement and out-migration of residents following Katrina coincided with trends of climate change and real estate.

A 2017 study published in Nature Magazine found that a six-foot increase in sea level by the year 2100 could see the

---

117 "Hurricane Katrina: A Nation Still Unprepared," (Washington DC: U.S. Government Printing Office, 2006): 41-42.

118 Plyer, Allison, Elaine Ortiz, Margery Austin Turner, and Kathryn LS Pettit, "Housing Production Needs: Three Scenarios for New Orleans," Greater New Orleans Community Data Center and The Urban Institute, November 2009; Dani McClain, "Former Residents of New Orleans's Demolished Housing projects Tell Their Stories," The Nation, August 26, 2015.

displacement of 500,000 people in New Orleans alone (almost half of all residents displaced due to Katrina).[119] But as coastal cities adapt and respond to climate change, real estate speculation and development change as well. New measures to address resiliency and new developments oftentimes displace low-income residents and communities of color, many of whom may already be struggling to keep up with rising costs of living in cities. Furthermore, the demand for higher-elevation neighborhoods over neighborhoods closer to waterfronts can spell trouble for New Orleans. In the Lower Ninth Ward, a predominately Black neighborhood hit hard by Katrina, in-migration from whiter and more affluent families led to increases in property values.[120] The relationship between climate change and real estate has culminated in what scholar Jesse Keenan calls "climate gentrification."

Climate gentrification can happen in a number of ways, such as when folks move from high-vulnerability areas to lower-vulnerability areas, the cost of adaption or resiliency measures jacks up living cost, or when certain areas are only accessible and livable by wealthy folks who are able to pay for high-cost of things like beach-front properties.[121] The fallout from climate change and gentrification stand on top of existing environmental injustice in Louisiana. In the eighty-five-mile span between Baton Rouge and New Orleans, there are over 150 petrochemical and gas plants

---

119 Matthew E. Hauer, "Migration Induced by Sea-Level Rise Could Reshape the US Population Landscape," *Nature Climate Change* 7 (April 2017): 321-325.
120 "Climate Gentrification: Fact or Fiction?" We Sell NOLA, May 16, 2020.
121 Cory Schouten, "'Climate Gentrification' Could Add Value to Elevation in Real Estate," CBS News, last modified December 28, 2017.

that emit harmful toxins and chemicals. Located along the Mississippi River, this stretch is home to mostly Black communities, and has become known as "Cancer Alley" since the 1980s—the risk from getting cancer here is twice as high as the national average.[122]

ATL: EMBRACED REVITALIZATION

In 1962, the mayor of Atlanta ordered barricades to block off access to Peyton Forest, a white subdivision of Cascade Heights in the southwest part of the city. Even though the wall stood for less than a year, the wall—now known as the Atlanta Wall or the Peyton Wall—was a physical barrier as much as it was symbolic; it stood to keep Black citizens out of the white neighborhood. After the wall was torn down, white residents started selling their homes and leaving the area (an instance of white flight) and within ten years, the white population in Fulton County decreased by 190,000.[123]

Typically, economic development in urban areas is strongly correlated with migration patterns—that is, as people leave an area, they take their capital and spending power with them. Over time, populations, property values, and municipal revenues decline. In turn housing, infrastructure, and public services (like education) suffer. When areas are revitalized, prioritized, or gentrified, people and businesses start to move back into those areas—increasing spending, property values, and public services. And, at times, this

---

122 Trymaine Lee, "Cancer Alley: Big Industry, Big Problem," MSNBC, accessed May 19, 2020.

123 Kevin M. Cruse, "The Barrier Wall: The Berlin Wall of Atlanta in 1962," ArcGIS, 2005

revitalization attracts new types of people—sometimes leading to full-force gentrification. This is the case with two major projects in Atlanta: the 1996 Olympics and the Atlanta BeltLine project.

In pursuit of becoming a global city and reinventing their reputation, Atlanta bid to host the 1996 Olympics. After winning, the city proceeded to clear acres upon acres in downtown to construct mega stadiums and housing quarters. Within the six years leading up to the Olympics, thousands of residents and businesses were displaced. After the Olympics, most of the purpose-built infrastructure was repurposed into dorms and athletic stadiums, and the local economy saw a massive push toward high-income development. This paved the way for new real estate speculations, white flight back into the city, and gentrification over the past two decades. This not only points to the unsustainability of the Olympic Games, but also the willingness of cities to decimate their communities in favor of global recognition and economic redevelopment.[124]

In 1999, Ryan Gravel, a master's degree candidate at Georgia Tech at the time, had a plan to repurpose old rail corridors into a network of trails and park connections. With the help of his two colleagues, Gravel was able to mail copies of his idea to influential Atlantans (city councilors, neighborhood associations, business leaders, etc.). Eventually, the BeltLine gained enough momentum to become a reality. Upon completion, it will span over thirty miles of multi-use trails, parks,

124 Mary G. Rolinson, "Atlanta Before and After the Olympics," Perspectives on History, November 1, 2006; Seth Gustafson. "Displacement and the Racial State in Olympic Atlanta," Southeastern Geographer 53, no. 2 (Summer 2013): 198-213.

and transit corridors—connecting over forty neighborhoods in the process.[125]

While the entire BeltLine vision is yet to be completed, those parts that have been finished have already transformed the city. So far, it has added hundreds of acres of greenspace, and treated hundreds more for environmental remediation. It has also added hundreds of jobs, created billions in revenue, and allocated thousands of affordable housing units, public displays of art, new rail transit, and improved streetscapes.[126]

But the BeltLine's promises opened doors to real estate developers to buy land in low-income areas and build high-class, luxury-style living developments. In Atlanta—where rents are increasing three times faster than the national median— BeltLine developers are required to spend 15 percent of any public funds they receive on affordable housing. But of the 5,600 affordable housing units promised by 2030, less than 1,000 were built before 2019, with hundreds more expiring or reaching market rates.[127] Moreover, new housing projections estimate that upward of 10,000 affordable housing units are now needed, partially due to the growing unaffordability brought by the BeltLine. Between 2011 and 2015, homes within a half mile of the BeltLine saw property values

---

125 Ethan Davidson, "History of the Atlanta Beltline Project in Public Roads Magazine," *Atlanta Beltline*, December 2, 2011.

126 "Wherever You Want to Go, Atlanta Beltline Takes You There," *Atlanta BeltlLine*, accessed June 14, 2020.

127 Patrick Sisson, "Atlanta's Beltline, a Transformative Urban Redevelopment, Struggles with Affordability," Curved, October 3, 2017; Mariano, Willoughby, Lindsey Conway, Anastaciah Ondieki, "How the Atlanta Beltline Broke its Promise of Affordable Housing," AJC, December 13, 2017.

increase 18-26 percent.[128] The BeltLine is Atlanta's way of bringing the city together, especially considering Atlanta's history of segregation and lack of transit options, but it also goes to show what can happen when cities aren't proactive or thoughtful.

NASHVILLE: HISTORIC PRESERVATION

For many cities, history is captured within physical buildings, infrastructure, and landmarks. Sometimes, the act of preserving a sight or landmark can serve as a sign or warning for gentrification; historic designations in some New York neighborhoods were founded to decrease affordability for renters.[129] At the same time, historic preservation can and has been used to preserve affordability in places like Golden Belt in Durham and Pilsen in Chicago.[130] This works by protecting properties, people, art, and culture. But in order for preservation to truly work, advocates have to see themselves as activists, fighting not only for protection of physical structures in historic neighborhoods, but also the people connected to those neighborhoods.[131]

---

128 Dan Immergluck, "Sustainable for Whom? Green Urban Development, Environmental Gentrification, and the Atlanta Beltline," *Urban Geography* 39, no. 4 (August 2017): 546–562.

129 Brian J. McCabe, and Ingrid Gould Ellen, "Does Preservation Accelerate Neighborhood Change? Examining the Impact of Historic Preservation in New York City," *Journal of the American Planning Association* 82, no. 2 (2016):134-146.

130 Amanda Abrams, "Using Preservation to Stop Gentrification Before It Starts," Bloomberg CityLab, December 14, 2016; Lori Rotenberk, "Can Historic Preservation Cool Down a Hot Neighborhood?" Bloomberg CityLab, June 20, 2019.

131 Katherine H. Hatfield, "How The Music City is Losing Its Soul: Gentrification in Nashville and How Historic Preservation Could Hinder the

Heritage tourism, which involves tourists staying longer and spending more time experiencing historical sites and artifacts, is a critical component of how cities gain their reputation and demonstrates the need for some form of preservation. But even if historic preservation prevents certain buildings from being redeveloped, it also means that things like renovations and extensions are off limits. Preservation is also a factor in increasing the value of property (and therefore property taxes). At the same time, restricting renovations for these homes may result in lost capital and opportunity for residents wishing to expand.[132] It all presents a very conflicting narrative on the idea of preservation, which is all the more reason to be cautious and methodical in pairing affordability and zoning measures.

In South Nashville, historic preservation in Edgehill has been a recent topic of interest. Edgehill was the sight of two Union forts and a contraband camp during the Civil War. After the war, formerly enslaved folks remained in the neighborhood and created and maintained a successful community.[133] However, the construction of I-65 and I-40 secluded the neighborhood, and urban renewal and the Music Row expansion contributed to the neighborhood's decline. For the past few

---

Process," (master's thesis, Middle Tennessee State University, May 2018), 74-78.

132   Dan Bertolet, "When Historic Preservation Clashes with Housing Affordability," Sightline, December 19, 2017; Siri Mackenzie Olson, "Overlapping Historic Preservation and Affordable Housing: Successful Outcomes in New York City and San Francisco," (master's thesis, Columbia University, May 2018): 17-23.

133   Michelle Ness. "A Short History of Edgehill," The Edgehill Neighborhood Coalition, January 2015; "Edgehill NCZO Design Guidelines," Metropolitan Historic Zoning Commission, accessed June 28, 2020.

years, the city has been considering a preservation and con-servation zoning overlay for Edgehill, which has split public opinion. On one hand, doing so would protect the neighbor-hood's integrity and character. On the other, it would prevent barriers related to affordability and the desires of residents, about 30 percent of whom are over the age of sixty-five.[134]

Brian McCabe, a sociologist at Georgetown, comments of the phenomenon of preservation-induced gentrification: "After a neighborhood is designated, in the coming years and decades, we see a definite increase in the socioeconomic status of the neighborhood relative to nearby neighborhoods: Wealthier people are moving in people with a higher level of college education. [...] But we actually don't see any evidence of racial turnover in those neighborhoods. This remains an interest-ing, puzzling finding for us because typically socioeconomic change and racial change in cities go hand in hand."[135]

* * *

RESOLUTIONS

Nashville, despite producing countless musicians, isn't a superstar city. And it shouldn't try to be. It has built a rather diverse economy around healthcare, tourism, education, entertainment, and logistics. But as economic activity and

---

134 J.R. Lind, "Historic Buildings in Nashville's Black Neighborhoods Are Disappearing," The Nashville Scene, September 24, 2020; "Edgehill State of Emergency," The Edgehill Story Project, accessed June 28, 2020; Sandy Mazza, "South Nashville community bitterly split over plan to restrict development," The Tennessean, last modified August 3, 2018.

135 Jack Denton, "Is Landmarking a Tool of Gentrification or a Bulwark Against It?" Pacific Standard, July 3, 2019.

industries such as tech and finance pick up, the potential for increased inequality and gentrification become more real.

To combat this, Nashville should focus on its local community to educate and empower. Projects and organizations like the temporary Build Better Tables exhibit (which drew attention to the effects of urban development and gentrification on community wellness), Stand Up Nashville, and Homes For All are a few different examples of community education and empowerment. Policy-wise, the city should look to build more affordable housing, focus of connecting neighborhoods and transit, and commit to mixed-income communities.

Atlanta is already on the right track by thinking about and investing in connected spaces. While equity and speculative real estate development have already proved to be an issue, the city is in a position to do more good than bad, especially since it's expected to grow in population. A focus on expanding walkable neighborhoods, public transit, and updating zoning and financing laws are a few key ways Atlanta can combat displacement. Another major hurdle the city faces is how to properly incorporate lessons from the BeltLine's earlier stages in the future, such as tax allocation districts. The Grove Park Foundation, the Partnership for Southern Equity, Gangstas to Growers, and the Community Movement Builders are a few of the many neighborhood and community development organizations working toward empowerment.

New Orleans, of course, is a resilient city. It has one of the most vibrant and unique atmospheres of all American cities, and should look to maintain that. To control the impact of tourism, the city should continue to limit short-term rentals and invest and protect low- and moderate-income communities. Above all, a focus on place-keeping and local empowerment is crucial. Leading this charge is design firm Colloqate Design and organizations like Jane Place Neighborhood Sustainability Initiative and 504 Ward.

* * *

For most of the country's history, the South has been entrenched in extreme segregation, racism, discrimination, and tension. Economic turmoil following the Civil War were exaggerated in South and, year by year, more southerners—both rich and poor, Black and white—left in pursuit of a better life. They relocated to the north and to the west, with many settling in the middle of the country. As they left, they brought with them their cultures, traditions, and ideals, which gives insight into the feel of the Midwest.

6

THE MIDWEST

———

When I first moved to Indiana for college, I was utterly disappointed. Beyond my own ignorance and naïveté, I expected the Midwest to be more substantial; but to me the landscapes were desolate, the architecture bland, and the people confusing. I welcomed the slower pace of life, accepting that the move was temporary and voluntary, but it soon became too slow for my liking. The Midwestern life felt like a more relaxed and progressive version of the South: lots of agriculture, even more pride, and Midwestern niceness. And for every Midwestern city I'd visit, I always detected an unexplainable nostalgia for the "glory days" by residents. Coming from the confrontational and vocal Northeast, I found the Midwest to be nuanced, conservative, and prevaricated.

The Midwest encompasses much of the Great Plains region and the states surrounding the Great Lakes. The mostly flat land is traversed by the Mississippi, Ohio, and Missouri Rivers, which all helped spur economic development and industrialization in the eighteenth and nineteenth centuries. Even before European settlement, farming and agriculture were common. This earned the Midwest the title "America's Breadbasket." Today the Midwest is responsible for an overwhelming share of corn, soybean, wheat, and barley production, as well as livestock. In addition to agriculture, the region has had a fair share of cities specializing in manufacturing and industrial production and, for this reason, is also referred to as the "Rust Belt."

* * *

CHICAGO, ILLINOIS

Chicago, the biggest and most famous Midwestern city, got its jump as the transportation and distribution hub for the entire region, and grew rapidly as European immigrants settled in. The Great Chicago Fire in 1871 decimated around 18,000 buildings and left over 100,000 residents without a home, but it allowed for a construction boom that jumpstarted the economy and population growth.[136] The city's close ties to agriculture and regional manufacturing further cemented Chicago's authority in the national and global economy. Their economy has since expanded to include finance, commerce, technology, and education, among others. Within this growth, Chicago has become known as the city of neighborhoods and has gained a reputation for crime and corruption. Today, Chicago has one of the wealthiest and most diversified economies in the world, coupled with an alarming gap in economic and social inequality.

---

136 "Chicago Fire of 1871," *History.com*, last modified August 21, 2018.

MINNEAPOLIS/TWIN CITIES, MINNESOTA

Situated between the Mississippi, Minnesota, and St. Croix Rivers, the Twin Cities area is home to over 3.5 million people, sixteen of the Fortune 500 companies, an interlinked Skyway system for pedestrians, and the best park system in the country.[137] Together, Minneapolis and St. Paul form the Twin Cities. Minneapolis is the most populous city in Minnesota, and St. Paul the state capital. Minneapolis was started by Scandinavian immigrants who used the nearby St. Anthony Falls to power saw and flour mills, and St. Paul grew around small settlements that had access to a harbor and eventually, railways. The draw of Fort Snelling gave settlers another reason to come, yet the two cities stood for and attracted different types of settlers: Minneapolis attracted younger, Lutheran, Scandinavian, and relatively liberal folks; St. Paul attracted older, more conservative Catholics and Irish immigrants and entrepreneurs.[138] This difference in ideologies blossomed into tension and rivalry between the cities up until the 1960s and encapsulated the individual character and histories of each city. This runs hand-in-hand with the "Minnesota paradox," a term describing the giant racial disparities that exist today.

DETROIT, MICHIGAN

Detroit was founded by the French in 1701 as a fur trading post and was populated by French colonists who came from Louisiana and Canada (many lured by French promises of

---

137 David Johnson, "These American Cities Have the Best Public Park Systems in the Country," *Time*, May 25, 2018; "Data Comparison: Minneapolis, MN & St. Paul, MN," DataUSA.io, accessed May 20. 2020.

138 Joy K. Lintelman, "Swedish Immigration to Minnesota," MNOpedia, last modified October 7, 2019

free land). Detroit was strengthened as a fort during the French & Indian War in 1756 before being transferred to British rule after defeat. It was further developed after the Iroquois Confederacy was defeated and routes developed through the Allegheny Ridge were utilized to encourage westward travel. In the eighteen hundreds, Detroit grew from industry and commerce, its strategic location, and influx of immigrants. In the nineteen hundreds, the rise of the automotive industry and manufacturing granted Detroit the title "Motor City." Despite its role in the Civil Rights Movement and strong entertainment culture, Detroit has had a strong history of segregation (for example, the 1941 construction of the Detroit Wall). Recently, the city experienced one of the largest declines in the history of cities, due to growing disparities, concentrated poverty, and deindustrialization.

* * *

THE GREAT MIGRATION(S)

Again, the Great Migration can be divided into two waves. The first, from 1916 to 1940, saw 1.6 million Black Americans left the South. The second, from 1940 to 1970, saw an additional 5 million Americans leaving the South.[139] But folks were leaving the Reconstruction-era South even before the Great Migration technically started, and in 1919 more than thirty-five cities across the country had seen race riots stemming from ethnic tensions and white supremacist terrorism. The summer of 1919 became known as the Red Summer,

---

139 "The Great Migration," History.com, last modified January 16, 2020.

as hundreds of Black Americans were lynched, burned, or killed.[140] At the time, the country was coming out of the Red Scare (widespread fear of communism and anarchism) and World War I, and white America was anxious and fearful of any changes in the status quo.

The introduction of Black southerners into northern cities did mark a pivotal moment in the history of urban settings, however. In the Midwest, southerners moved to Michigan, Ohio, Illinois, and Indiana more than anywhere else; these states offered new industrial and manufacturing jobs that supported wartime services. It represented a time in which—despite constant *de jure* and *de facto* segregation—the right to vote, learn, work, and earn better wages were extended to newcomers. The Great Depression stunted the flow of southerners, but that inital influx was sustained for decades to come.

The decades following the war were also marked by interstate highways, suburbanization, white flight, rise of the automobile, and American consumerism. As Leah Boustan, a professor of economics, writes in a 2007 paper about the connection between postwar suburbanization and white flight in the wake of the Great Migration, "The best causal estimates imply that each black arrival led to 2.7 white departures."[141] This correlation has more to do with the residential freedoms and restrictions of white and Black residents respectively than it does with Black folks displacing white folks in cities.

---

140 Jesse J. Holland, "Hundreds of Black Deaths During 1919's Red Summer are Being Remembered," PBS.org, July 23, 2019.

141 Leah Platt Boustan, "Was Postwar Suburbanization 'White Flight'? Evidence From the Black Migration," National Bureau of Economic Research, October 2007.

In another paper, Boustan, this time with economics professor Robert Margo, found that 26 percent of the national increase in Black homeownership rates can be attributed to white flight and suburbanization.[142] By the 1980s, the effect of the Great Migration had shown itself in racial splits within metropolitan areas: 33 percent of white families lived in central cities, compared to 72 percent of Black families. Aside from just cities, the geographic spread of Black families was drastically different—47 percent of Black families lived in the northern and western parts of the country, a huge increase compared to the 90 percent living in the South before the migration.[143]

RACIALLY RESTRICTIVE HOUSING COVENANTS

Throughout the country, racially restrictive covenants were intentionally included in property deeds as a way to maintain neighborhood demographics. And while the degree of discrimination varied from city to city, they all were designed to prevent certain ethnic groups from entering an area. In 1910, Minneapolis became the first city to enact such covenants, writing, "premises shall not at any time be conveyed, mortgaged or leased to any person or persons of Chinese, Japanese, Moorish, Turkish, Negro, Mongolian or African blood or descent."[144] Eventually, this type of language was worked into deeds across the city, and as a result, minority populations,

---

142 Leah P. Boustan, and Robert A. Margo, "A Silver Lining to White Flight? White Suburbanization and African-America Homeownership, 1940-1980," Boston University, August 2013.

143 Isabel Wilkerson, "The Long-Lasting Legacy of the Great Migration," *Smithsonian Magazine*, September 2016.

144 "What are Covenants?" Mapping Prejudice, accessed April 29, 2020.

especially Black folks, were cornered into a handful of neighborhoods, setting up the framework for racial segregation and spatial patterns of belonging.

The advent of the Homeowners Land Owners Corporation and redlining soon fueled the use of these covenants to promote segregation and neighborhood stability. By 1940, every federally funded housing development was required to include racial restrictions. As J.T. Wardlaw wrote in the Minneapolis Star in 1944, these covenants pushed minorities into areas that were once redlined, eliminating any chance for financing to buy or rent property: "the already inflated price is made higher for Negro prospects ... [the policies] are the tools used to depress homeownership among Negroes."[145] By 1946, 60 percent of Minnesota residents surveyed felt that Black people should not be permitted the freedom to live anywhere, and 64 percent would decline a sale to them, even if they offered more money than white buyers.[146]

But Black folks weren't the only targets of these covenants and discriminatory sentiments. Restricted housing locations also cornered Jewish residents into certain parts of the city. This is known as **racial steering**—a practice that still happens today—and refers to the racially motivated decisions by brokers and real estate agents to steer buyers toward or away a certain neighborhood. Northern Minneapolis became one of the only places where Jewish

---

145 Ibid.
146 "The Negro and His Home in Minnesota," The Governor's Interracial Commission, June 1, 1947.

residents and businesses were allowed to exist.[147] This barrier from integration and community led to Minneapolis being crowned the "capital of anti-Semitism in the United States" in 1946.[148]

It wasn't until World War II and the 1948 case *Shelley v. Kraemer* that these restrictions were ruled unconstitutional. But it's worth noting that many covenants remained in place until the 1968 passage of the Fair Housing Act. With the new ruling and changing attitudes, discrimination against and restriction of non-whites within neighborhoods was prohibited and unenforceable—but that didn't mean a complete integration could take place. Despite the reversal of the covenants on paper, the move was essentially symbolic. Decades' worth of these practices had already segregated Minneapolis and abolishing prior rules didn't automatically abolish the issue at hand. Patterns of residential segregation that existed in the mid-nineteen hundreds still remain in place today: Black Americans in the Twin Cities have the lowest rate of homeownership in the country, at 23 percent in 2015—down from 29 percent in 2005 and 35 percent in 1990.[149]

As real estate remains one of the primary ways families accumulate wealth in America, racially restrictive covenants and discriminatory real estate practices have contributed to the huge wealth gap in America. The wealth

---

147 Hannah Jones, "In 1930 Minneapolis, Not Just Anyone Got to be White," CityPages, July 24, 2018.

148 Kirsten Delegard, "'Gentiles Only'," Historyapolis, March 6, 2015.

149 Jim Buchta, "Already-Low Homeownership Rates of Twin Cities Minorities Fall Further," *StarTribune*, August 10, 2017.

of the average Black household is about one-tenth of that of white households. Exclusion from "intergenerational access to capital and finance," as a report out of Duke University writes, is a critical component in the wealth gap and disparity of homeownership that exists in the country today.[150]

Another practice that contributed to the housing gap was **contract buying**, occurring when real estate agents would sell homes to Black families with high down payments and interests rates. These families then had to make monthly payments and could be evicted at any time. Perhaps worst of all, buyers gained no equity on their homes; the homes and deeds did not belong to them until the contract was paid off and all other conditions were satisfied—only worsening the state of housing in America.

Contract buying was especially common on the West Side of Chicago, where as much as 95 percent of homes sold to Black families in the 1950s were sold on contract, with an average price markup of 84 percent. In neighborhoods like North Lawndale, the demographic split went from 87 percent white in 1950 to 91 percent Black in 1960, and one report found Black families in the 50s and 60s lost $3 to $4 billion dollars in wealth due to contract buying and other predatory housing terms.[151]

---

150 Darity, William Jr., Darrick Hamilton, Mark Paul, Alan Aja, Anne Price, Antonio Moore, and Caterina Chiopris, "What We Get Wrong About Closing the Racial Wealth Gap," Samuel Dubois Cook Center on Social Equity, April 2018.

151 "Contract Buying and Blockbusting," The Newberry, accessed May 12, 2020.

ZONING LAWS

The introduction of zoning in the United States enabled the calculated development of the American landscape. Separation of commercial and industrial areas from residential areas is a product of land use regulation, but such regulation has also been the playground for segregation and institutionalized discrimination. Zoning, a term sometimes used interchangeably with land-use planning, is the specific regulation of the types of activities permitted on land (as well as the size, placement, and development-type on specific parcels of land). Simply put, zoning is a part of land-use planning.

To help spur the development of cities and alleviate tensions between business owners and residents, the introduction of government planning was favored over free-market and unrestricted development. Adoption of government planning and zoning also facilitated ordinances for police jurisdictions and budgeting purposes across varying levels of government.[152] One of the first major documents to talk about zoning was the 1924 State Standard Zoning Enabling Act (SZEA), which laid the foundation for states to draft and implement their own zoning laws.

But as states and local governments began implementing comprehensive zoning ordinances, the influence of redlined maps made by the Home Owners Landowners Corporation and fraudulent political and social interests began taking form in the zoning policies themselves, as seen by the work of

---

152 Barlow D. Burke, *Understanding the Law of Zoning and Land Use Controls* (Newark: LexisNexus, 2002); Kurt H. Schindler, "Zoning and Police Power Ordinances are Not the Same, and Should Not Be Mixed Together," Michigan State University Extension, June 19, 2014.

influential and racist city planner Harland Bartholomew.[153] As urban planner and activist Yale Rabin found in his research, "While northern Progressives were enacting zoning as a mechanism for protecting and enhancing property values, southern Progressives were testing its effectiveness as a means of enforcing racial segregation."[154]

In the 1917 case *Buchanan v. Warley*, the Supreme Court ruled a racial zoning ordinance in Louisville, Kentucky (that prohibited the sale of property to Black folks in white neighborhoods) was unconstitutional by the Fourteenth Amendment. In lieu of this ruling, many states and local governments started employing "expulsive zoning," which was a legally defensible way of allowing disruptive and incompatible land uses (such as dump sites and treatment facilities) into Black neighborhoods. This transition established a zoning legacy that placed adverse and discriminatory impacts on Black and, soon, other minority and low-income neighborhoods. As time went on, this race-based planning manifested into things like the siting of public housing projects, discriminatory real estate practices, slum clearing, highway construction, and physical barriers between neighborhoods.

This racialized way of thinking is still happening today. It lends itself to toxic and heavy industrial sites choosing the path of least resistance (in other words, poor and minority communities) in determining new plant locations. They seek this path out because residents are less likely to have

153 Diana Budds, "Will Upzoning Neighborhoods Make Homes More Affordable?" Curbed, January 30, 2020.

154 Christopher Silver, "The Racial Origins of Zoning in American Cities," Arizona State University, accessed May 15, 2020.

the resources and power to contest their construction. Researchers from the University of Michigan and the University of Montana analyzed data about the placement of hazardous waste sites in America, finding "a consistent pattern over a thirty-year period of placing hazardous waste facilities in neighborhoods where poor people and people of color live." This is troubling because facilities emit toxic chemicals, contaminate local water and resource supplies, and intentionally look to operate in low income and minority communities. Another study from the same researchers found that more than half of people that live within three kilometers of a hazardous waste facility are people of color.[155]

Oftentimes, residents and developers alike favor single-use zoning (as opposed to mixed-use zoning), which is when parts of a city are blocked off for a singular development type—residential, commercial, industrial, etc. Jenny Schuetz, a housing expert at the Brookings Institute, commented on this desired homogeneity: "It was 'single-family neighborhoods should only have single-family detached homes' and a lot of this is about preserving the property values of those homes. [Single-family residential zoning] was about keeping away things that are considered undesirable uses, which might lower property values. There was also some pretty blatant intent to exclude lower-income families, renters, and non-white families." Awareness surrounding expulsive and racialized zoning—especially as it pertains to the proximity of toxic and hazardous facilities—has amplified the need for

---

155 Jim Erickson, "Targeting Minority, Low-Income Neighborhoods for Hazardous Waste Sites," University of Michigan News, January 19, 2016.

and movement of environmental justice and Indigenous sovereignty.

This intent to prevent encapsulates the very framework of **NIMBYism** (short for Not In My Backyard), a viewpoint which consists of stark opposition by residents of a neighborhood to local development. NIMBYism is cut from the same cloth used to deter certain industries, land uses, and residents of color from a desirable neighborhood. This card is played by homeowners and renters who support strict land regulation and oppose new housing developments, infrastructure projects, and social and rehabilitation services in their neighborhoods. Many researchers have found it to be a sort of insurance for homeowners and business owners, as it's common among all age groups, political parties, and demographics.[156] The power of NIMBYism is not to be underestimated; a simple Google search for news related to it will reveal its pervasiveness.

Reasons for staunch opposition stems almost entirely from self-interest and desire to preserve communal identity. These reasons include fear of increased noise, light, and air pollution, traffic, adverse effects on local property values, business, and neighborhood character, and an influx of lower-income, dangerous, and demographically different groups of people. Multiple studies have found that stricter land use regulations are common and preferred among whiter and more affluent communities. In fact, in many neighborhoods across the country, wealthier residents

---

156 Emily Badger, "The Bipartisan Cry of 'Not in My Backyard'," *New York Times*, August 21, 2018

voluntarily choose to pay additional fees and taxes to partake in things like Homeowners' Associations (which work to maintain uniformity, enforce strict guidelines and land uses, and limit individual expression).[157]

* * *

Zoning, in many ways, enables the foundational understanding of a city for us. This understanding is reflected in unspoken rules that dictate which neighborhoods we avoid, where we go to shop, the "way to work," and even the desire for tourists and visitors to stay in certain neighborhoods. Our perception of which neighborhoods belong to which land use and/or racial group many be useful in some ways, but problematic in others.

A study by Maria Krysan from the University of Illinois in Chicago and Michael Bader from the University of Michigan looked at racial blind spots in community knowledge. They interviewed white, Black, and Latinx residents in the Chicago Metropolitan Area on their perceived barriers to residential mobility. They found that community knowledge varies by race, which is to say that the mental maps of residents—which are formed by social networks, media, and personal experiences—reflect the perception of where residents can and would live.[158] Having such blind spots poses a threat of

---

157 Jessica Trounstine, "The Geography of Inequality: How Land Use Regulation Produces Segregation," *American Political Science Review* 114, no. 2 (May 2020): 443–455.

158 Krysan, Maria, and Michael D. M. Bader, "Racial Blind Spots: Black-White-Latino Differences in Community Knowledge," *Social Problems* 56, no. 4 (2009): 677–701.

reinforced discrimination and stereotyping, especially as a result of lacking or misinformed knowledge.

At the same time, knowledge of specific neighborhoods might imply there is something noteworthy about them. In the case of ethnic enclaves or majority-minority neighborhoods, the sense of belonging can stem from being surrounded by folks with similar ethnic or personal backgrounds. Such might be the case with Detroit, where almost 80 percent of the city's population is Black.

MAJORITY-MINORITY LANDSCAPES

In 2019, I attended a conference in Detroit and, aside from the professional aspects, I was excited to experience the great city my friends had boasted about. The conference was for the National Society of Black Engineers (NSBE), an organization I spent four years of leadership with, and all attendees had access to a digital guidebook. To my surprise, the most useful thing about the guidebook wasn't the agenda, but the list of Black-owned restaurants, shops, and services in the city. Here was an example of connecting local for-us, by-us businesses with thousands of visitors. In between workshops and sessions, we were able to pull out the guidebook, pull up on a Black-owned spot, and choose to circulate our hard-earned coin into the local economy.

The idea of Black-owned everything was a staple in NSBE, but even then it varied by city. For example, supporting Black businesses in Detroit was easier than in Indianapolis, and part of that reason has to do with the demographics and identity of the city. And as cities and neighborhoods change—either because of in-migration, out-migration, gentrification, or what-have-you—the fate and strength of Black and other minority-owned businesses are left in limbo.

An influx of any group brings changes to a community. As mentioned in Chapter 4, college-aged residents desire dining and leisure establishments, whereas residents of a particular ethnic background might desire grocery stores and services that pertain and cater to them. In Detroit, pressures from a changing population and economy are coming down on Black business owners in the downtown core, and considering that Detroit has the fastest growing suburbanization process among Black residents, Black businesses in the central city may continue to face financial troubles.[159]

The principle of giving tax breaks to major corporations and institutions, in some cases, has been shown to increase taxes on small and minority-owned businesses, many of whom may already be struggling and playing catch-up.[160] As more companies and wealthier residents move into a neighborhood, the cost of running a business, in addition to cost of

---

159 Deirdre McPhillips, "A New Analysis Finds Growing Diversity in U.S. Cities," US News, January 22, 2020; Joe T. Darden, "Black Access to Suburban Housing in America's Most Racially Segregated Metropolitan Area: Detroit," University of Toronto, Centre for Urban and Community Services, June 27, 2014.

160 Alyssa Wiltse-Ahmad, "Study: Gentrification And Cultural Displacement Most Intense in America's Largest Cities, And Absent From Many Others," National Community Reinvestment Coalition, March 18, 2019; Amy Saltzman, "New Research Illustrates the Struggles Facing Black Entrepreneurs in the South," ProsperyNow, July 20, 2017; Khanyi Molomo, "The Unique Challenges Faced By Black Business Owners," Big Cartel (blog). February 18, 2020.

living, can increase. Cultural establishments in Detroit such as Spectacles, Mo' Better Blues, the Tangerine Room, and Café D'Mongo's Speakeasy have already started feeling the heat from rising rents, evictions, and fraudulent lease agreements.[161] Still, in a country where the number of Black-majority cities has almost tripled since 1970, consequences from things like white flight, suburbanization, population growth, and displacement present an uncertain future for Black-owned business.[162]

A 2020 report from the Brookings Institute found that top-rated restaurants in Black neighborhoods accumulate revenue growth at slower paces that those in different neighborhoods—resulting in as much as $3.9 billion in unrealized annual revenue. The study pulled from Yelp's public database and the National Establishment Time Series database to find correlations between Yelp reviews and growth. Businesses in Black neighborhoods receive both fewer and lower Yelp reviews than other neighborhoods, a link that helps to explain not only why these businesses appear to struggle more, but also demonstrates how much weight Yelp reviews carry. Andre Perry, a lead author, remarks, "Our sense of location is so tainted by our associations with race, we're missing out on investing in neighborhoods that already have good food, good services, good retail."[163]

161 Kimberly Hayes Taylor, "Gentrification of Detroit Leaves Black-Owned Businesses Behind," *NBC News*, November 1, 2015.
162 Perry, Andre and David Harshbarger, "The Rise of Black-Majority Cities," The Brookings Institute, February 26, 2019.
163 Perry, Andre M., Jonathan Rothwell, and David Harshbarger, "Five-Star Reviews, One-Star Profits: The Devaluation of Businesses in Black Communities," Brookings Institute, February 18, 2020.

Still, Detroit remains a hotbed for new startups, especially for Black entrepreneurs, and is ranked fourth in the country for Black-owned businesses. The redevelopment and revival of Midtown and Cass Corridor is welcomed and encouraged by many, but has allowed for new business owners, employers, and residents to side-step and ignore the city's history and culture. This has given rise to a tale of two Detroits: one that is full of new developments and construction, trendy startups, and urban farming driven by white, wealthy young folks in redeveloped city centers and outer suburbs, and another that is struck with poverty, crime, neglect, and migration to closer suburbs, driven mainly by Black folks.[164]

DEINDUSTRIALIZATION

A large portion of the Midwest falls into the Rust Belt, which extends past Ohio and Pennsylvania into parts of New York. This stretch of the country got its push when small centers of manufacturing began large-scale production and transportation of goods and raw materials. The manufacturing of things like cars, weapons, and industrial parts was enabled by easy access to raw materials like iron ore (from Minnesota, Wisconsin, and Michigan), coal (from Appalachia), and steel (made using iron and coal). Proximity to the Great Lakes and road, water, and railroad networks allowed Rust Belt cities to expand their access to wider markets.[165] Factories soon opened all across the region, which became known as the

---

164 Francesca Spigarolo, "A Tale of Two Cities: Detroit, Between Collapse and Renaissance," August 29, 2016. Laboratory for the Governance of the City as a Commons, August 29, 2016; Joseph P. Williams, "A Tale of Two Motor Cities," *U.S. News*, January 22, 2020.

165 James Chen, "Rust Belt." Investopedia, last modified August 25, 2020.

industrial hub of America, and workers from the South and immigrants from Europe provided required labor.

After WWII, companies like Standard Oil, U.S. Steel, and General Motors (based in Cleveland, Pittsburg, and Detroit, respectively) walked the line of monopoly status, resulting from large market shares and lack of competition. In 1950, the Rust Belt was home to 43 percent of all jobs and half of all manufacturing jobs; market shares for Rust Belt auto, steel, and rubber industries hovered near 90 percent.[166] As a result, these corporations had little incentive to continue innovating or increase productivity of their factories. In addition, most of the states and industries in the Rust Belt had large labor unions, such as the United Steelworkers and the United Auto Workers, advocating for better wages and working conditions—both of which increased production costs for companies. Along with rising labor costs, industrial automation, reduced demand for steel and iron, and relaxed foreign trade policies, the decline of these industrial and manufacturing centers was well under way.

Part of the weak competitive environment that existed in the Rust Belt was due to companies and their unions lobbying the government to protect them from competition.[167] Research shows that the longer an industry lacks competition, the weaker that industry eventually becomes. As com-

---

166 Lee E. Ohanian, "Competition and the Decline of the Rust Belt," Federal Reserve Bank of Minneapolis, December 20, 2014.

167 Holmes, Thomas J., and James A. Schmitz, "Competition and Productivity: A Review of Evidence," *Annual Review of Economics* 2, no. 1 (2010): 619-642; Alder, Simeon, David Lagakos, and Lee Ohanian, "The Decline of the U.S. Rust Belt: A Macroeconomic Analysis," Center for Quantitative Economic Research, August 2014.

panies lacked the desire to innovate and improve, foreign players increased their share of the markets. By the 1980s, decline had shown itself in a number of ways—but none more indicative than September 19, 1977, also known as Black Monday, when the closure of Youngstown Sheet and Tube in Ohio resulted in over 40,000 jobs being lost overnight.[168]

I got a chance to sit down with Pete Saunders, a journalist who has written extensively about cities in the Rust Belt, and more importantly, is a proud champion of the Midwest. On speaking about why midwestern cities fell and remain behind other cities, he notes, "Our cities have lagged because our economies have lagged, and they have not made the full transition to the global knowledge economy that coastal cities have. And I also think that they are tied by their legacy of segregation, that is actually very different from what southern cities experience, but it's just as debilitating."

In Detroit, the decline was especially devastating. Around the time of the second world war, Detroit had already established itself as the Motor City, with companies like Ford, General Motors, and Chrysler all based in the city. The postwar economic boom increased demand for cars—which brought a population boom to the city—but when production of parts shifted to the South and overseas in the 1970s and 80s, so too did the vast majority of workers. This economic and population decline created a spiraling effect for Detroit; over 600,000 residents left the city between 1950 and 1980.[169]

---

168 Vince Guerrieri, "On The 40th Anniversary Of Youngstown's Black Monday, An Oral History," *BeltMag*, September 19, 2017.

169 Scott Beyer, "Why Has Detroit Continued To Decline?" *Forbes*, July 31, 2018.

EDS AND MEDS

On the other hand, some Rust Belt and Midwestern cities were able to adapt to the decline by diversifying their economies. Some also utilized the presence of anchor institutions, which play a central role in their local communities and economies. In fact, many American cities leverage higher education institutions and medical facilities—also known as eds and meds—to supplement their local economies. In cities like DC, San Diego, Philadelphia, and Memphis, eds and meds make up more than half of employers in the city. The presence of these institutions helps create jobs, attract businesses, recruit educated and higher-income residents, improve local knowledge bases, and beef up a city's reputation, allowing them to have a greater influence in how a community and neighborhood evolves.[170]

For example, the University of Chicago, located in Hyde Park in the South Side of the city, has been a driver of sorts for the community. UChicago, which enrolls about 15,000 students and employs 17,000 faculty and staff, opened a public medical center in 1927, forged partnerships with several research laboratories, and started the Laboratory Schools in 1896 for K-12 education.[171] And while its impact has been mostly limited to its direct campus and surrounding area, the university has taken steps to expand its influence.

---

170 Ira Harkay and Harmon Zuckerman, "Eds and Meds: Cities' Hidden Assets," The Brookings Institution, Center on Urban & Metropolitan Policy, August 1999; Timothy J. Bartik, and George Erickcek. "The Local Economic Impact of 'Eds & Meds'," Metropolitan Policy Program at Brookings Institute, December 2008.

171 Meagan M. Ehlenz, and Eugenie L. Birch, "The Power of Eds and Meds" University of Pennsylvania Institute for Urban Research, July 2014.

In 2012, the university launched a revitalization effort for the 53rd Street retail district. As David Greene, Executive Vice President for UChicago, stated in a *New York Times* interview: "Over the years and particularly in the 1950s and 60s, there was a lot of development aimed at creating a barrier around the campus. We're now trying to reverse that trend."[172] UChicago committed resources to redevelop the area, which now includes Harper Court (a mixed-use development with 77,000 square feet of retail, office space, a parking garage, and a hotel), Harper Theater (a redeveloped cineplex with two restaurants, four theaters, and a hub for the school's Innovation Exchange), and the Akira Building (a redeveloped two-story building with a gastropub, entertainment venue, yoga studio, and retail space). But stories of success, like the one of East 53rd Street, are a stark comparison of the university's influence in the past.

The Great Depression and housing shortages during WWII changed Hyde Park's demographics. Affluent, white families started leaving the soon blighted and overcrowded neighborhood, just as Black families moved in. In the 1950s, the Hyde Park-Kenwood Community Conference and the South East Side Commission (two organizations affiliated with the university) worked with city officials to designate almost 900 acres for urban renewal. By the mid-60s, the Black population had declined by 40 percent and median incomes rose by almost 70 percent. This change was enabled by amendments to the 1954 Housing Act, which allowed universities in urban renewal efforts.

---

172 Robert Sharoff, "University of Chicago Works on Its Neighborhood," *New York Times*, October 23, 2012.

Today, however, UChicago has spearheaded community and civic engagement efforts in Hyde Park through initiatives for public safety and community health, arts and culture, economic opportunities and leadership training, and integrated education and development. The power of eds and meds is evident across the Midwest—such as Cleveland Clinic and Case Western Reserve University in Cleveland, the Central Corridor Anchor Partnership in the Twin Cities, or the University of Michigan in Ann Arbor—and play a key role in how cities and neighborhoods change.

* * *

RESOLUTIONS

Many Rust Belt cities that declined in the late-twentieth century should take measures to foster development, entrepreneurship, and competition within industries. For minority-owned businesses, cities should look to offer things like tax abatement programs and services to education and entrepreneurs. Furthermore, cities in the Midwest should cherish and utilize their anchor institutions. Not only do they attract industry, working-class, and educated populations, but they also have significant resources and offerings to help support the community. Many anchor institutions make use of what's known as PILOTs (payment in lieu of taxes). This means they forego paying property taxes and instead offer charitable payments, municipal services, technical assistance, and partnerships—many of which are less than the comparable real estate taxes. For this reason, along with lobbying for project support, cities need to ensure that the values of institutions align with city values (while being careful to not become too dependent on these types of institutions).

Supporting local hiring efforts by these anchor institutions is also critical. Omar Blaik, CEO and founder of U3 Ventures, highlighted the importance of doing so in an interview with NextCity, "In Detroit, the average family income of Midtown was $20,000. The average salary of the anchor institutions was $50,000. What does that mean? Everybody that works there lives elsewhere, and there's no connection to the place they are in. The more you hire from the local community or buy from your city or encourage people to live around you, the more those two numbers will not be as far apart as they are now."[173] Blaik also went on to point out that of the $1.7 billion procurement of institutions in Detroit, 95 percent was sourced from outside the city—meaning these institutions were spending a vast majority of their money on services and goods that came from far away instead of from within the local ecosystem.

In Chicago, initiatives such as the Folded Map Project (which utilizes the city's symmetrical grid plan to introduce residents with corresponding addresses), Borderless, the Sweet Water Foundation, the Pilsen Alliance, the Institute of Community Empowerment, and the Chicago Housing Initiative are a few examples of organizations dedicated to empowerment, education, and equity in Chicago.

---

173 Bill Bradley, "The Evolving Role of Eds and Meds," NextCity, October 14, 2013.

In the Twin Cities area, the Center for Urban and Regional Affairs (CURA) at the University of Minnesota (which hosts a dozen of programs and sponsored research such as the Artists Neighborhood Partnership Initiative and the Kris Nelson Community-Based Research Program), the Center for Economic Inclusion, and the Housing Justice Center are examples of local organizations working to help the community.

In Detroit, where residents aren't being as displaced like in other cities, efforts to promote economic development and investing in low-income communities should be of utmost priority, as there isn't a housing shortage in metro Detroit.[174] The Motor City has an affordability and opportunities problem, and its concentration of poverty requires a deeper look into ways of reversing patterns of economic decline. New industries and companies are returning to Detroit, and projects and organizations such as Invest Detroit, Data-Driven Detroit, Community Development Advocates of Detroit, Interboro, and the Kresge Innovative Projects are spearheading equitable change in the city.

* * *

The Midwest serves as the backdrop for many phases throughout American history: the American Revolution, the Civil War, the Great Migration, growth of cities, and decades of change following both World Wars. For the most part,

---

174 "Growing Detroit's African-American Middle Class," Detroit Future City, February 2019; "American Neighborhood Change in the 21st Century: Gentrification and Decline," University of Minnesota, accessed May 13, 2020.

however, early American history did not extend to the western half of the country. There, development and evolution of the landscape differs from much of the country, which might help explain why it remains distinguished in its atmosphere and share of urban challenges.

7

THE WEST

———

"To live in a contemporary gentrifying city is simultaneously to experience the packaging of place as well as the loss of it. There is, simultaneously, there and the loss of there."

RACHEL BRAHINSKY [175]

———

My life changed when I first heard Kendrick Lamar's *Section.80* in 2011. The album revolved around the stories of two young women, delicately weaving commentary about racism, the crack epidemic, and drug dependency.[176] *Section.80* piqued my interest in the history of drugs, economics, housing, and a new type of hip-hop. Prior to that period, I was listening to newer, more mainstream hip-hop music. It wasn't until a bit later that I dug deeper into West Coast rap—Death Row records, G-Phunk, and Gangsta Rap—that I saw how music reflected larger social,

---

175 Rachel Brahinsky, "The Story of Property: Meditations on Gentrification, Renaming and Possibility," *Environment and Planning: Economy and Space* 52, no. 5 (January 2020): 837-855.

176 Kendrick Lamar, *Section.80*, recorded 2011, Top Dawg Entertainment, compact disc.

political, and economic attitudes. The resurgence of political and social themes in hip-hop in the past decade is a continuation of subject matter from Golden Era artists and groups like Public Enemy, Gil Scott-Heron, Common, Black Star, the Geto Boys, Killer Mike, Lupe Fiasco, Ice Cube, 2Pac, and Biggie.

During one of my first visits to LA I passed by Inglewood and Crenshaw, two neighborhoods I associated with Snoop Dogg and Nipsey Hussle. At once, I threw my favorite records on (to complete my urban experience). But as I got closer into Downtown, I passed by hundreds and hundreds of tents, all situated on the sidewalks of Skid Row. But these tents weren't like the ones sneakerheads and hypebeasts set up to wait for new sneakers or streetwear releases. These tents were permanent, and belonged to houseless folks.

Skid Row, as I later learned, has one the largest stable populations of houseless folks in the country, recently reporting an 11 percent population increase between 2018 and 2019.[177] LA county itself has an unsheltered population of 60,000 people and, despite efforts to improve conditions, Skid Row and houselessness remains. This isn't something new; houselessness has persisted in every decade since the Great Depression, and probably even before then. But just like the continuum of political and social themes in hip-hop music, houselessness is a facet that stems from this country's same troubling history and, like many other issues, is engrained into our urban fabric.

---

177 Nicholas Slayton, "Number of Homeless People on Skid Row Spikes by 11%," *Los Angeles Downtown News*, August 12, 2019.

* * *

This chapter focuses on three cities on the West Coast: Seattle, San Francisco, and Los Angeles. Together these three cities capture a lot of what the western half of the country has to offer: warm weather, beautiful nature, and tons of industry. Compared to the rest of the country, the West Coast's history isn't rooted in English colonization as much as it is in American expansion and postwar development, facilitated by things like gold, oil, and uncharted territory.

SEATTLE, WASHINGTON

Seattle's first major industry was timber and lodging, largely due to its proximity to tree stock. Its geographic location allowed it to be a major port city and shipbuilding center in the late-eighteen hundreds, which attracted many residents. As Chinese workers provided cheap and heavy industrial labor, increased racial tensions sparked a series of anti-Chinese riots in the 1880s. The Great Seattle Fire of 1889 destroyed much of the central business district, and while the fire triggered a rebuilding phase, a drop in gold reserves just four years later caused a citywide panic.[178] The Klondike Gold Rush ended the Panic of 1893, and led to the formation of many iconic American brands. Seattle got another economic boost from shipmaking during WWI, and the start of the Boeing Company around World War II brought airplane manufacturing into the local economy. Today, Seattle remains home to some of the biggest technology companies

---

178   Gregory Lewis McNamee, "Seattle," Brittanica, last modified September 21, 2017.

in the world, such as Microsoft and Amazon. Seattle has also been instrumental in nurturing early jazz and grunge rock music scenes.

SAN FRANCISCO, CALIFORNIA (SF)

San Francisco, together with Oakland and San Jose, forms the Bay Area, and serves as the heart of Northern California. SF got its independence from the Spanish in 1821 and was ceded to America after the Mexican-American War in the 1840s. The California Gold Rush in 1849 and influx of Forty-Niners into the area transformed it economy and landscape. A subsequent boom in other industries—such as banking—followed the rush. A disastrous earthquake in 1906 destroyed 75 percent of the city and left half the city on the streets, propelling the city into a period of rebuilding and major infrastructure projects, such as the Streetcar system in the 1920s and the Golden Gate Bridge in 1937.[179] During WWII, San Francisco became a popular port and base for soldiers before being shipped out to war. After the war, opposition to the Vietnam War and liberal attitudes pushed San Francisco to become the center of counterculture, the hippie movement, the sexual revolution, and the peace movement. The rise and presence of major banking and technology companies starting in the 90s added a new dimension to the Bay Area's liberal and cultural reputation. Today, SF has the highest salaries, disposable income, and median home values anywhere in the world.[180]

---

179 "San Francisco," History.com, last modified August 21, 2018.
180 Riya Bhattacharjee, "San Francisco Unseats Zurich as City with Highest Salaries and Most Disposable Income," NBC Bay Area, last modified May 22, 2019.

LOS ANGELES, CALIFORNIA (LA)

In 1542, Los Angeles was claimed by the Spanish empire during an expedition from Central America. By the late seventeen hundreds, LA became the largest Roman Catholic Archdiocese in the country. Much like the rest of California, the city remained under Spanish and Mexican control until the mid-1850s. Completion of railroad lines connected the city to the rest of the country and, along with the LA Aqueduct in 1913, helped support the city's growing population. In passing the country's first municipal zoning ordinance in 1908, the city designated three residential and seven industrial zones, which served to prohibit industries like oil-drilling, slaughterhouses, and tanneries from residential areas. The rise of Hollywood in the early nineteen hundreds kept the city afloat during the Great Depression, and shipbuilding and aircraft manufacturing during WWII brought the city an economic boom. Since then, Los Angeles has sprawled out into San Fernando Valley and grown to incorporate multiple townships and areas. Today, the Los Angeles area is the second most populous city in America, after New York City.

* * *

THE GOLD RUSH

In 1848, the discovery of gold in Coloma, California triggered a huge interest in large-scale gold production. Within a few years, upward of 300,000 people from across the world moved to the West in search of gold.[181] Effects on nearby

---

181 "California Gold Rush, 1848-1864," Learn California, accessed May 17, 2020.

towns were astronomical; the population of San Francisco jumped from 200 in 1846 to 36,000 in just six years.[182] But much of the greed surrounding the Gold Rush manifested itself in driving out Indigenous groups who worked with the lands to hunt, fish, and gather food. This influx of settlers was accompanied by capital, and required the construction and expansion of roads, transportation networks, agriculture, and public services (such as schools and churches). This rapid movement of people also led to narrow streets, something that still strains some cities today.

During this time, demand for railroad networks increased significantly, and desire to connect the West to the rest of the country steered railroad companies to hire thousands of new workers. But upon realizing the white labor pool was too scarce, companies started hiring Chinese workers (originally believed to be too weak for the job.)[183] Between 1863 and 1865, up to 20,000 Chinese workers helped build the Transcontinental Railroad—all were paid less and given worse housing accommodations than white workers. But as cities like San Francisco grew, so too did crime, corruption, and anti-immigrant sentiment; Committees of Vigilance often bullied city officials, kidnapped immigrants, and even lynched residents.[184] These attitudes

---

182 Amy Graff, "Boomtime: What San Francisco Looked Like at the End of the Gold Rush," SF Gate, last modified October 3, 2019.

183 Lesley Kennedy, "Building the Transcontinental Railroad: How 20,000 Chinese Immigrants Made It Happen," *History.com*, last modified April 30, 2020; Nadja Sayej, "'Forgotten by society' – How Chinese Migrants Built the Transcontinental Railroad," The Guardian, June 18, 2019; Hilton Obenzinger, "Geography of Chinese Workers Building the Transcontinental Railroad," Stanford University, 2018.

184 "San Francisco Gold Rush," SF Info, accessed June 14, 2020.

eventually culminated into race riots, exclusion acts, and harsh ideas of police and patrolling.

GHOST TOWNS, HOOVERVILLES, AND HOUSELESSNESS

Eventually, gold and mineral reserves in the West started to run dry, forcing miners and business to abandon settlements in search of better and more consistent work. These abandoned towns are physical reminders of our patterns of migration, especially those induced by economics and capitalism. These "ghost towns" can also result from things like flooding, decommissioned industrial works, and other economic or population downfalls. Ghost towns can be found around the world, and some, with surviving buildings or landmarks, have even become tourist attractions.

The Great Depression, as mentioned in Chapter 3, shook the country to its core. In fact, it seeped so deeply into the lives of Americans that new developments of tents, makeshift, and houseless communities popped up across the country. Scrambling for a place to stay, thousands of Americans huddled into shantytowns—also known as "Hoovervilles." Some of the biggest Hoovervilles, like the one in St. Louis, established churches, social institutions, and an organizational structure.[185] By 1960, many Hoovervilles, lodging houses, and other houseless settlements were destroyed as part of economic recovery and housing programs. But the issue of houselessness still remains in most American cities,

---

185 "Hoovervilles and Homeslessness," University of Washington, accessed
      May 17, 2020; "Great Depression Poverty," United States History for Kids,
      accessed May 17, 2020.

a testament to how far cities and the government have to go. Today, there are three types of houselessness:[186]

- chronic (those who have been houseless or in shelters for longer periods of time and may suffer from disabilities, old age, or substance abuse problems),
- transitional (those who are houseless for a short period of time and between life events, due to sudden or catastrophic upheaval), and
- episodic (those who float in and out of houselessness, likely due to chronic unemployment, mental and physical health issues, or substance abuse problems).

Other factors—domestic violence, environmental disasters, poverty, mental health, etc.—are prevalent in houselessness discussions. Evicted renters, returned veterans, and victims of abuse are among those who have and still remain in houseless communities—some in cities (like Skid Row), some in tent cities (like Camp Quixote in Olympia, Washington), and some in abandoned or unused buildings (known as squatters). Compounded with increased medical costs, strict zoning laws, shortage of affordable housing and shelter units, and anti-homeless laws (such as sit-lie, panhandling, and right-to-shelter laws), millions of Americans are left stranded on the streets every night.[187]

Some cities have turned to "hostile architecture," a term to describe benches, seating, bus stops, lighting, and other tactics intended to deter houseless folks, drug users, and

---

186 "Homelessness in America," National Coalition for the Homeless, accessed May 17, 2020.
187 Benjamin Schneider, "CityLab University: Understanding Homelessness in America," Bloomberg CityLab, last modified July 6, 2020.

loitering teenagers. Things like uncomfortable benches, seat dividers, anti-sleeping spikes in storefronts, and loud classical music are a few examples.[188] These semi-permanent structures disincentivize and discourage folks from interacting with a public space, and represent ill-adapted use of design.

Almost every major city employs what is called Greyhound therapy, or patient dumping, in which unsheltered populations are put on a bus and transported to other cities. Between 2010 and 2017, more than 20,000 houseless folks were bussed across the country.[189] Sometimes, cities use the guise of family reunification to justify this, but most cities fail to follow up and track where they're sending folks. As cities look to attract new developments and spur economic revitalization, they tend to evacuate, hide, and criminalize unsheltered folks. In doing so, they fail to address to the root issues of houselessness, which include a lack of affordable housing, social work and welfare, adequate employment and wages, and access to rehabilitation and treatment centers.

It isn't just cities and developers though. Every day, people consciously avoid looking, passing, and interacting with the houseless as they traverse a city, producing an "out-of-sight, out-of-mind" effect. But where ghost towns represent people abandoning the cities, houselessness presents almost the opposite phenomenon: it's cities abandoning its people. Now

---

188 Roman Mars, and Selena Savic, "Unpleasant Design & Hostile Architecture," August 5, 2015, In *99% Invisible*. Produced by Mars Roman. Podcast, MP3 audio, 18:49.
189 "Bussed Out: How America Moves Its Homeless," *The Guardian*, December 20, 2017.

the two aren't complete opposites, but both present a disconnect between supply and demand; between what's available and what's not.

GHETTOIZATION + PUBLIC SPACES

For almost every city I've been to, I've been warned about what areas to avoid. They were too Black, too violent, or too ghetto. It took a few years to really grasp that no matter the city, there always seemed to be an area that was worse than others. But how did something like ghettos become so common?

Prior to the Civil Rights Movement, collective action racism isolated minorities and poor communities, but the persistent concentration of these populations into ghettos wasn't a coincidence. Some researchers have found that as cities become bigger and denser, they can become more segregated, partly due to voluntary assembly and partly due to continued segregation and discrimination.[190]

But in LA, like many others, I had an internal association of ghettos with street gangs, and most of this can be attributed to portrayals in the media. I knew more about the Bloods, Crips, and Pirus in California than I did about gangs, mobs, and mafias in places I've actually lived. Regardless, the prevalence and influence of gang culture in LA is notorious and pronounced.[191]

---

190 "The Rise and Decline of the American Ghetto," National Bureau of Economic Research, accessed May 29, 2020.

191 Brown, Gregory Christopher, James Diego Vigil, and Eric Robert Taylor, "The Ghettoization of Blacks in Los Angeles: The Emergence of Street Gangs," *Journal of African American Studies* 16, no. 2 (2012): 209-25.

Foundation of street gangs in America lies at the intersection of education and resources (or lack thereof), poverty, and racism. Following the American Revolution, groups of mainly European immigrants emerged to contest various socioeconomic and political conditions (such as the Ku Klux Klan, the Forty Thieves, and the Spook Hunters). As migration patterns brought more immigrants (and thus, racial tensions) into cities, more gangs formed and organized. With advances in the Civil Rights Movement, the rise in social conscientiousness triggered a minor decline in gang activity among Black and minority populations. Groups like the Brown Berets and Black Panther Party replaced street gangs as organized movements that called for more strategic responses to brutality and racism.[192]

In the 1970s, politicians and police forces became increasingly threatened by these community groups and launched a series Counter Intelligence Programs to spy on, dismantle, jail, and assassinate important members. As these groups lost members and influence, street gangs picked back up, this time lacking the leadership and mobilization skills of the Black Panthers and Brown Berets.

Continued struggles for power, the War on Drugs, and disregard for officials paved the way for gangs to become more violent and territorial. Gang violence gained traction in the

---

192 James C. Howell, and John P. Moore, "History of Street Gangs in the United States," National Gang Center Bulletin, May 2010; James C. Howell, and Elizabeth A Griffiths, "History of Gangs in the United States," in *Gangs in America's Communities, 3ʳᵈ Edition.* (Thousand Oaks, California: SAGE Publications, 2019): 1-29; Gary Brown, "Los Angeles Gangs: The Bloods and the Crips," Socialist Alternative, accessed June 3, 2020.

80s, and the impacts on communities became more apparent: Blocks were subdivided, neighborhoods were separated, and territories were marked. The built environment in these areas reflected the harsh realities for folks living in them—both by strengthening a communal identity and protecting against outsiders. The story of modern gangs is the story of trying to belong, first in a space with a tarnished history, second in a neighborhood with a lack of resources, and third within a subdivided territory.

* * *

The famous 1992 riots in South Central LA crystallized tensions between police forces, justice systems, and the people. Following the acquittal of four offers who were filmed brutally beating twenty-five-year-old Rodney King after a traffic violation, and the failure of Judge Joyce Karlin to imprison a storeowner after the shooting of fifteen-year-old Latasha Harlins in Koreatown (despite the jury recommending sixteen years in prison), a wave of riots erupted in Los Angeles. Starting in South Central, businesses were looted, destroyed, and set afire. Drivers passing by the intersections of Florence and Normandie were stopped, pulled from cars, and beaten. Bystanders and victims account that cops had driven right by the riots and—despite calls about the unrest—LAPD wasn't officially deployed or mobilized for three whole hours.[193]

Eventually, a state of emergency was declared by the mayor, and 2,000 National Guard troops were called in by the

---

193 Anjuli Sastry and Karen Grigsby Bates, "When LA Erupted in Anger: A Look Back At The Rodney King Riots," *NPR*, April 26, 2017.

governor. After five days of tension, fifty people were killed, 2,000 more injured, 6,000 arrested, over 1,000 buildings destroyed, and a billion dollars-worth of property damaged.[194] In an interview with *NPR*, civil rights lawyer and activist Connie Rice spoke about prejudice within the LAPD in the 90s: "What we had was aggressive paramilitary policing with a culture that was mean and cruel, racist and abusive of force in communities of color, particularly poor communities of color."[195] Unsurprisingly, just twenty-seven years earlier, the 1965 Watts riots painted a similar portrait of police misconduct.

After 1992, there was a drop in homicides and gang violence, as groups had established truces and cooperation. But extensive over-policing and criminalization in the twenty-first century, especially in gentrifying areas, led to many communities being displaced and disbanded. Furthermore, many gang members were funneled into the prison-industrial complex (a phenomenon that describes the capitalist incentive to over-police, overcriminalize, and exploit members of society for corporate and political profit).

Still, as monumental as the LA riots were, they were constrained in a spatial context. Because the city is so sprawled out, car dependent, and devoid of central meeting places, it was difficult to produce a citywide demonstration. In many western cities like Phoenix, Salt Lake City, and Las Vegas,

---

194 Jeff Wallenfeldt, "Los Angeles Riots of 1992," Brittanica, last modified July 23, 2020.

195 Greene, David, Steve Inskeep, and Karen Grigsby Bates, "Connie Rice: Conscience Of The City" January 12, 2012. In *NPR Author Interviews*. Podcast, MP3, 7:19.

the low urban density, lack of public transit, and auto-dependent design stunts the traction of protests. And this lack of visibility is further entrenched by unconnected street networks, which can lead to increased detentions and police traps for participants.

Protest settings have always been public and symbolic. Cities involved in the Arab Springs had their plazas and squares, Athens had its agoras, and Rome its forums. Given these settings, the power of citizenship and democracy raises a question about the use and access of public space. These public spaces are what connect us to each other, allowing us to discuss, congregate, grieve, and demand.

In the past few years, the Black Lives Matter movements has redefined what it means to take to the streets. But it has also tested cities on their ability to foster civic discourse and enable collective action. The power of public demonstration lies in the ability of the people to fill public spaces—parks, highways, streets, walkways, etc.—in a show of what Kyle Shelton, deputy director for the Kinder Institute for Urban Research, calls "infrastructural citizenship."[196] But when design has long been in the language of the oppressor, there is little space for folks to exist—both physically and metaphorically. And when cities are sprawled out and inconducive to resistance, our voices are drowned out by the surplus of boxy buildings and rumbling cars.

---

196 Christele Harrouk, "Public Spaces: Places of Protest, Expression and Social Engagement," ArchDaily, June 10, 2020; Peter Schwartzstein, "How Urban Design Can Make or Break Protests," Smithsonian Magazine, June 29, 2020; Kyle Shelton, "Protests, Public Space and the Remaking of Cities," Kinder Institute for Urban Research, June 15, 2020.

The history of policing and the prison industrial complex in particular have always been troublesome. What started as a way to police property and crime has snowballed into centuries of abuse and misconduct by law enforcement and corporations. As parts of the country grew more diverse, racist sentiments surfaced in things like advertisements, housing discrimination, and policing. These ties have undoubtedly altered the built environment and urban landscapes we experience today.

CONFLICTING SETTLEMENT PATTERNS

Unlike much of the rest of the country, the West was spared from Northern European colonization efforts. Booming new industries that brought American settlers to the West—railroad construction, manufacturing, tunneling, mining, and agriculture—all required manual labor. But even before these industrial booms, many Asian groups (Filipinos, Chinese, Japanese, Indian, and Korean) had migrated to work on plantations in Hawaii. Soon, these workers made their way to the West coast to fill these roles and were instrumental in clearing lands, building cities, and providing infrastructure and labor for growth that would follow for decades to come.[197]

Unsurprisingly, white lawmakers, officials, and residents became threatened by the presence of Asians, citing things like unemployment, and the "unclean" and "uncivilized" nature of the workers. This ushered in a wave of anti-Asian

197 "Chinese Immigration and the Chinese Exclusion Acts," United States Depart of State, Office of the Historian, accessed June 5, 2020; "Immigration to the United States, 1851-1900," Library of Congress, accessed June 4, 2020

sentiment and legislation, the most notable being the Chinese Exclusion Act of 1882. This act prohibited immigration of all Chinese labor workers and was an extension of the Page Act of 1875 (which prohibited Chinese women from coming to America).[198] Attitudes stemming from the "yellow peril" led to race riots and massacres across the country, exemplified in the West by the Tacoma riot in 1885, the Seattle riot in 1886, and the Hells Canyon Massacre in 1887. This hostility continued well into the nineteen hundreds, with the 1907 Pacific Coast Riots and the 1943 Zoot Suit Riots, as well as Japanese internment camps in the 1940s, and residual racism from the First and Second Red Scares, in the 1920s and 1950s, respectively.

* * *

Since its formation, Seattle has always been a predominately white city. Despite waves of immigration and a diversified economy, only recently has it seen an increase in non-white populations and, even then, it remains the fifth-whitest big city: it went from 94 percent white in 1950 to 64 percent white in 2016.[199] But even in neighborhoods with the most diversity, the demographic breakdown of residents has changed dramatically. For example, the Central District, a majority Black neighborhood in 1970, lost 60 percent of Black residents and gained 50 percent more non-Hispanic white residents. Similarly, neighborhoods on the south side that used to be

---

198 "Chinese Exclusion Act," African American Policy Reform, accessed June 6, 2020; "The Great Arrival," Library of Congress, accessed June 6, 2020.

199 Gene Balk, "Seattle is Less White Than It has Ever Been in Modern History, New Census Data Show," *Seattle Times*, last modified September 14, 2017.

predominately white in the 1970s and 80s are now seeing increases in non-white residents.[200]

Given this breakdown, gentrification and displacement present enormous potential for further economic segregation. A study from the Federal Reserve Bank of Philadelphia found that Seattle was the third most gentrifying city between 2010 and 2014, with 36.6 percent of census tracts gentrifying.[201] Neighborhoods that used to be majority non-white, such as Beacon Hill, Bellevue, Renton, and Kent, are seeing an influx of whiter and wealthier residents. The study also found that the effects of gentrification can actually be positive, especially for original residents who are able to stay in those neighborhoods.

Research from Stanford sociologist Jackelyn Hwang found that immigration from Asian communities into neighborhoods with high Asian populations shifts pressures of gentrification to lower-income and Black neighborhoods. She writes that "increased immigration to a city with a tight housing market may have unintended consequences on black urban neighborhoods," and that "because black urban residents may disproportionately face displacement and subsequent disadvantages on the housing market, the

---

200 Yoon, Anna, Brian Lam, Gihoon Du, Jiang Wu, and Yurika Harada, "Mapping Race in Seattle/King Country 1920-2010," University of Washington, Spring 2017; Manson, Steven, Jonathan Schroeder, David Van Riper, and Steven Ruggles, IPUMS National Historical Geographic Information System: Version 12.0 [Database]. Minneapolis: University of Minnesota.

201 Brummet, Quentin and Davin Reed, "The Effects of Gentrification on the Well-Being and Opportunity of Original Resident Adults and Children," Federal Reserve Bank of Philadelphia, July 2019.

findings have implications for the future prospects of housing for blacks."[202] These findings challenge the common notion of gentrification—in that gentrification and displacement occur independently of outside neighborhoods and demographics, and represent unforeseen housing shortages and pressure can be brought by any group, regardless of intent to gentrify or displace.

ETHNIC ENCLAVES

Despite racist and supremacist attitudes in America, immigrants from across the world make their way to cities on the West Coast. LA, in particular, has an extremely diverse economy, established cultural networks, and desirable weather—all key in attracting immigrants. In fact, LA county has some of the highest ethnic diversity per capita. In 1960, close to 80 percent of the population was composed of non-Hispanic whites. But due to things like white flight, suburbanization, and sprawl, that number dropped to less than 30 percent in 2010.[203] Now, Latinx folks make up close to 50 percent of LA's population, Black folk almost 10 percent, Asian folks another 15 percent, and Native, Hawaiian, and other races about 5 percent collectively.[204]

Just by looking at a map of LA, one can see this diversity reflected in the names of some neighborhoods: Koreatown,

---

202 Melissa De Witte, "Tight Housing, Immigration are Shifting Pressure onto Seattle's Black Neighborhoods, Stanford sociologist finds," *Stanford News*, August 28, 2019.

203 James P. Allen, and Eugene Turner, "Ethnic Change and Enclaves in Los Angeles," American Association of Geographers, March 3, 2013.

204 "QuickFacts: Los Angeles County, California," US Census Bureau, accessed June 3, 2020.

Little Ethiopia, and Little Armenia. But other neighborhoods are also ethnic enclaves, like West San Gabriel Valley, Olvera Street, and Boyle Heights, and the stories of these enclaves is a reflection of larger trends in the economy and America's immigration policy.

The Dust Bowl, the Great Migration, and ongoing industrial booms were instrumental in bringing people out West, with aspects like restrictive covenants, zoning laws, and white flight limiting where they settled. The end of *de jure* segregation in the 1950s allowed for middle-class Black families to move out of South Central and into areas like Inglewood and Baldwin Hills. Likewise, urban renewal in the old Plaza and Downtown displaced Mexicans to the East Side. And where enclaves like Chinatown and Little Tokyo at one point hosted many residents and businesses, they now mostly serve as centers for tourism and commerce, largely due to suburbanization and out-migration of original residents. With over eighty neighborhoods, LA has myriad contributing identities. But it's the ethnic enclaves that provide stitching for the quilt that covers LA and gives it its undercurrent.

THE RENAMING OF NEIGHBORHOODS

Typically, the names of our neighborhoods are rooted in history. And even though neighborhoods change throughout time, the names typically remain—perhaps to offer some type of solace and familiarity. The names of our neighborhoods tell a story, just like the patterns of migration and infrastructure that compose them; one needs to look no further than the naming of the New England by English colonists, Seattle after the Duwamish leader, or Pleasant Plains in

Washington, DC. The names of our neighborhoods play into our identity of a place, not only helping us mentally map our cities, but also framing the narrative of our lived experiences into a spatial relationship with the outside world.

For the real estate industry (which is based on the very idea of selling a home and a neighborhood) the framing of a neighborhood is part of the game. But sometimes, real estate professionals abuse their influence by renaming neighborhoods—repackaging and marketing them in order to appeal to newer audiences. These attempts are indicative of attitudes that surround gentrification; in order to direct more attention and make money, one must disregard existing status quo and make something new. But to repackage and rebrand an existing community walks the line of erasure and disregard.

In the Bay Area, there have been numerous attempts to bend the boundaries of neighborhoods and assign new names. Some of these changes propose grouping neighborhoods together (the "quad" composing Dolores Park and parts of Inner Mission, Castro District, Mission Dolores, and Noe Valley) and splitting other neighborhoods to reach new renters and buyers (Noe Valley being given new boundaries; adding Yerba Buena, Candlestick Point, and Little Hollywood).[205]

In 2018, Google Maps grouped Rincon Hill, South Beach, and South of Market and packaged it as East Cut, and because Google Maps is used by hotel sites, dating apps, ride sharing platforms, and more, the name quickly entered the lexicon.

---

205 John Wildermuth, "S.F. Neighborhoods Change Names to Map Out New Identity," SF Gate, last modified March 23, 2014.

Soon it was being used in news reports and real-estate listings. Unsurprisingly, this sparked outrage and confusion among its people, especially since the area is a Community Benefit District. With continuous updates and usage by thousands of users, websites, and apps, Google Maps has tremendous influence. In the case of East Cut, the ripple effect created by its cartographers shows just how much power is vested in tech companies.[206]

Other renaming attempts include changing Bayview—Hunter's Point Shipyard to San Francisco Shipyard, and packing East Bay's collection of neighborhoods in North Oakland, Berkeley, and Emeryville into NOBE. Both neighborhoods have longstanding histories of urban struggle and economic restructuring. Hunter's Point has a prominent history with ties to early naval and military history, along with many working-class immigrants who used to live in the neighborhood.

The call for NOBE, an acronym few locals use themselves, is almost like a blanket term that groups together the North Beach neighborhoods that consists of microneighborhoods like Bushrod, Santa Fe, Gaskill, and Lorin. This area is tied to the formation of the Black Panther Party, as Huey Newton and Bobby Seale attended a community college that was once at its center. These neighborhoods managed to attract new businesses, residents, and investments into the area, possibly signifying that the renaming process is successful in gaining traction—and erasing important reminders of local history.

---

206 Jack Nicas, "As Google Maps Renames Neighborhoods, Residents Fume," *New York Times*, August 2, 2018.

Oftentimes, attempts to subdivide and rename neighborhoods by newer, richer, and whiter residents stem from the desire to distance neighborhoods from their previous socioeconomic class and race, which itself speaks to the need to legitimize and establish a sense of place and identity.[207] This is what happened when new residents in northern Fillmore began using the name "Lower Pacific Heights" to disassociate with Fillmore's "ghetto" reputation after redevelopment.[208] Sarah Schulman writes of something called "gentrification of the mind," and describes the clearing of consciousness and identity that accompanies gentrification.[209] People, businesses, and cultures that are displaced or gentrified are stripped of their ability to foster belonging. And when an area is rebranded and repackaged, claims and memory of the prior title are just those—claims and memories.

WHAT'S WITH ALL THE TECH COMPANIES?

The impact of technology companies on housing and affordability in cities is frequently cited in conversations surrounding gentrification. As big tech companies (Amazon, Facebook, Apple, Google, etc.) recruit and hire more knowledge workers from outside the city, demand for housing skyrockets, coinciding with an influx of educated, wealthier, and typically whiter residents. Eventually, rents rise because of high demand and low supply, and because property and business owners realize that these

---

207 "When Big Businesses Attempt to Take Over and Rename Neighborhoods," *US News*, April 22, 2019.

208 "Fillmore Timeline 1860 - 2001," PBS.org, accessed May 30, 2020.

209 Sarah Schulman, *The Gentrification of the Mind: Witness to a Lost Imagination* (Berkeley: University of California Press, 2012).

new residents earn more, they increase the cost of rent, food, goods, and other services.

As this happens, existing residents (many of whom are long-time residents, service, or blue-collar workers) can't keep up with the rapid change of pace, and therefore are priced out of their neighborhoods. This is a defining story of Silicon Valley—the stretch of land that encompasses the Bay Area, Palo Alto, San Jose, and San Mateo. But the story of how tech companies came to be and why they cluster together has been decades in the making.

In the 90s, the rise and promise of the World Wide Web showed businesses and investors that the internet could revolutionize how we live our lives. As consumers started buying more PCs and advances in software and network capabilities were made, some companies and startups began emerging primarily on the internet. Hundreds of dot-com companies appeared, unprecedented amounts of capital started flowing, and thousands of people signed on; within two years, AOL saw a 500 percent increase in users, from 200,000 to 1 million.[210]

By 2000, many startups were burning through their funds, overspending on marketing and advertising, and neglecting profitable business strategies. Combined with overspeculation by investors, stock overvaluation, and investor tendencies to ignore key metrics, the dot-com bubble burst, sending companies and the stock market tumbling. For simple

---

210 Steve Case, "Steve Case: The Complete History Of The Internet's Boom, Bust, Boom Cycle," *Business Insider,* January 14, 2011; Adam Hayes, "Dot-com Bubble," Investopedia, last modified June 25, 2019.

measure, NASDAQ, the stock index containing most major tech companies, fell almost 80 percent between 2000 and 2002, resulting in the loss of $5 trillion dollars. Soon enough, hundreds of companies ceased to exist.[211]

After the burst, tech companies slowly started up again, like Facebook, Cisco, and Intel. Despite a few hiccups in the 2008 financial crisis, tech and social media companies have permeated almost every aspect of our daily lives. And with the rise of the app and gig economy, companies like Uber/Lyft, WeWork, and Airbnb have further disrupted existing concepts around economic models and traditional startups. Throughout the internet's entire history, the backdrop of San Francisco as a haven for hippies and open-mindedness paints a clashing story between social ideologies and their respective economic impacts. How could a city that was once so weird and welcoming be overcome by tech companies with such little regard for a city and its people?

Aside from fueling the housing crisis, tech companies (and governments) are notorious for avoiding taxes that could help many cities. Despite financial contributions in the billions, big tech's measures and promises do very little to ease the area's housing issues.[212] Coupled with outdated zoning laws and unsustainable growth, SF and similar areas have debilitated themselves in the pits of what professor, author, and acclaimed urban scholar Richard Florida calls winner-take-all urbanism. By dominating certain industries, cities

---

211 Brian McCullough, "A Revealing Look at the Dot-com Bubble of 2000—and How It Shapes Our Lives Today," TED Ideas, December 4, 2018.
212 Ankita Rao, "Tech Giants Want to Solve the Housing Nightmare They Helped Create," *Vice*, January 25, 2019.

often funnel an overwhelming flow of knowledge capitalism into their neighborhoods.[213]

As tech companies centered themselves around talent, resources, and other tech companies, so too did investors looking for the next big startup. In SF, four neighborhoods alone (Palo Alto, Rincon Hill, Pontero Hill/Dogpatch/South Beach, and SoMa/Mission District) account for almost $4 billion in venture capital (VC) investment, with the entire Bay Area accounting for almost half of all investment in the country.[214] Despite the Bay Area adding about 882,000 jobs (mostly in or related to tech) between 2010 and 2018, only 177,000 new apartment units were created, inflicting housing cost burdens for every income bracket in the area.[215]

AIRBNB

Airbnb, the company that specializes in global short-term home rentals, started in San Francisco in 2008. The home-sharing platform works like this: Hosts list spaces in their apartments or houses on Airbnb, and guests can book these listings for a predetermined cost (of which the company takes a cut). Within a decade, Airbnb became the largest provider of accommodations globally and a torchbearer for

---

213 Richard Florida, "Tech Made Cities Too Expensive. Here's How to Fix It," *Wired*, April 26, 2017.

214 Richard Florida, "America's Leading Startup Neighborhoods," Bloomberg CityLab, June 14, 2016.

215 Chris Mills Rodrigo, "Tech Firms Face Skepticism Over California Housing Response," The Hill, November 12, 2019; Noah Buhayar, and Christopher Cannon, "How California Became America's Housing Nightmare," Bloomberg CityLab, November 6, 2019.

travel in the digital age. It functions both as a vehicle for tourism and as a battering ram to affordability in cities.

As the use of Airbnb increased, property owners realized the potential for larger profits, especially those with listings in more popular neighborhoods. As listings became more expensive and demand for those areas increased, actual rent and housing costs increased as well, prompting some wealthier folks to purchase additional housing with the sole intent of listing it on Airbnb. As a result, more housing stock is being converted into short-term rentals for guests, decreasing housing supply and properties available for full-time residents. By taking affordable housing and rent-controlled apartments off the market in favor of more profitable listing types, Airbnb contributes to increased costs of living and displacement of existing and low-income residents.[216]

CREATIVE EXODUS & RESIDENTIAL SPILLOVER

Gentrification inevitably places pressures on lower-income residents. As folks leave big and expensive cities for smaller, more affordable ones, a host of knowledge, talent, social capital, and creativity leaves with them. This loss in knowledge has earned the term of "creative exodus," which represents the artists, musicians, actors, and other creatives who are

---

216 Dayne Lee, "How Airbnb Short-Term Rentals Exacerbate Los Angeles's Affordable Housing Crisis: Analysis and Policy Recommendations," *Harvard Law & Policy Review* 10 (February 2016): 229-253; Alastair Boone, "There's New Research Behind the Contention that Airbnb Raises Rents," Bloomberg CityLab, August 2, 2017.; Monica Bernardi, "The Impact of AirBnB on Our Cities: Gentrification and 'Disneyfication' 2.0," Laboratory for the Governance of the City as a Commons, October 2, 2018.

priced out of cities they once called home.[217] This is a different side of displacement, one that isn't necessarily families
of color, service or public workers, or those suffering from
systemic racism and discrimination.

In Seattle, the influx of tech companies and their workers
has created a dichotomy within cities. Similar to San Francisco's backdrop of liberals and hippies, clashes of different
social groups have become more pronounced, as seen by an
uptick in hate crimes against people of color and members of
the LGBTQIA+ community.[218] Struggling creatives move to
more affordable Washington cities, like Spokane and Tacoma,
contributing to mini cultural resurgences in those areas, as
part of something that's known as "residential spillover."[219]

The work of artists—John Criscitello, Tom Van Deusen,
Emnet Getahun, and Yeni Sleidi, for example—protests big
tech's invasion and gentrification of their neighborhoods,
many of which were formed as places of refuge from capitalist and homophobic residents.[220] Indeed, the role of art and
artists in neighborhood change and gentrification should
not be ignored. Although further discussed in Chapter 11,
it's important to note that art has been long believed to
be a driver of gentrification, as artists tend to use certain

217 Denisa Krásná, "Metamorphosis of the West Coast Cities: Gentrification,
Displacement, Homelessness, and Racial Discrimination," *Reviews Magazine*, September 15, 2019.

218 Gene Balk, "Hate Crime Reports Against Blacks, LGBT People Double
in Seattle," *The Seattle Times*, last modified June 24, 2016.

219 Paul Constant, "I'm From Seattle. Here's What Amazon Will Do To New
York City," *Buzzfeed News*, November 15, 2018.

220 Corrine Chin, "Culture Clash: 'We Came Here to Get Away From You,'
Says Capitol Hill Art," *The Seattle Times*, last modified March 13, 2015.

neighborhoods to build their portfolio, attract high-end art galleries, and sell to higher-income tourists, residents, and businesses.[221] While this may be the case in some neighborhoods in some cities, other reports found that art is actually helpful in revitalizing neighborhoods, making an area suitable for attention and investment. All in all, the role of art—like gentrification itself—is different in every city, and any attempts to generalize its impacts prove to be difficult and multi-faceted.

* * *

RESOLUTIONS

General solutions for these three cities include focusing on affordable housing, expanding alternative modes of transportation, and leveraging geographic location and nearby industries to promote more equitable urban environments. All three cities have the potential and resources to transform their spaces into havens for urban agriculture, as well as the drive to experiment with progressive policies surrounding policing, houselessness, transportation, and social equity. Things like transit-oriented development and community empowerment should be focused on by all three cities.

Seattle is uniquely positioned to continue improving its reputation. The Urban Village initiative, adopted in 1994, seeks to

---

221 Peter Moskowitz, "What Role Does Artists Play in Gentrification?" Artsy, September 11, 2017; Grodach, Carl, Nicole Foster, and James Murdoch III, "Gentrification and the Artistic Dividend: The Role of the Arts in Neighborhood Change," *Journal of the American Planning Association* 80, no. 1 (July 2014): 21-35.

enable a sustainable future for neighborhoods by providing housing and employment opportunities that are connected to public transit routes.[222] Things like community gardening, the Equitable Development Initiative, and the Africatown Community Land Trust will be key to creating a more inclusive city. The Fair Housing Center, Housing Development Consortium, Sharing Our Stories project, and Shelf Life Community Story project are a few examples of necessary uplifting movements.

In San Francisco, big tech needs to take responsibility and accountability for exacerbating the housing crisis. They can start by working with local officials and developers to build more affordable housing, better public transit, and extend equitable support, treatment, and recruitment of local service workers. Expanded public transit could ease affordability difficulties, as it would connect outlying areas and commuters to the city, alleviating housing demand in the city proper. Lastly, the city should continue leveraging the presence of tech and knowledge firms to devise innovative solutions (as seen with the city's Smart City and mobility initiatives). Organizations like Brass Liberation Orchestra, FoundSF, Causa Justa :: Just Cause, and the Anti-Eviction Mapping Project are a few working toward empowerment.

In Los Angeles, the need for affordable and low-income housing and car and traffic alleviation are of utmost priority. The city and developers have a longstanding history of choosing to ignore and disregard its unsheltered residents. The city should not only make use of local knowledge and talent, but

222 "Urban Village Element," Seattle Comprehensive Plan, January 2005.

also the Title V Program of the McKinney-Vento Homeless Assistance Act, which would allow any underutilized or surplus property to serve houseless folks. Firms and organizations working toward equity and empowerment include Destination Crenshaw, LA Más, the Civil Rights Project at UCLA, Housing Rights Center, Serve the People, and Take Back the Boulevard.

* * *

The polarities that exists in America—such as ones between the East and West Coasts—are indicative of our different yet simultaneous evolutionary paths. Aside from character, these polarities are captured in our attitudes, entertainment, culture, food, development, industry, geography, and more. But there are still extensive similarities that exist between our cities. Patterns of expansion and investment, neglect, and the intersectionality of urban settings enable hundreds of experiential nodes across the country. But beyond the physical ramifications of discrimination and segregation, there are even more forces that explain how and why our cities look the way they do. Among others, these include economics, culture, identity, psychology, science, and education.

PART III

SEAMS OF THE URBAN FABRIC

8

ECONOMICS PART 1: THE GROWING GRADIENT

"White society is deeply implicated in the ghetto. White institutions created it, white institutions maintain it, and white society condones it."[223]

The Long, Hot Summer of 1967 refers to the wave of race riots that took place across the country, in cities like Boston, Atlanta, Buffalo, Newark, Detroit, Tampa, and Milwaukee. In more than 150 total cities, riots between Black folks and the national guard, police officers, and army troops took place—resulting in over eighty fatalities, thousands of injuries, and millions of dollars in damaged property.[224]

---

223 "REPORT OF THE NATIONAL ADVISORY COMMISSION ON CIVIL DISORDERS," New York: Bantam Books, 1968, pp. 1-29.
224 Kelly Gonsalves, "The 'Long, Hot Summer of 1967,'" *The Week*, accessed April 15, 2020.

The above quote was taken from the Kerner Report, published in 1968. Chaired by Illinois Governor Otto Kerner, a committee of eleven politicians and executives set out after the riots to answer three main questions posed by President Lyndon B. Johnson: What happened? Why did it happen? What can be done to prevent it from happening again?

White racism and discrimination, they found, led to the civil unrest. Police misconduct, economic inequality, and segregation of housing and education was not the exception for Black Americans, it was the norm; the passage of the Civil Rights and Voting Acts (in 1964 and 1965, respectively) had done little to immediately ensure protection to Black Americans.

The Kerner Report dispelled any existing theories and accusations of Black inferiority popularized by white Americans, and found that white southerners set the precedent of violent acts of defiance, chiefly in attacks against the Freedom Riders. The Kerner Commission advocated for things still being advocated for today: Public integration, increased government assistance, equal opportunities, and investment in minority neighborhoods and education. It also set the stage for executive ignorance and disagreement with experts, a phenomenon that unfortunately still exists today. Despite the commission's findings, which surprised Johnson, its recommended actions were not taken.

* * *

The term gentrification was coined by British sociologist Ruth Glass in the 1960s. It was used to describe the influx of upper-class "gentry" into lower-income neighborhoods in London, displacing some of the "original" residents.[225] As explored in Chapter 4, gentrification is a combination of many things revolving around neighborhoods and economics.

With constant economic cycles and migration patterns, the flow of residents and businesses can understandably change the feel of a place. Cities and neighborhoods are bound to experience fluctuations in residents, ethnic composition, businesses, establishments, infrastructure, and character. Yet as space in most places is limited, some residents are displaced—either voluntarily or involuntarily. But displacement alone is not gentrification.

Displacement is in and of itself a separate facet of economic segregation, connected to issues like evictions, demolitions, cultural replacement, and legal disputes; it does not necessarily fulfill other trademarks of gentrification (which often show up in the data prior to neighborhood changes). This mislabeling of out-migration as "gentrification" not only dismisses the real issues and communities where gentrification is actually occurring, but also distorts conversations that exist at the intersection of economic inequality and poverty.

A common argument for how gentrification is beneficial lies in improvement of public services (such as schools, trash collection, police presence, etc.) and increase in home values. While this is the case for many gentrifying neighborhoods,

225 "Ruth Glass and Coining 'Gentrification,'" The Bartlett, accessed May 16, 2020.

there's still an uneven breakdown of benefits reaped by renters and homeowners across all income classes. It seems that in-migration by wealthier folks can bring positive changes and that, more often than not, these positive changes can be fruitful for those that manage to stay in the neighborhoods. A 2010 study out of the University of Colorado-Boulder found that while incomes and median home values increased nationwide in the 1990s, much of these increases went to white college graduates under forty and white families, respectively. [226]

There are other reports that suggest gentrification isn't as bad as it's made out to be. A 2019 study conducted by the Federal Reserve Bank of Philadelphia looked at original, low-income residents of central city neighborhoods in the hundred largest metropolitan areas using data from the 2000 census. Researchers then tested this data against American Community Survey data from 2010 to 2014 and found that while gentrification does cause out-migration from neighborhoods, the difference between rates of out-migration in gentrifying neighborhoods versus non-gentrifying ones is only 4 to 6 percent. The reports reads: "Cross-neighborhood migration over the course of a decade is high (70 percent of less-educated renters and 80 percent of more-educated renters move to another neighborhood), allowing neighborhoods to change quickly primarily through changes to the composition of in-migrants, not the direct displacement of incumbents." [227]

---

226 McKinnish, Terra, Randall P. Walsh, and Kirk White, "Who Gentrifies Low Income Neighborhoods?" *US Census Bureau Center for Economic Studies Paper No. CES-08-02*, (January 2008): 17-26.

227 Quentin Brummet and Davin Reed, "The Effects of Gentrification on the Well-Being and Opportunity of Original Resident Adults and Children,"

It also found that gentrification can be overdetermined as a direct cause of displacement, which highlights the difficulty in determining links between the two. This is in addition to multiple studies that found that as neighborhoods gentrify, low-income residents relocate at a rate similar or less than those in non-gentrifying neighborhoods—presumably because of services and establishments in gentrifying neighborhoods.[228] Lack of significant, widespread evidence that gentrification causes direct displacement has led to the realization that while gentrification *is* happening, it certainly isn't happening nearly as much as we think it is. To me, it seems that the idea of gentrification has become a scapegoat for unfavorable change and conditions for original residents within neighborhoods. But perhaps these frustrations speak more to a lack of community engagement, widespread inequalities, and an inability of cities to adapt and maintain a sense of place.

THE STATE OF INEQUALITIES

Across the country, the lasting effects of redlining and discriminatory lending practices are evident: 74 percent of neighborhoods that were redlined in the 1930s are low-to-moderate income (LMI) neighborhoods today, while 64 percent of redlined neighborhoods remain minority-dominated.[229] Coupled with reverse-redlining (the practice of

---

Federal Reserve Bank of Philadelphia, July 2019.

228 Jacob L Vigdor, "Does Gentrification Harm the Poor?" *Brookings-Wharton Papers on Urban Affairs* 2002 (2002): 133-182; Lance Freeman, and Frank Braconi. "Gentrification and Displacement New York City in the 1990s," *Journal of the American Planning Association* 70, no. 1 (2004): 39-52.

229 Bruce Mitchell, "HOLC "Redlining" Maps: The Persistent Structure Of Segregation And Economic Inequality," National Community

charging minorities inflated and unfair credit and lending terms) and predatory lending tactics (like loading loans with fees and penalties, negative amortization, loan flipping, balloon payment loans, etc.), banks and other financial institutions have been disenfranchising folks for decades.[230]

Gentrification in a few areas is associated with neighborhoods that were previously redlined, as "decades of depressed home values" might have stunted typical home value appreciation and increases. Residential segregation engineered by the federal government was further compounded when minority communities were denied equal access to public services, healthcare, car loans, lines of credits, and access to education.

In 2013, the US Census Bureau data showed the median net worth for Black and Latinx families was $9,000 and $12,000, respectively. Meanwhile, median net worth for white families was found to be more than tenfold both these figures, at $132,000.[231] On the other hand, 2019 data from the Federal Reserve Bank showed that the median wealth of typical white families in 2019 was eight and five times that of Black and Hispanic families.[232] The lack of assets and liquid capital by

---

Reinvestment Coalition, March 20, 2018.

230 Mary Szto, "Real Estate Agents as Agents of Social Change: Redlining, Reverse Redlining, and Greenlining," *Seattle Journal for Social Justice* 12, 1 (2013): 28; Asma Husain, "Reverse Redlining and the Destruction of Minority Wealth," Michigan Journal of Race & Law, November 2, 2016.

231 "Wealth, Asset Ownership, & Debt of Households Detailed Tables: 2013," U.S. Census Bureau, 2013.

232 Bhuttan Neil, Andrew C. Chang, Lisa J. Dettling, and Joanne W. Hsu, "Disparities in Wealth by Race and Ethnicity in the 2019 Survey of Consumer Finances," Federal Reserve Bank, September 28, 2020.

Black and other minority families stems from longstanding disenfranchisement and discriminatory housing and financial policies.

In Boston, these figures are even more alarming: Black households had an average net worth of just eight dollars, compared to $247,500 for white households. This was found in a report published by Duke University and the Federal Reserve Bank of Boston, which calculated net worth by subtracting total household debt from total assets.[233] But it's important to realize that even if we look at present values and net worth for families, we are actually looking at the sum of generational wealth patterns, and that decades of disenfranchisement are embedded in almost any statistic we look at.[234]

* * *

A study titled "Racialized Costs of Banking" found that banks charge Black communities more to open and maintain bank accounts than compared to white communities. The average white person needs to deposit about 3 percent of a paycheck to open a checking account and keep 28 percent of it in their account to avoid fees or closures. For the average Black person, those values jump to 6 percent and 60 percent; for the average Latinx person, those values are 6 percent and 54 percent.[235]

233 Muñoz, Ana Patricia, Marlene Kim, Mariko Chang, Regine O. Jackson, Darrick Hamilton, and William A. Darity Jr, "The Color of Wealth in Boston," Federal Reserve Bank of Boston, March 25, 2015.

234 Martin C. Pederson, "Bryan C. Lee on Design Justice and Architecture's Role in Systemic Racism," Common Edge, June 18, 2020.

235 Jacob Faber and Terri Friedline, "The Racialized Costs of Banking," NewAmerica, last modified June 21, 2018.

But it's not just checking accounts. When adjusted for socio-economic similarities, minorities across the country are significantly more likely to be denied a home loan than white folks. John Taylor, president and CEO of the National Community Reinvestment Coalition, touched on the impact of discriminatory policies on wealth disparities: "Homeownership is the number-one method of accumulating wealth, but the effect of these policies that create more hurdles for the poor is a permanent underclass that's disproportionately minority."[236]

Rates of homeownership, like many things in America, vary based on race and ethnicity. White, Asian, and Native American populations compose the highest rates of homeownership in the US; Latinx and Black populations make up the lowest. This discrepancy can largely be attributed to gaps in education and income, predatory lending practices, and housing policies by both the government and private institutions.[237] Things such as redlining, reverse-redlining, and racial discrimination are just a few examples—all of which factor into distrust by people of color for financial systems and barriers to seeking credit.[238]

Some studies have found that, compared to schools with impoverished students, schools in wealthier areas are more

---

236 Tracy Jan. "Redlining was banned 50 years ago. It's still hurting minorities today," *The Washington Post*, March 28, 2018.

237 Chris Salviati, "The Racial Divide in Homeownership," Apartment List, August 21, 2017.

238 Richard Rothstein, "A Comment on Bank of America/Countrywide's Discriminatory Mortgage Lending and its Implications for Racial Segregation," Economic Policy Institute, January 23, 2012; Lori Teresa Yearwood, "Many Minorities Avoid Seeking Credit Due to Generations of Discrimination. Why That Keeps Them Back," *CNBC*, last modified September 5, 2019.

likely to improve all-around, mostly because of social capital and richer tax bases present in these neighborhoods. Likewise, underperforming schools are more common in areas of greater income inequality and economic segregation, part of which has to do with the cycle of poverty.[239] This is all in addition to the fact that state and local school funding in thirty-six states declined between 2008 and 2014, despite increases in student enrollment.[240]

THE CYCLE OF POVERTY

In 2016, over 40 million Americans—almost 14 percent of the population—were living under the poverty line. That comes out to about one in five households.[241] Poverty, aside from lack of money or wealth, is a complex web of factors that touches on virtually all aspects of life. There are five drivers of poverty: chronic unemployment, addiction and trauma, debt, family breakdown, and education gaps.[242] As you might guess, falling to one of these categories often leads to falling into additional categories.

Today, 43 percent of minors come from low-income families, creating a cycle of poverty than can—and most likely will—transcend generations. In fact, most children born into poverty end up spending large portions of their childhoods

---

239 Ann Owens, "Income Segregation Between School Districts and Inequality in Students' Achievement," *Sociology of Education* 91, no. 1 (2017): 1-27.
240 Turner, Cory, Reema Khrais, Tim Lloyd, Alexandra Olgin, Laura Isensee, Becky Vevea, and Dan Carsen, "Why America's Schools Have A Money Problem," *NPR*, April 18, 2016.
241 "Quick Facts United States," U.S. Bureau, accessed June 14, 2020.
242 "What Drives the Cycle of Poverty," Stand Together Foundation, July 26, 2017.

and even adulthoods remaining in poverty.[243] Even within generations, it is extremely difficult to break out of poverty, and much of that has to do with how dependent public services are on our geographic location.

If a family has a low household income, they likely live in a low-income neighborhood and thus, a housing unit with low property value. These neighborhoods are statistically less likely to attract businesses and new developments. They may already suffer from high unemployment, crime, and a lack of adequate public resources. These lower-income residents then pay lower state, federal, and property taxes, which results in lower funding for things like schools, community development, and job creation. And as household leaders struggle to find work or juggle multiple jobs, they are less likely to spend time with their families; their children may suffer from lack of oversight, care, and development, which translates into poor academic performance. And because public school funding is largely dependent on property taxes and social capital bases, this renders young folks less likely to receive a good education and career—ultimately playing back into the same cycle.

This cycle is concentrated in cities across the country. More than one in four poor Black residents and one in six poor Hispanic residents live in neighborhoods of extreme poverty, compared to just one in thirteen poor white residents. Moreover, the number of people living in high-poverty areas almost doubled, from 7.2 million in 2000 to 13.8 million in

243 Caroline Ratcliffe, and Signe-Mary McKernan, "Childhood Poverty Persistence: Facts and Consequences," The Urban Institute, Brief 14, June 2010.

2015.[244] These areas are stricken with poverty and disinvestment, but are still very different than neighborhoods that end up gentrifying.

WHERE GENTRIFICATION DOESN'T HAPPEN

The threat of gentrification only reaches "gentrifiable" neighborhoods (those that are good enough for prospective residents). In other words, gentrification has a tendency to bypass neighborhoods of extreme poverty. A 2015 study by two Harvard sociologists looked at gentrified neighborhoods in Chicago and found that those "that are more than 40 percent Black gentrify much more slowly than other neighborhoods," indicating that folks (or "gentrifiers") prefer neighborhoods with lighter-skinned residents, meaning that poor Black neighborhoods are likely to remain poor and Black. This apparent unwillingness of other ethnic groups to move into and invest in predominantly Black communities therefore perpetuates the segregation and inequality that already exists in our country today.[245]

A 2014 report from urban policy think tank City Observatory analyzed 1,100 census tracts from 1970 that were located within ten miles of business districts in the fifty-one largest cities with high levels of poverty. They found a few things. First, two-thirds of neighborhoods in poverty in 1970 remained so in 2010, and another 25 percent of neighborhoods

244 Paul Jargowsky, "Architecture of Segregation," The Century Foundation, August 7, 2015.
245 Jackelyn Hwang, and Robert J. Simpson, "Divergent Pathways of Gentrification: Racial Inequality and the Social Order of Renewal in Chicago Neighborhood," *American Sociological Review* 79, no. 4 (2014): 726-751.

remain beneath the federal poverty line. Second, the amount of people living in extreme poverty had doubled, and the number of high-poverty neighborhoods had jumped from 1,100 to 3,100. Lastly, only three cities—New York City, Chicago, and Washington, DC—composed a third of the tracts that saw declines in poverty rates.[246]

WHY GHETTOS LOOK THE WAY THEY DO

The word ghetto has mysterious etymological roots, but was first used to describe Jewish quarters in European cities. In the late-eighteen hundreds, the term was applied to some American cities. Then, as cities passed zoning ordinances and segregated Black and white folks, the term was used to describe Black neighborhoods. Later, ghettos were established in Nazi Germany to isolate and deprive Jewish folks from outside contact and resources.[247]

Following WWII and things like white flight, suburbanization, and urban renewal, the term resurfaced, becoming synonymous with the inner-city neighborhoods that housed Black and minority populations. With the 1965 publication of Kenneth Clark's *Dark Ghetto*, the link between ghettos and Black folks further cemented the word's newfound association—even though the book was highlighting that ghettos were bleak neighborhoods, devoid of faith and promise.[248]

---

246 Joe Cortright, and Dillon Mahmoudi, "Lost in Place: Why the Persistence and Spread of Concentrated Poverty—Not Gentrification—is Our Biggest Urban Challenge," CityObservatory, December 2014.

247 Daniel B. Schwartz, "How America's Ugly History of Segregation Changed the Meaning of the Word 'Ghetto,'" *Time*, September 24, 2019.

248 Currie, Elliot, Tim Goddard, Randolph R Myers, "The *Dark Ghetto* revisited: Kenneth B Clark's Classic Analysis as Cutting Edge Criminology,"

As public housing projects began construction in the 1930s and 40s, Black projects were purposely placed in segregated and already-depressed neighborhoods, both to further concentrate low-income families and to appease conservative lawmakers (who didn't want them in the middle of cities, along public corridors, or sight-lines).[249] Coupled with decades of institutional segregation and discrimination, this state-sponsored racism and containment has rooted itself into the persistent and prevalent presence of ghettos.[250]

Today, signs of ghetto may include missing street furniture, piles of rubble, missing street lights, building-less blocks, boarded-up windows, spiraling fences, lawns blanketed with litter, and decaying building facades.[251] But where ghettos might only represent the urban side of poverty, trailer parks, shantytowns, and informal settlements might represent more rural and exurban depictions. And of the topics we associate most with ghettos, crime is the one that has been reinforced time and time again in popular media/culture and news outlets.

* * *

The history of crime and civil unrest is about as American as it gets. As cities grew bigger during the nineteenth century, offenses related to property damage, larceny, and

Theoretical Criminology 19, no. 1 (2014): 5-22.

249 Jamelle Boule, "How We Built the Ghettos," *Daily Beast*, last modified July 12, 2017.

250 Richard Rothstein, "Black Ghettos are No Accident—How State-Sponsored Racism Shaped US Cities," Directed by Mark Lopez. AEON, June 6, 2019. Video, 17:42.

251 Jane Holtz Kay, "Ghetto Architecture: An Exhibition of Makeshift Design," The Christian Science Monitor, October 7, 1983.

robbery increased. The arrival of poorer immigrants and economic pressures during the late eighteen hundreds and early nineteen hundreds are often pointed to as a reason for this increase. The rise of organized crime before Prohibition started as illegal prostitution and gambling, before evolving to include bootlegging, political corruption, and racketeering. The Great Depression brought a wave of nonviolent crime offenses and after WWII there was not only a boom in population, but a boom in crime, riots, and protests.

The War on Crime, decreed by President Johnson in 1965, was an attempt to reduce crime. But by 1970, property crime rates increased 147 percent and violent crime rates by 126 percent.[252] In addition, the War on Drugs during the 1970s unleashed a tsunami of mass incarceration and exacerbated tensions surrounding the use and regulation of drugs. Since then, the government has managed to incarcerate and overpolice its citizens at such an alarming rate that—despite holding only 5 percent of the world's population—the US now hold 25 percent of the world's imprisoned population.[253]

Both the War on Crime and the War on Drugs are built around the broken windows theory, which states that visible signs of crime and disorder (vandalism, public intoxication, etc.) encourages more crime and disorder. Some

---

252 James Vorenberg, "The War on Crime: The First Five Years," *The Atlantic*, May 1972.

253 Wagner, Peter, and Wanda Bertram, "'What Percent of the U.S. is Incarcerated?' (And Other Ways to Measure Mass Incarceration)", Prison Policy Initiative, January 16, 2020.

studies have validated the concept in clinical experiments, but where the broken window strategy works in theory and controlled environments, it fails in practice and opens the door to racial profiling and bias, police misconduct, and overpolicing of Black and Brown communities. The theory has lent itself to New York's stop-and-frisk policy, which allows police forces to detain, question, and search residents—often young Black and Latino men—for weapons, contraband, or drugs.

George Kelling, one of the criminologists who wrote and advocated for the broken window theory in 1982, recently touched on the theory's shortcomings, misapplication, and false credibility in an interview with *NPR*: "It's to the point now where I wonder if we should back away from the metaphor of broken windows. We didn't know how powerful it was going to be. It simplified, it was easy to communicate, a lot of people got it as a result of the metaphor. It was attractive for a long time. But as you know, metaphors can wear out and become stale."[254]

Increased presence and overpolicing has reinvigorated distrust of the police. And as one report that looks at police perception in high-crime, low-income communities puts it: "Perhaps not surprisingly, areas with high levels of mistrust tend to be those that are heavily policed, where police use tactics such as pretextual stops that damage their relationship with the people they are charged to protect." The report continues, "the people most likely to experience

---

254 Vedantam, Shankar, Chris Benderev, Tara Boyle, Renee Klahr, Maggie Penman, Jennifer Schmidt, "How A Theory Of Crime And Policing Was Born, And Went Terribly Wrong," *NPR*, November 1, 2016.

high rates of violence and heavy police presence in their communities have limited resources, social capital, and political voice."[255]

Recent calls for defunding the police are stacked with legitimate and accurate evidence, citing astronomical police budgets, entrenched racial bias and profiling, aggressive force, lack of training, and stagnant levels of civil and criminal offenses, among many others. So why do we rely on police forces to fix so many of our problems?

Considering most dispatches are nonviolent and procedural (investigating premises, traffic accidents, city ordinances, etc.), we end up asking the police to do more than what they're actually trained for. But by shifting responsibilities away from police forces and into the hands of trained and more appropriate professionals, we could transition to a safer future, with community-based organizations, coalitions, and support.

In an interview with *Vox*, Princeton sociologist Patrick Sharkey discusses potential changes to the policing system, noting that "we've never thought of [institutions driven by residents and local organizations] as the central actors responsible for creating safe streets, so we've never given them the same commitment and the same resources that we give to law enforcement and the criminal legal system. When we talk about how to respond to violence, the default

---

255 La Vigne, Nancy, Jocelyn Fontaine, and Anamika Dwivedi, "How Do People in High-Crime, Low-Income Communities View the Police?" The Urban Institute, February 2017.

response in the US is always to focus on the police and the prison."[256]

* * *

Last year, Minneapolis approved a measure requiring crime prevention through environmental design (CPTED) tactics for all new developments. Popularized in the 1950s and 60s, CPETD is a group of strategies that includes natural surveillance (ensuring visibility of residents and guests), natural access control and natural territorial reinforcement (controlling entrances/exits, fences, lighting, and landscaping to differentiate public and private spaces), maintenance, and activity support (communicating regular activities in a neighborhood).[257]

Related to CPETD is the concept of "defensible space" which was first explored by architect Oscar Newman in 1972, and connects ideas of crime prevention through architectural and environmental design. The concept argues that sense of ownership and responsibility can make a space safer, and that empowering residents to ensure their security is key to reducing crime. There are five factors of a defensible space: territoriality, natural surveillance, image, milieu, and safe adjoining areas.[258]

---

256 Roge Karma, "We Train Police to be Warriors—and Then Send Them Out to Be Social Workers," *Vox*, July 31, 2020; Roge Karma, "How Cities can Tackle Violent Crime Without Relying on Police," *Vox*, August 7, 2020.

257 "Best Practices For Using Crime Prevention Through Environmental Design in Weed and Seed Site," National Crime Prevention Council, 2009.

258 Patrick G. Donnelly, "Newman, Oscar: Defensible Space Theory," University of Dayton, eCommons, 2010; Oscar Newman, "Creating Defensible

But (like the broken windows theory) defensible space and CPTED sound great as an ideology and can help in certain areas, but still tend to criminalize Black and Brown communities by relying on racist stereotypes and tendencies that call for unwarranted police intervention. More broadly, these tactics focus on community surveillance rather than community empowerment, promoting an elitist view of public space.[259] And after all, what good is surveillance if you and your neighbors are racist?

* * *

Our perception of social disorder is key to how we view crime. In fact, many experts think that both social and physical disorder stem from certain neighborhood characteristics, such as concentrated poverty and absence of social resources (which both may factor into low incomes), high unemployment, and lack of investment potential.[260] Researchers Robert Sampson and Stephen Raudenbush found that people perceived more disorder in a neighborhood with Black folks than one without, even if the two neighborhoods had the exact same amount of graffiti, litter, and loitering.[261] But any upticks in crime and violence stems from America's failure

Space," U.S. Department of Housing and Urban Displacement, April 1996

259 Bryan Lee Jr, "America's Cities Were Designed To Oppress," Bloomberg CityLab, June 3, 2020.

260 Robert J. Sampson, and Stephen W. Raudenbush, "Disorder in Urban Neighborhoods— Does It Lead to Crime?" National Institute of Justice: Research in Brief, February 2001.

261 Robert J. Sampson and Stephen W. Raudenbush. "Seeing Disorder: Neighborhood Stigma and the Social Construction of 'Broken Windows,'" *Social Psychology Quarterly* 67, no. 4 (2004): 319-342.

to address its poverty, racism, discrimination, mass incarceration, and obsession with law and order.

RESOLUTIONS

As simple as it may sound, a lot of these issues can be abated by economic stimulation, job creation, increased investments, and funding for low-income communities. By cultivating a sense of ownership, empowerment, and self-sufficiency within and by these communities, the cycle of poverty can be severed. There should be state-sponsored focus on things like healthcare, education, mobility options, local businesses, the arts, recreational services, and community development, with sources of funding including grants and taxes, coupled with a diversion from excess police and crime spending.

Roughly speaking, the federal government contributes less than 10 percent of total funding for public schools, with state and local governments contributing about 45 percent each. But of the contributions by local government, almost 36 percent comes directly from property taxes.[262] Because of this, a reallocation of funds from state tax pools could help underperforming schools. And diversifying funding sources for public schools could help to improve education across municipalities. Accompanying policies regarding property taxes, rent control, zoning, and public funding should be revisited and improved.

---

262 Andrew Reschovsky, "The Future of U.S Public School Revenue From The Property Tax," Lincoln Institute of Land Policy, July 2017; Matthew Chingos and Krisin Blagg, "How Do School Funding Formulas Work?" The Urban Institute, November 29, 2017.

* * *

What was "urban" a thousand, a hundred, or even fifty years ago may not be what we consider urban today. The plight of ethnic and colored folk has changed what we, in America, think about when we hear the term. In the past thirty years or so, urban has become an umbrella term when referring to low-income communities, inner-city youth, and Black and Brown folks. It has also been used to describe music, fashion, and the rebellious nature of young people. But in doing so, it diminishes the individual components that comprise what it truly means to be urban.

The Kerner Report confirmed the narratives of those living in the communities where the riots took place, and foreshadowed the current state of race relations today. Things such as police brutality (and its connection to police nervousness) were trademarks of the summer of 1967 and, as the report found, National Guardsmen would haphazardly and recklessly fire their weapons after hearing gunshots. A flawed and biased justice system, voter suppression, and unethical housing and credit practices were issues central to riots back then, and remain central to calls for racial justice to this day.

Needless to say, the character of our neighborhoods is not set in stone (or cement, asphalt, or brick and mortar for that matter). Urban settings can be extraordinary places, but the urban umbrella can't remain a euphemism for Black and Brown cultures. Generational differences are what distinguish us from our parents and grandparents. But they are also what bring each individual generation together. So when our children are protesting and rioting in the streets, we must ask ourselves—are we willing to share our umbrellas?

8.6

ECONOMICS PART 2: ARE WE MISSING SOMETHING?

———

"A developed country is not when the poor have cars. It is when the rich use public transportation."

GUSTAVO PETRO, FORMER MAYOR OF BOGOTA, COLUMBIA

———

Growing up on the East Coast, I grew accustomed to taking public transportation. It was mostly reliable, relatively afford-able, and always fun. Most folks, regardless of class or status, used public transit, making it a normal part of life. Plus, when I missed a bus, I could always run and catch another one, helping me feel like I fit into the urban system.

But when I moved to Indiana, I quickly learned that public transit was seen as a welfare program. Not only did buses not run on Sundays, but if you missed your bus during the week, you'd have to wait for the same bus to come back around. So when you showed up late to something, people either didn't believe you or felt bad because they thought you were poor. What compelled folks to think they were better than others, simply because they owned a car? And if public transit was made for the public, why was there such a stigma around using it?

* * *

PUBLIC TRANSPORTATION

By the nineteen hundreds, many American cities had public transit in the form of trolleys, omnibuses, carriages, and especially streetcars. In fact, there were over 17,000 miles of streetcars and a majority of Americans used them. Unlike government-owned transit agencies that exist today, these streetcars were privately funded and operated. Because of this, cities and companies formed contracts and policies that kept fares shockingly low—around a dollar (in today's valuation) per trip. (Some companies even locked into permanent five-cent fares, which ultimately factored in their demise.)[263]

Soon, the rise of personal cars around WWI disrupted the efficiency and operating schedules of streetcars, as cars now drove on streetcar tracks, increasing traffic and gridlock. Rising maintenance costs furthered the economic disaster streetcars were headed toward, and the Great Depression put the nail in the coffin for companies across the country. By 1932, the president of General Motors founded the National

---

263 Joseph Stromberg, "The Real Story Behind the Demise of America's Once-Mighty Streetcars," *Vox*, May 7, 2015.

Highway Users Conference (now referred to as the American Highway Users Alliance) as a way for private corporations and industry groups to advocate for federal funding toward highways and transportation policies.

As car manufacturers advocated and lobbied for more cars, streetcars became unprofitable and unpopular, and were soon being converted into buses.[264] In his book *Fighting Traffic: The Dawn of the Motor Age in the American City*, Peter Norton writes, "There was a really successful effort by people with a stake in the automotive industry to characterize road-building as a public responsibility."[265] Norton also points out that the automotive industry actually worked to create and criminalize the notion of "jaywalking," as a way for car and insurance companies to deflect blame from drivers onto pedestrians—something that remains a petty crime and results in biased criminalization and enforcement in low-income areas. The Highway Users group was also instrumental in scrapping the ubiquity of toll roads in favor of "free roads" or "freeways." By using a tax on gasoline, they argued, the public and the federal government would be more willing to support and use highways.

The federal government, in a 1939 report titled "Toll Roads and Free Roads," formally identified the feasibility and master plan for a transcontinental highway system.[266] Originally,

---

264 Jay Young, "Infrastructure: Mass Transit in 19th- and 20th-Century Urban America," Oxford Research Encyclopedia, March 2015.

265 Joseph Stromberg, "Highways Gutted American Cities. So Why Did They Build Them?" *Vox*, last modified May 11, 2016.

266 U.S. Congress. House of Representatives. *Toll Roads and Free Roads*. 76th Cong., 1st sess., 1939. H. Doc. 272.

toll roads were used to generate revenue from drivers, then these taxes were used to fund new infrastructure projects. (The use of toll roads and user fees dates back to colonial America and the Turnpike Era after the American Revolution; recent trends of congestion and electronic toll collection (ETC) technology have renewed interest in toll roads.)[267]

And because American politics and economics (unlike most other developed countries) supported a more car-centric future, problems surrounding public transit started ramping up. In Canadian, European, and Asian cites, residents and officials treat public transit like a public utility, not as a political or welfare issue. Those governments invest heavily in transit systems, citing benefits in health, economy, and service to their residents, and ridership, service, and fares are usually higher than they are here.[268]

In the US, most public transit is funded through a mix of fares, taxes, and government funds—but oftentimes there's a disconnect between different levels of government, resulting in transit development being more capital-intensive than it needs to be.[269] Where American cities depend on fares to cover 30 to 40 percent of operating costs, European transit

---

267 "Toll Roads in the United States: History and Current Policy," US Department of Transportation, Federal Highway Administration, accessed April 15, 2020; Changju Lee, and John S. Miller, "Lessons Learned from the Rise, Fall, and Rise of Toll Roads in the United States and Virginia," Virginia Department of Transportation, accessed April 15, 2020.

268 David Levinson, "How To Make Mass Transit Financially Sustainable Once and for All," Bloomberg CityLab, June 5, 2014; "Why and How to Fund Public Transportation," Arizona PIRG Education Fund, March 2009.

269 Ben Adler, "The Koch Brothers Just Kicked Mass Transit in the Face," *Grist*, February 3, 2015.

systems have more help from grants, municipal government, and the public sector.[270] And where America separated cities with highways and lost money to support transit, other cities abroad connect suburbs by transit and invest in their systems to maintain services. David King, professor of urban planning at Columbia University notes: "Transit in the US is caught in a vicious cycle. [...] We push for low fares for social reasons, but that starves the transit agency, which leads to reduced service."[271]

Also contributing to this cycle is the operational nature of transit in America. Here, agencies operate with infrequent trips and closely spaced bus stops (which means trains and buses run slower between stops). Meanwhile, systems outside the US typically have frequent trips with spaced out stops, sometimes using buses to service the in-between areas, making them faster and more reliable. The layout of transit systems here can also make transfers between routes difficult, as most cities direct major routes into a central hub within the city. This is opposed to having a more decentralized and redundant layout of routes that would facilitate transfers, ease traffic and congestion, and save money and emissions.

In 2019, the city council of Kansas City, Missouri voted unanimously to offer free bus service—making it the first major city to offer free transit (their light rail system was already

270 Jonathan English. "Why Public Transportation Works Better Outside the U.S." Bloomberg CityLab, October 10, 2018; Giles Bailey, "How Europe's Free Public Transit Movement Tries to Rebalance Fare Use," *Metro Magazine*, October 23, 2019.

271 Joseph Stromberg, "The Real Reason American Public Transportation is Such a Disaster," *Vox*, last modified August 10, 2015.

free). The move was pushed by Mayor Quinton Lucas, who tweeted: "We want this city to be as efficient as possible…we want to make it a city where a pedestrian has an opportunity to get to where they need to go." This fare-free approach is being explored in multiple cities (such as Boston and LA), and helps to increase access to jobs, education, healthcare, business, and other parts of the community.[272]

Numerous reports highlight the benefits of extending public transit across community types, as it connects residents to jobs and spurs economic activity.[273] Data from Transportation For America found that for every $1 billion invested in public transit, there's a $3.5 billion increase in new business sales, a $1.8 billion increase in GDP, a $1.6 billion increase in labor income, $472 million generated in tax revenue, and a creation of 35,600 new jobs.[274]

But unfortunately, public transportation remains a partisan issue in America, hindering the development and full potential of transit. That—in addition to the fact that transit is seen as a welfare program for poor folks—severely threatens the rate and path of change American cities need to take. And as rural interests are often given more attention and per-pupil spending (due to the electoral college and representation), things like transit (which are seen as urban interests) are sacrificed. Another deterrent to increasing and expanding

---

272 Abigail Hess, "Americans Spend Over 15% of Their Budgets on Transportation Costs—These US Cities are Trying to Make it Free," *CNBC*, last modified March 2, 2020.

273 Kyle DeMaria, and Alvaro Sanchez, "Accessing Economic Opportunity," Federal Reserve Bank of Philadelphia, December 2018.

274 The Basics on How Public Transit is Funded," Transportation for America, accessed April 13, 2020.

public transportation in America lies in the ways capitalism and politics has commandeered our lives. To this day, lobbying by big companies and capitalist groups fuel car dependency, especially by advocating for car industry subsidies and for cheaper gas.

C.R.E.A.M. (CARS RULE EVERYTHING AROUND ME)

Some folks are indifferent to public transportation, given that cars have become so cemented in our lives. Take a moment to reflect on how much space we give to cars and how much time we actually spend driving. There are parking garages, parking lots, street-side parking, underground parking, car dealerships, auto shops, roads, streets, highways, parkways, and so much more.

Now, consider these three statistics: Cars are parked about 95 percent of the time, about 53,000 Americans die from vehicle pollution every year, and about 76 percent of Americans drive to work alone every day.[275] In terms of idling alone, Americans waste an average sixteen minutes a day—totaling 1.8 billion lost gallons of gas and 15.8 million metric tons of carbon emitted every year.[276]

Traffic and congestion are two problems that persist in almost every city, but the two aren't exactly the same. Traffic

---

275 Paul Barter, "'Cars are Parked 95% of the Time.' Let's Check!" Reinventing Parking, February 22, 2013; Adie Tomer, "America's Commuting Choices: 5 Major Takeaways from 2016 Census Data," The Brookings Institute, October 3, 2017; Edward Humes. "The Absurd Primacy of the Automobile in American Life," *The Atlantic*, April 12, 2016.

276 Tom Jacobs, "American Idling: The Ecological Cost of Keeping The Engine Running," *PS Mag*, last modified June 14, 2017.

is simply the hold-up of users (drivers, bikers, pedestrians, etc.), whereas congestion is the accumulation of users. Every year, congestion costs drivers around a hundred hours in lost time and $1,400 in wasted fuel, and each car emits an average of 4.6 metric tons of carbon dioxide every year.[277] Moreover, researchers have even linked traffic congestion to stunted economic growth in some metropolitan areas.[278]

Much of the traffic and congestion we see arises because of *how* we've built our cities. By separating land uses and using a hierarchal road network (local streets feed into collector streets which feed into highways, etc.), we trip ourselves up by not creating redundancies and connected streets and neighborhoods. For example, having fewer collector streets prevents distribution of traffic load over multiple points, thereby increasing traffic and congestion on those fewer streets.[279]

* * *

For American families, the top two budget items are housing and transportation.[280] Increasing rates of urbanization and decreasing supply of housing presents an interesting dilemma for the storage of personal vehicles. In fact, this

---

277 "INRIX: Congestion Costs Each American 97 hours, $1,348 A Year," INRIX, February 11, 2019; "Greenhouse Gas Emissions from a Typical Passenger Vehicle," US EPA, accessed April 14, 2020.

278 Kent Hymel, "Does Traffic Congestion Reduce Employment Growth?" *Journal of Urban Economics* 65, no. 2 (March 2009): 17-135.

279 Anthony Downs, "Traffic: Why It's Getting Worse, What Government Can Do," Brookings Institute, January 1, 2004.

280 "Consumer Expenditures—2019," U.S. Bureau of Labor Statistics, last modified September 9, 2020.

imbalance has unleashed some data on how much space we devote to parking.

A 2018 report from the Mortgage Bankers Association looked at five cities—New York, Philadelphia, Seattle, Des Moines, and Jackson, Wyoming—and found that parking was worth $81 billion in these five cities alone.[281] Michael Kodransky, global research manager for the Institute of Transportation and Development Policy, notes: "As parking regulations were put into zoning codes, most of the downtowns in many cities were just completely decimated. [...] What the cities got, in effect, was great parking. But nobody goes to a city because it has great parking."[282]

This parking surplus reflects America's longstanding history car dependency. Eighty-five percent of all daily trips in America are made by driving, compared to just 50 to 65 percent in Europe.[283] Of course, there are a number of reasons and explanations for this disparity. Early American cities—those formed prior to the nineteen hundreds—were designed primarily for pedestrians, carriages, streetcars, and light rail. Then, the interstate highway system, suburbanization, and consumerism funneled tons of Americans behind the steering wheel; newer cities started skipping important street design principles, instead designing solely and primarily for automobiles.

---

281 Ali Ahmad, "RIHA Releases New Report: Quantified Parking - Comprehenize Parking Inventories for Five Major U.S. Cities," Mortgage Bankers Association, July 9, 2018.

282 Nate Berg, "Lots to Lose: How Cities Around the World are Eliminating Car Parks," *The Guardian*, September 27, 2016.

283 Ralph Buehler, "9 Reasons the U.S. Ended Up So Much More Car-Dependent Than Europe," Bloomberg CityLab, February 4, 2014.

This led to increased standardization (of speeds, signage, tunnels, etc.) across the country, with officials issuing favorable taxes and subsidies on cars and supporting industries. Eventually, the US would fully encouraging car dependency and ownership, to the point of not breaking even for roadway expenditures: gas taxes, polls, and registration fees have only contributed about 60 to 70 percent of roadway costs (the remainder being pulled from external tax and revenue bases).[284] This is a stark contrast to European countries, who collect more revenue from drivers, focus their planning efforts on shifting away from cars, and promote more sustainable and healthier modes of transportation.

* * *

Let's do a little thought exercise.

The US spends more on direct subsidies for fossil fuels than it does for education and renewable energy combined, and when you account for the social costs of carbon and other indirect subsidies that number is well over five times the amount we spend on defense.[285] A report released by the International Monetary Fund (IMF) estimates that global subsidies on all fossil fuels in 2015 was $4.7 trillion, of which the US contributed $649 billion. The IMF also calculated

---

284 Ibid.

285 Clayton Coleman, and Emma Dietz, "Fact Sheet: Fossil Fuel Subsidies: A Closer Look at Tax Breaks and Societal Costs," Environmental and Energy Study Institute, July 29, 2019; James Ellsmoor, "United States Spend Ten Times More On Fossil Fuel Subsidies Than Education," *Forbes*, June 15, 2019; "Oil & Gas Subsidies: Myth vs. Fact," Oceana, accessed May 7, 2020.

the yearly rate of increase to be $250 billion.[286] Adjusting these values for 2019, the global subsidies total can be assumed to be $5.7 trillion, and the US share can be assumed to be $787 billion.

Using the fact that the US accounts for 27 percent of the world's automobiles and 37 percent of the world's gasoline use (or 142.17 billion gallons), and that the average cost per gallon of gas in 2019 was $2.60, US subsidy on gas per gallon comes out to be $5.54. This means that without subsidies, the real cost of gas would be $8.14 per gallon.[287] And that estimate doesn't include associated social costs and impacts on traffic, pollution, global warming, and human health.

(It's important to note that the above figure is a simple calculation made with a few assumptions. Still, it is consistent with June 2020 global averages: A gallon of gas was $5.15 in the UK, $5.66 in France, $6.16 in Denmark, and $8.47 in Hong Kong).[288]

David Wessel, economic editor of the *Wall Street Journal*, highlighted the discrepancy with gas subsidies in an interview with *NPR*: "The result is that people here and abroad

---

286 Coady, David, Ian Parry, Nghia-Piotr Le, and Baoping Shang, "Global Fossil Fuel Subsidies Remain Large: An Update Based on Country-Level Estimates," International Monetary Fund, May 2, 2019.

287 "U.S. Average Retail Gasoline Prices in 2019 were Slightly Lower than 2018," Energy Information Administration, January 8, 2020; "How Much Gasoline does the United States Consume?" Energy Information Administration, last modified September 4, 2020; "The True Cost of Gasoline: $15 Per Gallon," Smart Cities Drive, accessed May 4, 2020.

288 "Gasoline prices, liter, 21-Sep-2020," Global Petrol Prices, accessed June 21, 2020.

use more energy than they would otherwise. So the IMF says that subsidizing energy or mispricing it aggravates budget deficits, crowds out spending on health and education, discourages investment in energy, encourages excessive energy use, artificially promotes capital-intensive industries, accelerates the depletion of natural resources and exacerbates climate change."[289]

The IMF, urban think tanks, economists, and environmental activists all recommend moving away from global gas and fossil fuel subsidies, diverting those funds to things like infrastructure, clean energy, and education (which would curb the effects of fossil fuels and combustion-engine vehicles on climate change). Reducing subsidies would have a downstream effect on some drivers and low-income residents, but many subsidies offered on fossil fuels aren't spread to these communities anyway, since these folks don't own as many vehicles or properties, and probably aren't using as much energy as richer folks. But even in the unlikely event that gas prices reflect a more accurate cost, things like direct vouchers and cash offsets could help alleviate burdens on low-income communities.

* * *

Generationally, there are differences in how folks live their lives. A 2019 report from MIT found that millennial and baby boomer households have almost the same rates of car ownership. Unsurprisingly, they also found millennials are

---

289 David Greene, "IMF: Gas Prices Don't Reflect True Costs," *NPR*, March 28, 2013.

less likely to marry before thirty-five and more likely to live in urban areas.[290] A 2011 study from Zipcar found that "millennials are increasingly embracing access over ownership" and that millennials are more likely to participate in "the sharing economy," which includes car, ride, home, and work-sharing services.[291] Perhaps the most interesting finding was that 55 percent of millennials have made an active effort to drive less, a 10 percent increase from participants in the same study a year prior.

Another deterrent from vehicle ownership is costs. According to NerdWallet, the average cost of owning a vehicle with more than 15,000 miles is $8,469.[292] On top of an unprecedented amount of credit card and student loan debt, buying a car may not be a top priority for young people, especially considering that over 87 percent of millennials want to own a home in the future.[293]

The desire to reduce carbon emissions remains a key reason millennials refrain from driving: About one-third of US greenhouse gas emissions comes from transportation, with about half of that coming from personal vehicles.[294] On the other hand, however, electric vehicles and alterna-

290 Knittel, Christopher R. and Elizabeth Murphy, "Generational Trends in Vehicle Ownership and Use: Are Millennials Any Different?" MIT Center for Energy and Environmental Policy Research, April 2019.

291 "Millennials & Driving," Zipcar, February 27, 2013.

292 Philip Reed and Nicole Arata, "What Is the Total Cost of Owning a Car?" NerdWallet, June 28, 2019.

293 Rob Warnock, "2019 Millennial Homeownership Report: More Millennials Are Preparing For A Life of Renting," ApartmentList, November 18, 2019.

294 "Inventory of U.S. Greenhouse Gas Emissions and Sinks: 1990 – 2016," United States Environmental Protections Agency, April 12, 2018.

tive fuel sources are still managing to entice millennials, but do little to curtail our dependence on cars and present additional ethical concerns related to mining and vehicle manufacturing.

Increasing availability of such services plays into the idea of **induced demand**, which represents a paradox for the economics of transportation. It states that increasing the supply of something (such as roads) increases demand for that same thing—creating a counterintuitive result when it comes to transportation offerings. For example, by making or expanding more roads, more people will be tempted to drive, creating more traffic and congestion, and therefore tricking people into wanting even more roads. This also helps explain why people in neighborhoods with more sidewalks are more likely to get physical exercise than those without.[295]

The theory works in reverse as well; when cities remove lanes or roads, traffic actually readjusts and congestion stays the same, because drivers utilize other routes or modes of transportation.[296] This is what happened when San Francisco demolished their Central Freeway in 2002 and built Octavia Boulevard in its place, which only carries half the freeway's

---

295 Sallis, James F., Heather R. Bowles, Adrian Bauman, Barbara E. Ainsworth, Fiona C. Bull, Cora L. Craig, Michael Sjöström, Ilse De Bourdeaudhuij, Johan Lefevre, Victor Matsudo, Sandra Matsudo, Duncan J. Macfarlane, Luis Fernando Gomez, Shigeru Inoue, Norio Murase, Vida Volbekiene, Grant McLean, Harriette Carr, Lena Klasson Heggebo, Heidi Tomten, Patrick Bergman, "Neighborhood Environments and Physical Activity Among Adults in 11 Countries," *American Journal of Preventative Medicine* 36, no. 6 (June 2009): 484-490.

296 Adam Mann, "What's Up With That: Building Bigger Roads Actually Makes Traffic Worse," *Wired*, June 17, 2014.

volume. Other examples of reduced demand took place in Atlanta, Seattle, Minneapolis, and Los Angeles.[297]

Placement of cars and highways at the center of urban planning is a disservice to the very idea of cities as livable spaces. Jane Jacobs, one of the most prominent figures in American urban studies, touched on highways and car dependency in her famous 1961 book *The Death and Life of Great American Cities*. She remarks, "Not TV or illegal drugs but the automobile has been the chief destroyer of American communities."[298] That was almost sixty years ago—yet her statement remains true today.

* * *

GENERATING WEALTH

Where we live makes a huge, huge difference in how we move on the social and economic ladder. For example, poor folks in Scranton, Pennsylvania are twice as likely to move into the middle class than poor folks in Rust Belt cities like Columbus, Ohio and South Bend, Indiana. Generally speaking, cities in the Northeast, the West, and the Great Plains are more primed for higher rates of mobility, whereas cities in the South and Midwest are not. Cities like Pittsburg, Seattle, Salt Lake City, and Boston offer higher rates for upward mobility than cities like Memphis, Atlanta, Raleigh, and Cincinnati.[299]

---

297 Joe Cortright, "Why Carmaggedon never comes (Seattle edition)," City Observatory, January 16, 2019.

298 Jane Jacobs, *Dark Age Ahead* (New York: Random House, 2005): 37.

299 David Leonhardt, "In Climbing Income Ladder, Location Matters," *New York Times*, July 22, 2013.

This upward mobility is dictated by things like occupation, family structure, education, income, and wealth, but is also influenced by things like geographic location, proximity to public transit, and quality of public services. Moreover, the presence of a geographically diverse and dispersed middle class, two-parent households, decent public education, and religious/community organizations also plays a part. For these reasons, mobility in some cities is much more attainable than others. But these gaps don't apply as much to upper-class families as they do low- and middle-income families.[300]

A report by four award-winning economists at Harvard University and UC Berkeley, titled "Where is the Land of Opportunity: The Geography of Intergenerational Mobility in the US," found five common characteristics in high-mobility cities: low levels of residential segregation, low levels of income inequality, greater social capital, quality of primary education, and family stability.[301]

It's important to note that these findings largely indicate correlation, not necessarily causation. Their report measured absolute mobility (how far up a low-income child will climb in their life) and relative mobility (the difference between rich and poor children coming from the same community). The Brookings Institute reports similar findings related to mobility of children born from unintended pregnancies and

---

300 Andrews, Rodney, Marcus Casey, Bradley L. Hardy, Trevon D. Logan, "Location matters: Historical Racial Segregation and Intergenerational Mobility," *Economic Letters* 158 (September 2017): 67-72.

301 Chetty, Raj, Nathanial Hendren, Patrick Kline, and Emmanuel Saez, "Where is the Land of Opportunity? The Geography of Intergenerational Mobility in the United States," *The Quarterly Journal of Economics* 129, no. 4 (2014): 1553-1623.

single parent households.[302] As a result, these factors—most of which are outside of our direct and individual control—end up shaping and predicting the trajectory of mobility for millions of Americans every day.

HOUSING

Housing is one of the biggest issues facing America today. Cities are facing massive housing shortages, losing affordable housing, and seeing increasing costs of living, as well as rising costs of construction and preferential treatment and policies for homeowners.[303]

The standard of affordability for housing in the US is 30 percent, meaning that families should be spending no more than a third of their income on housing. But that threshold is often surpassed; the 2006 American Community Survey found that 46 percent of renters, 37 percent of homeowners with a mortgage, and 16 percent of homeowners without a mortgage exceed this standard of affordability.[304]

The intersection of housing and finance was crystallized in the 2008 financial crisis, which resulted from a combination

---

302 Isabel V. Sawhill, and Joanna Venator, "Three Policies to Close the Class Divide in Family Formation," Brookings Institute, January 21, 2014.

303 Khater, Sam, Len Kiefer, Ajita Atreya, Venkataramana Yanamandra, "The Major Challenge of Inadequate U.S. Housing Supply," FreddieMac, December 5, 2018; Sisson, Patrick, Jeff Andrews, and Alex Bazeley, "The Affordable Housing Crisis, Explained," *Curbed*, last modified March 2, 2020.

304 Mary Schwartz, and Ellen Wilson, "Who Can Afford To Live in a Home?: A Look at Data from the 2006 American Community Survey," US Census Bureau, accessed April 30, 2020.

of skyrocketing debt and housing prices, deregulation of banks and financial services, and loose and predatory loans to buyers and homeowners. As thousands of Americans lost their jobs, homes, and savings, banks and investment firms seized upon foreclosed homes and mortgages, entering housing markets for rent-backed securities and bonds.[305] The 2008 financial crisis is incredibly complex but, through it all, it highlights the flaw of housing being a commodity in America, instead of a right or granted freedom. And even then, housing and wealth are inextricably connected through things like ownership, equity, and debt.

Equity—the value behind ownership of assets—is one of the biggest contributors to wealth. For homes, it is mainly built through mortgage payments and appreciation, and is calculated by subtracting any debts from current market value. But like many other things in America, building equity looks different for different groups of people, especially between white and Black families. Part of that is due to decades' worth of disenfranchisement of Black families, resulting in them having more debt, buying less expensive homes later in life, and owning those homes for less time. Disparities in things like homeownership and debt, as previously discussed, are present throughout the housing market and contribute largely to racial gaps in wealth, income, and education.[306]

---

305 Jeff Andrews, "10 Years After the Financial Crisis, is the Housing Market Still at Risk?" Curbed, August 29, 2018; McArthur, Colin, and Sarah Edelman, "The 2008 Housing Crisis," Center for American Progress, April 13, 2017.

306 Choi, Jung Hyun, Alanna McCargo, and Laurie Goodman, "Three Differences Between Black and White Homeownership that Add to the Housing Wealth Gap," The Urban Institute, February 28, 2019.

But even in places where people of different backgrounds have comparable incomes, their overall wealth may differ greatly due to debt and lack of assets (especially property). As cost of living goes up and labor markets change, the inability to afford rent or a mortgage can lead to residents being displaced or evicted—sometimes through eminent domain, in which building owners or the government seize property or housing units.

Combined with entrenched discrimination in housing and labor markets, those who fall victim to these pressures are often further penalized with things like tenant blacklists, poor references, and increased costs or burdens related to court fees and payments, as well as demerits to credit scores, which all present even more obstacles to socioeconomic mobility.

AFFORDABLE HOUSING

The realm of affordable housing plays a critical role in housing at large, and is typically monitored by housing authorities. These are usually governmental bodies that handle housing at the local level. Housing authorities receive federal funds from the US Department of Housing and Urban Development, and use those funds to help low-income residents find and afford rental housing. There are about 3,300 housing authorities across the country.

Part of affordable housing includes public and subsidized housing. Public housing is the situation in which an affordable housing unit is owned by a housing authority. Subsidized housing is when an affordable housing unit is owned and operated by private landlord, who receive subsidies from the government in exchange for renting to low- and moderate-income (LMI) residents.

Based on eligibility, tenants can obtain vouchers to use in the private market. Vouchers can also be given to owners of multifamily subsidized housing, who provide affordable housing to tenants in exchange. Section 8 of the Housing Act of 1937 authorizes the payment of rental housing at fair market rates, via subsidies and vouchers, directly to private landlords.[307]

Eligibility is mainly based on income. For public housing, tenants typically pay around 30 percent of their income on rent and utilities. Housing authorities use incomes to determine rent and any deductions/exclusions. For vouchers programs, tenants can pay up to 40 percent of their income on rent and utilities. For multi-family subsidized housing, rents can be calculated based on income, number of bedrooms, or even immigration status of family members.

After eligibility is confirmed, tenant screening and waiting lists are two ways housing authorities determine which families actually get public housing. Tenant screens can involve looking at previous landlord references, credit reports, and criminal records; waiting lists are kept by housing agencies and owners, and can be organized chronologically or via a lottery system.[308]

---

307 "United States Housing Act of 1937 as Amended by the Quality Housing and Work Responsibility Act of 1998 as of 3/2/1999," United States House of Representatives, March 2, 1999.

308 Maggie McCarty, "Introduction to Public Housing," Congressional Research Service, January 3, 2014.

Despite such a complicated system, we still fail to allocate sufficient funds and housing supply. As Valerie Schloredt writes, "Lack of funding means only one in four families that qualifies for public housing or housing vouchers gets help; more is spent every year on homeowner tax subsidies than on low-income housing assistance. The mortgage interest tax deduction costs the government $34 billion annually, and the deeply flawed housing voucher program that relies on private landlords costs another $20 billion."[309] A report for the Urban Institute found that for every one hundred "extremely low-income" households in 2012, only twenty-nine affordable rental units were available—a drop from thirty-seven in 2000.[310]

The many hoops families must jump through to obtain affordable housing shows how much we've normalized poverty and how deep we've descended into the affordability crisis. In 2017, New York City became the first city in the country to adopt a Right to Counsel (RTC) approach to housing evictions, which grants an attorney to families facing evictions that are 200 percent below the federal poverty line (currently $26,200 for a family of four).[311] In addition to the RTC program, NYC has adopted anti-harassment programs to protect renters facing harassment, pressures, or discrimination from landlords.

---

309 Valerie Schloredt, "Antidotes to Gentrification: Plans for Democratized, Affordable Housing," *Yes! Magazine*, February 19, 2020.

310 Erika C. Poethig, "Housing Assistance Matters Initiative," Urban Institute, accessed June 3, 2020.

311 "Federal Poverty Level (FPL)," US Healthcare, accessed June 17, 2020; Oksana Mironova, "NYC Right to Counsel: First Year Results and Potential for Expansion," Community Service Project New York, March 25, 2019

* * *

By and large, the way we think about housing and space in our cities is wasteful. According to an analysis done by the *New York Times*, detached, single-family homes account for 75 percent of all land zoned for residential use in Los Angeles; 94 percent in San Jose; 89 percent in Arlington, TX; 81 percent in Seattle; 77 percent in Portland, OR; and 70 percent in Minneapolis.[312] This overdevelopment and emphasis on single-family homes is baked into the idea of the American dream, and draws attention away from more diverse building and land uses, while posing a threat to housing affordability.

Another downside to zoning is minimum lot and building sizes, both of which encourage exuberant development and can be linked to things like sprawl, unaffordable housing, and housing and land shortages.[313] Some zoning rules also require certain mandates for parking, landscaping, and density of housing developments. These rules often force developers to make tradeoffs when making design decisions. For example, less than two-thirds of renters in the fifteen most populated metropolitan areas have access to balconies—a result of nonsensical and capitalist zoning policies. As Brent Toderian, a Vancouver-based city-planning consultant, points out, "If you build bigger balconies, it means

---

312 Emily Badger and Quoctrung Bui, "Cities Start to Question an American Ideal: A House With a Yard on Every Lot," *New York Times*, June 18, 2019.

313 Devin Michelle Bunten, "Untangling the Housing Shortage and Gentrification," Bloomberg CityLab, October 23, 2019; Matt Ohern, "Minimum Lot Size: What is it Good for? Absolutely Nothing," Jefferson Policy Journal, July 21, 2010.

you would have to build less internal space, and almost no developer would be willing to make that trade. Hence you get small balconies."[314]

Recent approaches to zoning have been focused on promoting integrated and livable areas. One of these ways is through something called inclusionary zoning, which requires housing developers to allocate funds or a certain percentage of total housing units to low and moderate-income families. But even measures like this can have negatives outcomes, such as rising costs of living (by shifting costs onto developers and thus, residents), reducing construction, smaller housing units, and evasion of building any units at all (as developers sometimes avoid cities with such policies altogether).[315]

* * *

The Community Reinvestment Act (CRA), passed in 1977, was a piece of legislation that sought to address banking and credit needs of LMI neighborhoods by scoring banks on how well they serve their communities. Part of the CRA's purpose was to tackle the issue of urban blight and reverse the effects of redlining, but despite forty years and numerous updates to the act, disparities between homeownership rates and financial

---

314 Linda Poon, "A Lesson from Social Distancing: Build Better Balconies," Bloomberg CityLab, April 20, 2020.

315 Joe Cortright, "The 0.1 Percent Solution: Inclusionary Zoning's Fatal Scale Problem," CityObservatory, April 245, 2017. Robert Hickey, "After the Downturn: New Challenges and Opportunities for Inclusionary Housing," Center for Housing Policy, February 2013; Lance Freeman and Jenny Schuetz, "Producing Affordable Housing in Rising Markets," Federal Reserve Bank of Philadelphia, September 2016.

well-being still persist.[316] Banks, in their obligation to lend money to community members, disproportionately gave out money to white newcomers and denied loans to long-time Black residents. For example, TD Bank denied loan applications from Black and Latinx folks more than any other major bank in 2015 and 2016, turning down applications at a rate three times the national average.[317]

The power of the CRA lies in the opportunity and mission to promote equity and access. Things like a low-income housing tax credit (LIHTC), community land trusts, limited equity co-ops, right of first refusal, tenant opportunity to purchase, and split rate taxes are just a few examples of measures to promote affordability.[318] A focus on community-based organizations, fair lending, and improved context analysis and regulations of CRA exams should be emphasized.

* * *

The Tax Cuts and Jobs Act, passed in 2017, created something called Opportunity Zones (OZs).[319] These are low-income and economically distressed census tracts that are submitted

---

316 Kriston Capps, "It's Time to Rewrite Fair Lending Rules. (Just Not Like This.)," Bloomberg CityLab, August 31, 2018; Kriston Capps, "What Mike Bloomberg Got Wrong About Redlining and the Financial Crisis," Bloomberg CityLab, February 13, 2020.

317 Aaron Glant, and Emmanuel Martinez, "Gentrifying became low-income lending law's unintended consequence," *Reveal News*, February 16, 2018.

318 "The Community Reinvestment Act," National Community Reinvestment Coalition, December 2016; Scally, Corianne Payton, Amanda Gold, and Nicole DuBois, "The Low-Income Housing Tax Credit," The Urban Institute, July 2018.

319 "Opportunity Zones Frequently Asked Questions," Internal Revenue Service, accessed July 8, 2020.

by each state, in which certain investments may qualify for preferential tax treatment. They incentivize long-term investment (either through real estate or business) in exchange for zero capital gains on any profit returns and temporary deferral of reinvested profits. There are over 8,700 opportunity zones across the country, and they can provide benefits for all classes and demographics.

OZs do prevent certain private and commercial development—such as country clubs and gambling facilities—but they also allow some establishments that don't meet the intentions of job creation and economic development to pass, such as luxury condos and self-storage centers. Furthermore, it's not uncommon for developers and investors to take advantage of favorable tax treatment to build high-scale businesses and developments that don't serve the community at-large. Moreover, OZs can be unregulated and unchecked, meaning that lack of community involvement and engagement furthers the focus on investment rather than impact.[320]

IMMIGRANT ENTREPRENEURSHIP

The sight of immigrants as entrepreneurs is one that can be seen across the country. It is reflected in stereotypes (Brown folk as owners of bodegas and convenience stores, Asian folk as laundromat and salon owners, etc.), local and regional

---

320 Ayesha Rascoe, "White House Touts Help For Poor Areas—But Questions Endure Over Who'll Benefit," NPR, July 8, 2019; Morgan Simon, "Opportunity Zones: We're Doing It Wrong," *Forbes*, September 3, 2019; Alex Wittenberg, "The Biggest Problems With Opportunity Zones," Bloomberg CityLab, June 25, 2020; Morgan Simon, "What You Need to Know About Opportunity Zones," *Forbes*, March 30, 2019.

business landscapes, and stories of the American dream. Compared to their American-born counterparts, immigrants are twice as likely to start their own business. In fact, one in five American entrepreneurs is also an immigrant.[321] Furthermore, refugees have a higher rate of entrepreneurship than both regular immigrants and US-born residents. Altogether, immigrant businesses account for over a trillion dollars in annual revenue, employ almost 8 million workers, and contribute over $400 billion in annual tax revenue.[322]

Reasons for high rates of entrepreneurship among immigrants vary. Some suggest that better saving and financial habits help secure loans, while others point out job and labor discrimination and similar cross-cultural experiences. Whatever the reasons, a few things remain certain: immigrant businesses and entrepreneurship spur economic activity, neighborhood development, and connection among community members.[323]

RESOLUTIONS

Cities and towns across the country need to update their zoning regulations if they wish to be affordable. Things like single-use zoning (and single-family residential zoning),

---

321 "New Data Shows Immigrant-Owned Businesses Employed 8 Million Americans; Immigrants Wield $1.1 Trillion in Spending Power," New American Economy, March 12, 2019.

322 "Immigrants Create Billions For The US," Immigrant Business, October 8, 2019.

323 Sari Pekkala Kerr, and William R. Kerr, "Immigrant Entrepreneurship in America: Evidence From the Survey of Business Owners 2007 & 2012," National Bureau of Economic Research, last modified July 2019; Dan Kosten, "Immigrants as Economic Contributors: Immigrant Entrepreneurs," National Immigration Forum, July 11, 2018.

minimum parking requirements, and exclusionary zoning should be left in the past. Moving toward things like mixed-use zoning, upzoning (with appropriate measures for production and protection of affordable housing), car-free zones, updated street design standards, and transit-oriented development should be prioritized.[324]

In terms of mobility, cities should look to develop and improve public transportation and alleviate car dependency as much as possible. By doing so, cities can become healthier, more sustainable, more affordable, more equitable, and more connected—all of which come with additional benefits. For central city districts, things like congestion pricing (a fee added to drivers in certain parts of a city during peak times) offer great value and returns. Furthermore, treating public transit like a public utility will ease transition to a better future, as will more funding and dedicated transportation revenues to aid operations and offerings. Strategies like land value capture and competitive tendering, and incentives and vouchers for ridership will help as well. Some American cities have already adopted bus priority lanes and Bus Rapid Transit (BRT) systems, which dedicate and prioritize entire lanes to buses.

In terms of America's looming automobile problem, it helps to know that personal car ownership rates may see its peak soon, and is expected to drop significantly in the coming decade.[325] Not only will this reduce the amount of cars on the road, but it'll free up valuable space in cities and cut down

---

324 Anna Kramer, "The Unaffordable City: Housing and Transit in North American Cities," *Cities* 83 (December 2018): 1-10.

325 Charlie Johnson, and Jonathan Walker, "Peak Car Ownership Report," Rocky Mountain Institute, 2016.

on wasted gas and emissions. Cities can speed the split from wasted space by reducing parking minimums, eliminating free or low-priced parking, and limiting the number of cars on the road. Two other measures cities and governments can take are to increase gas taxes (a short-term solution that would help in areas of high combustion gas vehicles) and to explore toll roads (which more equitably distribute costs for driving).

Local, state, and federal governments can start supporting small and local businesses, especially those that play an instrumental role in maintaining and preserving a place's cultural identity. Certain tax incentives for these types of businesses not only help circulate capital within the community, but prevent against invasion from large corporations (which can spur displacement and rising costs of living). Cities and governments need to be proactive in creative, affordable housing and holding supporting services and institutions accountable. Things like LIHTCs, stabilization vouchers, land value taxes, and rent control measures can help incentivize equitable investments and housing profiles across cities.

* * *

The places we live in and the ways we physically move through a space are reflections of our history. Some communities have wide ranges of housing types, income levels, and ethnic backgrounds, tied together with multi-modal methods of transportation. Other communities are homogeneous in housing type, income level, and racial composition, and are serviced predominately by cars and roads.

Ease of access to transportation and its connection to livability and residents' happiness is not something to overlook. Residents who live in connected, walkable, affordable, and transit-accessible neighborhoods are more likely to be healthier and happier.[326] And aside from modes of transportation in neighborhoods, communities with established characteristics play a huge role in our satisfaction, contentment, and feelings of belonging in a physical space.

---

326 Eric Jaffe, "Living Near Good Transit May Make You Happier," Bloomberg CityLab, September 12, 2013; David Charron, "Walkable Neighborhoods Provide Health, Environmental and Financial Benefits," The Washington Post, October 9, 2017; Daniel A. Cox, and Ryan Streeter, "The Importance of Place: Neighborhood Amenities as a Source of Social Connection and Trust," American Enterprise Institute, May 20, 2019.

9

COMM-UNITY / A GLASS WALL

"The character of a place, its identity, and its people's sense of rootedness are shaped by interactions within the place and with other places."[327]

Taking a regional bus from Boston to New York is something I must have done a hundred times. In junior high, my mom and I used to take the bus to link up with her friends in Long Island or Queens. Every time we went to Queens, in fact, we would always go to Jackson Heights. Starting around 37th and Roosevelt, Little India was an oasis for South Asians. There were grocery stores, sweet shops, restaurants, jewelry stores, films stores, boutiques, and more. It created the strongest sense of community I'd ever seen, which included being able to speak and communicate in our native tongues.

---

327 "The Importance of Place and Connectedness," National Research Council, 2002. *Community and Quality of Life: Data Needs for Informed Decision Making.* Washington, DC: The National Academies Press.

Street vendors sampled lychees and sold samosas. Cases and cases of staple food products and spices waited on sidewalks. Storefronts were littered with tacky mannequins dressed in jewelry and formalwear, and the merchandise of knick-knacks and rip-off designer goods would extend past the sidewalks. People walked in the streets with no regard for their lives (a common sight in South Asian countries) and would intrude into your personal bubble. Here, people called anyone older over-thirty "auntie" or "uncle"—regardless of kinship status—which always brought an unwelcomed sense of familiarity. Above all, the air was thick, heavy with the scent of incense and body odor.

Being in an enclave (or ethnoburb, if outside a city) is a multi-sensory experience. There are things you see, hear, smell, feel, and sometimes taste. These areas can be found in countries around the world and represent geographic areas with a particular cultural identity and concentration. This is why we might be able to gather information about a neighborhood during our first visits, just by looking at things like signage, advertisements, restaurants, architecture, and ornamentation. Hanging banners, light fixtures, roof structures, mythical statues, native vegetation and gardens, smells, music—it all comes together as a manifestation of a place's larger thematic presence.

All of the things I remember about Jackson Heights still stay with me, just like every other special place in my life. Being in a city is a multi-dimensional experience: If time can be considered a dimension, then the physical, three-dimensional form of a city is no longer static. This change is reflected via time of day (i.e., a city during the day is different than at night) but also in longer spans of time as neighborhoods change throughout the months and years.

* * *

The role of food in the multi-dimensional experience of cities—and our lives—is paramount. Things like food trucks, street food, and fast food are all important and relevant to how we identify and classify cities. As mentioned in Chapter 5, cities become synonymous with the foods they champion: bagels in New York, Italian pastries, and seafood in Boston, beignets in New Orleans, and deep-dish pizza in Chicago are a few examples. But our regional differences in specialty foods is largely due to two factors: the types of immigrants who settled there, and local/available agriculture. Just like the European colonists who brought their architectural identities to America, food and culinary expertise goes hand-in-hand with migration and settlement patterns.

Street food (which has been around since ancient times) and food trucks can be found across the country, typically selling items that are quick, cheap, and convenient. Elsewhere in the world, street food gives a glimpse into local cultures, history, and class stratifications. In America, we commonly see small carts and food trucks that sell all types of foods and drinks, giving more clarity into the regional differences in food. For example, there are tons of BBQ- and Tex-Mex-inspired street foods in the Southwest; New York has food stalls that reflects its global immigration and cultural patterns; and California has lots of Asian- and Mexican-inspired street food and food trucks.

The foods of our countries, childhoods, and families bring us a special type of comfort. The foods we associate with places in our lives says a lot about how we interact with the spaces around us. These so-called comfort foods arise from positive associations we form with our caregivers, providing social connection and remedying feelings of isolation or rejection.[328] But beyond foods, the idea of comfort has been extended to things like architecture, music, textures, and clothing—and they all remind us that everyday items and settings have an impact on our moods and behaviors.

ETHNIC ENCLAVES

The passing of the Immigration Acts in 1921 and 1924, the Housing Act of 1949, and the Federal-Aid Highway Act of 1956 were all instrumental to the changing identity and character of many urban communities. As waves of immigrants came to America, they typically settled in certain cities and around each other. And as these areas developed, businesses opened to support those immigrants, which strengthened the pull for other new immigrants. Furthermore, the slew of housing covenants and discriminatory housing and zoning rules made it so that ethnic communities remained concentrated in certain neighborhoods. As time went on, some groups, such as Irish and Italians, began being phased out of status as "bottom" and "low-class residents" of a city, and anti-immigration sentiment instead shifted to groups from Latin America and the Middle East.

---

328 Bert Gambini, "Love the Cook, Love the Food: Attraction to Comfort Food Linked to Positive Social Connections," University of Buffalo, March 27, 2015; Cari Romm, "Why Comfort Food Comforts," *The Atlantic*, April 3, 2016.

These enclaves typically host their own local economies and are fueled by social capital spending, cultural commodities, food and grocery stores, and cultural services. They are self-sufficient communities that maintain strong social networks and valuable resources and knowledge, making them prime areas for new residents and immigrants. As members of particular groups leave their home communities to come to America, they rely on these resources and knowledge—employment opportunities, housing assistance, organizations, etc.—to aid the assimilation process, allowing the area to mimic a transplanted community.[329]

The lack of language and other sociocultural barriers in enclaves facilitates social cohesion, as it allows for more instantaneous connection and clustering among residents. It also enables these enclaves to accommodate higher employment, upward mobility, and migration networks for future residents. But at the same time, networks established in ethnic enclaves can sometimes hinder or limit assimilation and mobility of immigrants into the wider society and economy by erecting a glass ceiling on growth of newcomers. Nevertheless, things like religion and food remain key staples of ethnic enclaves, as they represent a group's important cultural and traditional values.

Oftentimes, the large presence of a particular group leads to high participation in religious and cultural institutions. Not only do houses of worship provide a sense of belonging within

329 Mark Abrahamson, "Urban Enclaves: Identity and Place in America," *Contemporary Sociology* 25 No. 6 (November 1996): 781-782; Liu, Michael and Kim Geron, "Changing Neighborhood: Ethnic Enclaves and the Struggle for Social Justice," *Social Justice* 35, no. 2 (112) (2008): 18-35.

communities, but they also serve as community centers and spaces for folks to congregate, organize, and socialize as part of enclave activism and social cohesion. This can be seen in the spatial positioning of communities and their respective religious centers: Buddhist temples in Asian enclaves, Hindu temples and mosques in South Asian enclaves, synagogues in Jewish enclaves, and so on. Access to certain cultural foods is another huge component of ethnic enclaves. Certain cuisines and cultures incorporate different products and spices (many of which aren't available in generic grocery stores). But in global markets and ethnic grocery stores, products from all over are brought to residents.

In Boston, the neighborhoods of Jackson Square in Jamaica Plain (JP) and Hyde Park, sometimes referred to as the "Latin Quarter," have experienced tremendous pressures of gentrification in the past couple decades. JP and neighboring Roxbury and Dorchester were redlined in the 1930s, and until recently have remained communities of color and low-to-moderate income neighborhoods. According to a report out of the University of Massachusetts, non-white populations in every municipality in the Greater Boston Area have increased since 1990, with a great deal of non-whites moving to the suburbs. But in most of Roxbury, JP, Dorchester, and the South End—all of which were historically immigrant and communities of colors— there appears a large influx of white residents in the past twenty years, coinciding with original non-white residents moving away from those areas.[330]

---

330 "Changing Faces of Greater Boston," The Boston Foundation, May 2019.

The closing of Hi-Lo Foods, an independent grocery store that served staple food products for its Latinx and Caribbean clientele, was a devastating blow for the community. Hi-Lo served as a social center, bringing together folks from around the Greater Boston Area. The use of Spanish in the store and products from Latin and Caribbean countries provided familiarity and comfort for the shoppers. But in 2011, Hi-Lo Foods closed and was reopened as a Whole Foods, a move seen by many as an early indicator for rising costs of living and displacement of residents.[331]

* * *

A stroll in any cultural enclave might bring you face-to-face with signs, flyers, and messages in a different language. The dialectical patterning of language surrounding enclaves is a special form of communication in cities. Within enclaves themselves, language provides a common ground for members of a group and, for those who aren't proficient in English, it provides a judgment-free zone. But the in-between space (which sometimes is geographically distributed and not actually in-between) can be filled with dialects and mixed languages, such as Spanglish, African American Vernacular English (AAVE), and the many Creole dialects. These types of dialects are progressions on the sociolinguistic continuum and demonstrate language's capabilities in culture and community.

A key strength of enclaves lies in the clustering of people and businesses, which works to create a symbiotic relationship:

---

331 Jen Douglas, "From Disinvestment to Displacement: Gentrification and Jamaica Plain's Hyde-Jackson Squares," *Trotter Review* 23, no. 1 (2016): 60.

The people support the businesses, and the businesses serve the people. But the idea of clustering isn't just common amongst ethnic groups. Certain industries often cluster together to capitalize on proximity and growth in a region. This type of clustering can be broken down into four categories, which can all span various industries:[332]

1. **Marshallian districts** are the typical clustering in a confined geographic area, as seen by the abundance of tech startups in Silicon Valley.

2. **Hub-and-spoke districts** can be understood as a branching out of auxiliary businesses and suppliers around a main business or industry, as seen by aerospace and defense contractors supporting Boeing in Seattle.

3. **Satellite platforms** are unconnected branches and businesses across regional boundaries, as seen in some suburbs and satellite towns, such as Waco, Texas and Valpariso, Indiana.

4. **State-anchored districts** are clustering of businesses and activities that support one or more institutions, as seen by college towns or governmental agencies in the DMV area.

According to economist Alfred Marshall, clustering provides access to innovation and technical dynamism and leads to increased returns on capital, potential to collaborate, and a compounding of regional advantages (such as tax policies and community benefits).[333] Similar to chain migration of residents, Marshallian clustering supports local supply and demand, accumulation of knowledge, and ease of access

---

332 Nicholas LePan, "Form and Function: Visualizing the Shape of Cities and Economies," VisualCapitalist, September 26, 2019.

333 Kent Hymel, "Does Traffic Congestion Reduce Employment Growth," *Journal of Urban Economics* 65, no. 2 (March 2009): 127-135.

to supporting goods and services; this is despite creating pressures of the bottleneck effect, high competition, and potential for economic inequality.[334]

COMMODIFICATION OF ENCLAVES

In her 2014 paper "Commodification of Transitioning Ethnic Enclaves," researcher Kathryn Terzano looks into two ways that enclaves change. One way is when people and businesses representing different demographics move into a neighborhood and contribute to diversity in the area. The other way is when people of a specific ethnic demographic move away from the enclave, yet businesses representing those demographics remain. This method makes way for the commodification of a cultural identity—oftentimes for tourism purposes. This presents an interesting dichotomy of business representation and residential representation. Spurring the outmigration of residents of that demographic, real estate brokers use the presence of those businesses to market and justify labeling a neighborhood as culturally diverse.[335]

Other takes on commodification of culture come from fashion and food. Signature styles of specific groups (such as streetwear and makeup styles) have permeated through to high fashion and mainstream culture in what we know as cultural appropriation. Furthermore, the use of ethnic food staples by western chefs and restaurants (such as turmeric

---

334 Dara Lind, "What 'Chain Migration' Really Means—and Why Donald Trump Hates It So Much," *Vox*, December 29, 2017.

335 Kathryn Terzano. "Commodification of Transitioning Ethnic Enclaves," *Behavioral Sciences (Basel, Switzerland)* 4, no. 4 (September 2014): 341-351.

and other "authentic" or "exotic" spices) have been subject to debates around cultural appropriation and fetishization.[336]

But to be clear, there is nothing trendy about culture. To imply otherwise minimizes the traditions and history of an entire group, and perpetuates cycles of white supremacy and appropriation. It's a striking and difficult feat to balance appreciation against appropriation—where does inspiration end and appropriation begin? Still, it's something that must be thought about, discussed, and made tangible as cities and neighborhoods continue to change.

* * *

GAYBORHOODS

Gay villages—also known as gayborhoods, gaytowns, gay ghettos, or gay districts—are small enclaves with high concentrations of residents and businesses that either are or support LGBTQIA+ communities. Similar to ethnic enclaves, most gay villages have been established by members of the LGBTQIA+ community who mobilized and organized to create a space within a larger city. Gayborhoods represent an oasis, a place of refuge from violence and discrimination at the hands of intolerant residents and businesses, and they thrive on the social capital. Therefore, gay villages contain establishments (such as bars, restaurants, and clubs) and symbolism (most notably the gay pride flag) that cater for and support LGBTQIA+ folks. Gay villages are present across

---

336 Maria Godoy, "When Chefs Become Famous Cooking Other Cultures' Foods," *NPR*, March 22, 2016; Sara Kay, "Yelp Reviewers' Authenticity Fetish Is White Supremacy in Action," Eater New York, January 18, 2019.

the country (such as Boystown in Chicago, Gayborhood in Philadelphia, and West Hollywood in LA) as well as across the world (like Green Point in Cape Town, South Africa and Canal Street in Manchester, England).

It wasn't until the late 1960s and 70s, when the gay liberation movement culminated in a wider sexual liberation and counterculture revolution, that America started seeing challenges to mainstream and authoritative ideals and beliefs. The police raid into the Stonewall Inn, a gay bar and establishment, and subsequent series of counter-riots in 1969 is largely seen as the inception of the gay liberation and pride movement. By the mid-70s, gay liberation and awareness swept across the country (and the world) along with early inceptions of gay villages.

But like many special neighborhoods, gayborhoods tend to have a high demand, which can decrease neighborhood affordability. This creates its own type of gentrification, in that higher-income residents and businesses are allured by the village, but end up driving out members of the community, who end up forming new villages as a result of overflow. This is what happened when gays left Greenwich Village in the 90s and moved to the Chelsea area, and in Chicago when gays left Boystown/Lakeview in favor of Andersonville. In many ways, the "stereotypes" of gentrification persist in gay villages: As more whiter, affluent, and educated/professional folks move into a neighborhood, they tend to displace the gay creatives, people of color, disabled, and lower-income residents who may not benefit from the same privileges.[337]

_____

337 Feargus O'Sullivan, "The 'Gaytrification' Effect: Why Gay Neighbor-hourhoods are Being Priced Out,"

In the early 2000s, Richard Florida wrote about the correlations between gay-friendly cities and upcoming tech hubs. He then spent years trying to understand this relationship, finding that the presence of LGBTQIA+ folks indicates a higher concentration of diverse residents, which is then linked to more robust economies. Soon, cities started positioning themselves to appeal to young knowledge workers and the "creative class," the third of us in professions that rely on innovation, knowledge, and ideation (STEM, the arts, design, healthcare, business, education, etc.).[338]

Cities and neighborhoods supportive and inclusive of LGBTQIA+ folks often benefit from having these communities and festivals centered around pride. Events like Pride Parades, marches, and gay games have long brought investment and tourists to support and participate. Oftentimes, the physical embodiment of pride—as seen in things like art murals, flag displays, and iconography—is severely underestimated in its role in creating a sense of place.

Public art is incredibly valuable and effective, sometimes even transforming our images of cities—think "The Bean" in Chicago, LOVE Park in Philadelphia, or the St. Louis Arch. Having good, accessible, and meaningful art can and should provide a humanizing, educational, and memorable identity of a place. Murals can lead viewers to self-awareness,

The Guardian, January 13, 2016.

338 Steven Malanga, "The Curse of the Creative Class," City-Journal, Winter 2014; Sam Wetherell, "Richard Florida Is Sorry," Jacobin Magazine, accessed June 16, 2020; Paolo Mercado, "The Creative Economy Gay Index: Why Tolerant Cities Attract Creative People," *Adobo Magazine*, June 18, 2018.

reflection, and discussion with other viewers. Colors and art reflect the history, aspirations, and culture of a place and unite residents and businesses that may seem to operate as individual cornerstones of a neighborhood. Aside from aesthetics, art and color offer cities opportunities to break the mundanity of the built environment, offering a free experience to all. But more importantly, it's a conversation between cities, artists, and the people, demonstrating the benefits of collaboration.[339] And in rapidly urbanizing cities with busy lifestyles, public art warrants viewers to stop, think, and reflect—all things that are grossly excluded from traditional city life.

I got the chance to interview Dr. Winifred Curran, a professor at DePaul University who researches different facets of gentrification, about the role of public art and street life in cities. She noted that a vibrant street life and strong ethnic identity (like in the Mexican neighborhood of Pilsen in Chicago) functions as a protective force that can help forestall the pressures of gentrification and displacement, mainly because folks understand the importance of historic architecture, food, and culture to the community. Still, vibrancy eventually becomes a commodity—through things like walking and art tours and food truck festivals—and begin being manufactured to appeal to outside visitors and investors.

The Porch Light Program, from the Mural Arts Program in Philadelphia, has focused on community health and well-being by connecting and creating partnerships and art between

---

339 Public Art Network Council, "Why Public Art Matters," Americans for the Arts, 2014; Public Art Network Council, "Why Public Art Matters 2018," Americans for the Arts, June 2018.

artists, youth, housing agencies, and residents facing houselessness and trauma. They worked with Yale School of Medicine to report their impact, finding that tangible benefits of the program included sustained **collective efficacy**, perceived neighborhood safety, economic revitalization in blighted areas, and increased awareness and resources for things like mental health and substance abuse.[340] Similar stories of success can be found with New York's Percent For All and Detroit's Power House Productions.

Collective efficacy is essentially the willingness of residents to take action to improve their neighborhoods. Based around the concept of social cohesion—which represents how residents think and feel about their neighbors—collective efficacy is physical (often unrequested) action taken to improve a neighborhood. It serves as a type of accountability for fellow neighbors and includes things like shoveling an elderly neighbor's yard, offering assistance in times of despair, and maintaining neighborhood safety.[341] Collective efficacy can promote a sense of community and belonging, but oftentimes fluctuates based on neighborhood demographics and migration rates, meaning our sense of community and belonging is as fluid as we allow them to be.

* * *

When it comes to choosing where we live today, we tend to have a laundry list of priorities and amenities we desire. For example, people who prefer to use public transit, walk, or

340 Tebes, Jacob Kraemer, Samantha L. Matlin, Bronwyn Hunter, Azure B. Thompson, Dana M. Prince, and Nathanial Mohatt. "Porch Light Program," Yale University School of Medicine, June 2015.

341 Brian R. Higgins and Joel Hunt, "Collective Efficacy: Taking Action to Improve Neighborhoods," National Institute of Justice, May 1, 2016.

bike often desire denser, more urban areas. Likewise, people who prefer bigger houses and to drive more frequently tend to move into less-dense, suburban, and rural areas. This idea is known as residential self-selection, which states that people choose where to live, based on how they live (or want to live).

Related to this is the idea of self-segregation, which represents an interesting dynamic in spatial settings. The idea states that folks from similar groups or backgrounds consciously and intentionally choose to separate themselves from other groups. Perhaps the best example of this can be seen in classrooms, when students of particular ethnic or social backgrounds congregate and separate themselves from other students. Increased freedoms, made possible through technology, individualism, and abundance of choices, represent a powerful liberty granted to groups to have more autonomy and direction in where they settle.

As it relates to Black, Indigenous, people of color, or queer-only spaces, self-segregation allows specific groups access to each other and themselves, free from the prejudice and oppression from other, more privileged classes. These spaces are important because they typically aren't established to exclude outsiders as much as they are to protect and heal insiders.[342] This self-segregation is the same track that flows through ethnic enclaves and gay villages, which serve as sanctuaries and spaces of refuge from the white,

---

342 Cao, Xinyu (Jason), "Residential Self-Selection in the Relationships Between the Built Environment and Travel Behavior: Introduction to the Special Issue," *Journal of Transport and Land Use* 7, no. 3 (2014): 1-3; Devah Pagar, and David S. Pedulla, "Race, Self-Selection, and the Job Search Process," *American Journal of Sociology* 120, no. 4 (2015): 1005-1054.

patriarchal spaces that have systematically oppressed minorities, women, and queer folks. These communities are common in most American cities and play a crucial role in the urban fabric.

THE ENTITLEMENT OF NIMBYS—"NOT IN MY BACKYARD"

The need for control in our neighborhoods, even when stemming from a well-intentioned place, creates an interesting paradigm when it comes to upward mobility and neighborhood control. This attachment is not illogical or irrational, however. The feeling of and longing for home and familiarity is one that cements us as social creatures. To be moved from place to place at someone else's request can be exhausting, and this type of relocation sparks an interesting psychological idea of territory and how we identify where we belong.

From its inception, America displaced thousands of Native Americans, many of whom had established spiritual, physical, and emotional ties to their land. The Transatlantic Trade took thousands of Black people and sold them into slavery, forcing not just relocation, but readjustment. Both cases brought psychological and physiological implications tied to spatial control. Now, gentrification raises the centuries-old question of belongingness and attachment to place.

Combined with findings that individuals who purchase more expensive homes are more likely to participate in local politics, NIMBYs use privilege and status as a means to protect the value of their homes and assets, more so than becoming engaged with their local communities.[343] This self-interest embodies the perils of entitlement when it comes to community spatial dynamics: If one owns a home and wishes to increase its value, they translate their selfishness into political action, projecting their desires unto the community beyond their property lines.

One study out of Boston University found that individuals who participate in local government (typically older, long-time residents and male homeowners) are more likely to oppose new housing developments.[344] Another, out of the University of California, found that "cities that were whiter than their metropolitan area in 1970 are more likely to have restrictive land use patterns in 2006," and that land use regulation has become another way to segregate communities.[345]

NIMBYs and their cousins—yes-in-my-backyard (YIMBYs), public-housing-in-my-backyard (PHIMBYs), not-against-my-business/industry (NAMBIs), not-in-my-neighborhood (NIMNs), and place-in-Blacks'-backyards (PIBBYs), to name a few—form a conflicting clash of interests that challenge the very idea of community and ownership. How can we balance people's efforts to engage themselves with a community and the desires and self-interests of residents themselves? This dilemma helps in understanding why there would be such

343 Andrew B. Hall and Jesse Yoder, "Does Homeownership Influence Political Behavior? Evidence from Administrative Data," Stanford University, March 26, 2019.

344 Einstein, Katherine Levine, Maxwell Palmer, and David Glick. "Who Participates in Local Government? Evidence from Meeting Minutes." *Perspectives on Politics* 17, no. 1 (2018): 28-46.

345 Jessica Trounstine, "The Geography of Inequality: How Land Use Regulation Produces Segregation and Polarization," University of California, Merced, July 2018.

polarized interests regarding certain developments, but also in questioning if where we live can be considered a community at all. Throughout the constant changes in urban politics, economy, and migration patterns, we tend to overlook the value of place-keeping in favor of place-making. This is to say we are looking for a place to speak to every part of us, instead of tuning our personal dials to fit into an existing community.

PLACE-KEEPING AND PLACE-MAKING

There are about 1,000 streets today named after Dr. Martin Luther King, Jr. They span forty-one states and exist in all types of areas. The act of designating a street after Dr. King is seen by many as a way to commemorate and spread the message of the late civil rights leader. But there have been many protests, boycotts, petitions, marches, and even lawsuits contesting the renaming process. Tensions between what streets or roads should be renamed present a complex issue for some cities. Should it be a major road or a small road? Should it go through Black neighborhoods? Should it just be a dedication? Should it be roads that connect different neighborhoods?

Some business owners and residents oppose renaming, citing loss of business and potential violence. Others support it for increased foot traffic and tourism. The symbolism of what streets are designated after Dr. King have been pointed out by many researchers. Even Chris Rock, famous comedian and actor, highlights in a stand-up special, "I don't give a fuck where you at in America, if you on Martin Luther King Boulevard, it's some violence going down."[346]

---

346 Bil David, "Chris Rock MLK Blvd," January 14, 2015, video, 1:10

On the topic of commemorative activism and place-making efforts, cultural geographer Derek Alderman has taken a keen interest in King Streets. Due to the lack of a national database of all the King Streets, Alderman writes, "Limited census-related research suggests that the majority of these streets have lower incomes and higher inequalities and levels of racial segregation than city-wide and national norms."[347] The spatial geography is correlated with physical markers of economic segregation—research out the University of North Texas found that residents in neighborhoods with MLK streets are almost $6,000 poorer than those without.[348]

The politics of belonging, as demonstrated by King Streets across the country, raise the issue of spatial place-making and place-keeping in urban communities. Some think King Streets are a testament to King's message, but others are quick to point out that concentrated crime and poverty on these streets are constant reminders of struggles and marginalization faced by Black folks.[349] Likewise, the renaming of streets and plazas for the Black Lives Matter movement has drawn both praise and criticism of performative allyship and support. In both examples, it begs two questions: At what point does a symbolic gesture become a taunt, and what does the name of a place mean if its root is performative?

---

347 Tanvi Misra, "The Remaking of Martin Luther King Streets," Bloomberg CityLab, November 23, 2015

348 "UNT Student Researches U.S. Streets Named for Martin Luther King Jr," North Texas eNews, January 5, 2011

349 Derek Alderman, and Joshua Inwood, "Street Naming and the Politics of Belonging: Spatial Injustices in the Toponymic Commemoration of Martin Luther King Jr," *Social & Cultural Geography* 14, no. 2 (March 2013)

* * *

Ethnic enclaves and gay villages are just two examples of places that serve a community. But there are many places across cities that can tie a community together: parks, community centers, town centers, etc. It's important for us to recognize the value of these places and to take steps to preserve and protect them. However, some might argue that place-keeping requires more maintenance and money. But through proper care and resources, places can be maintained and even operated by community volunteers. This provides not only a sense of place for users, but also a sense of ownership for residents, as seen in Houston with the Pasadena Trails, or the various community-owned mobile home parks and housing cooperatives across the country.

Community ownership models could also allow for collaboration with local artists and residents who can elevate these places with their respective knowledge and talents. Things like green spaces and landscaping, textures and functional spaces, and breakout rooms and collaborative spaces should be emphasized in buildings and urban design. Furthermore, when we design for communities, we must be cognizant, aware, and attentive in creating adaptable, human-centered services, amenities, and spaces.

The line between cultural appropriation and cultural appreciation is a thin one, so a key to creating coexisting networks within urban settings is communication. As a species, the idea of a home base and territory provides us with familiarity and routine. Places help us recognize where we are and influence our interpretation of livability. Our self-identified communities represent the settings for our interactions, as well as the groups of people we associate with. By removing the physical setting and environment of one's community, sense of belonging becomes dependent solely on the nonphysical.

Glass walls erected by different communities serve many purposes. First, they establish a home base for inhabitants, enabling a type of preservation that can't be attained elsewhere in a city. Second, they allow others to gaze into the life of that community, allowing for sound and brief interactions. Lastly, they push those within to become self-aware in space and time. They can sometimes force behavior adjustment—a switch in dialect or a transition in facial expressions. This change in behavior is largely attributed to how a place looks and feels different than others, and this perceived difference is largely a non-conscious one.

In writing about the underwater research of biologist Elizabeth Sherman, Akiko Busch writes, "Her belonging has less to do with an allegiance *to* a place than an absorption *by* a place."[350] This quote aptly lends itself to how humans interact with a space—or rather, how a space interacts with humans.

---

350 Busch, Akiko, *How To Disappear: Notes on Invisibility in a Time of Transparency.* (New York: Penguin Press, 2019): 75.

10

WHAT'S THAT CALLED?

———

"Place is security, space is freedom: We are attached to the one and long for the other."

YI-FU TUAN[351]

———

My high school was a prison complex. And I mean that in a quite literal sense. The brutalist building located on the west side of town was built in 1971, and aside from the non-architectural components—hallway patrols, bells signifying time changes, unjust detentions and punishments from authoritative figures—my high school has drawn comparisons to a prison for decades. The restrictive architectural properties of the building (such as lack of windows, chipped and monotonous paint, and crumbling fixtures and doorframes) made it difficult to learn and connect. When

---

351 Yi-Fu Tuan, *Space and Place: The Perspective of Experience* (Minneapolis: University of Minnesota Press, 1977): 3.

I entered other academic spaces, such as museums or college buildings, I felt more engaged and inclined to learn. Whether or not these things were placebos, I still felt like I was doing my brain an injustice by subjecting it to ugly and uninviting spaces.

In many contexts, spaces and places are used interchangeably. But they are very different. A space is a static gap, the skeletal confinement of unused area: a blank canvas. A place is a compiled collection of external stimuli, distinctive physical elements that direct connections for users; the intersection of bodily senses and perception of a physical environment. A space is devoid of meaning, such as a hotel room, and a place is full of meaning, such as a neighborhood restaurant. If places are the ones that mold us and our identities, then spaces are the ones that challenge us and our identities.[352]

Within our cities, there is nothing like a place—a park, a plaza, a street, a bridge—that feels like your own. It could be the street you grew up on, the park where you met your best friends, or a view front from which you saw countless sunsets. These places mean something to us, but they can also mean different things to others. The street could represent a bad car accident, the park a bad fight, the view front a tough conversation. In fact, the region of our brain most responsible for forming long-term memories, the hippocampus, is the same place that controls our spatial navigation and place recognition, which helps to explain why our memories are

---

352 Drew Moser, "Space vs. Place [and why it's important to know the difference]," DrewMoser.com (blog), July 12, 2016.

always tied to a place and why places from our childhood never fail to bring back certain memories.[353]

Within cities, it's important for planners to consider the duality of space and design, for these spaces help us heal, laugh, experience, reflect, and congregate. In addition to transforming and democratizing spaces to be more inclusive, it's also important to create spaces specifically for people of color, for marginalized communities, for disabled folks, for victims—not as a proclamation of self-segregation, but for self-expression and existence without surveillance or tokenization. Establishing different spaces within cities is critical to fostering a sense of place and belonging, and as far as gentrification goes, a sense of belonging is tied to both conscious and non-conscious cues.

* * *

For each of the cities and regions I discussed, there are two things contributing to the feel of cities beyond our control: climate and the naturally occurring colors (which are generally a reflection of the climate and geography). Climate (or long-term weather patterns) is the omnipresent babysitter for the geography and ecology of a place; it nurtures the physical landforms and bio-geophysical processes that crawl about them. This, of course, varies with respect to space (and time, but that takes years upon years, and in the case of climate change, human activity) and results in parts of the country

353 Martin Pedersen, "How Architecture Affects Your Brain: The Link Between Neuroscience and the Built Environment," ArchDaily, July 25, 2017.

looking and feeling different than others (notwithstanding the built environment).

For example, the Northeast, with its semi-mountainous terrain and elevation changes, experiences all four seasons, and thus has colors ranging from greens of spring and summer vegetation, to reds and oranges of the fall, to browns and whites of wintertime. The Pacific Northwest taunts colors from the greyscale—blacks from natural minerals and coals, greys from the cloudiness and rainy seasons, and whites from mountainous snowcaps—with flashes of green from its vast natural landscapes. In the hot and humid regions of Georgia and Florida, we think of browns and greens from swamps and warm colors such as oranges and reds from peaches.

We've incorporated this collective interaction with the physical world into our daily lives and cultures—from our language (the wind patterns due to flatness of the Midwest and proximity to Lake Michigan earned Chicago the moniker of "The Windy City"), our belief systems (palm trees signifying victory in Christianity, butterflies signifying dead loved ones), and even our music genres (such as the emergence of Swamp Rock in Acadiana, Louisiana, and Southeast Texas in the 1950s, and East Coast vs. West Coast rap).

These areas are of critical importance. We know the impacts of and connections between things like color, language, religion, and music, to our minds and identity. Moreover, these interactions, as well as the ubiquity of vernacular architecture (the use of local material and knowledge by local builders and workers) have made way for regional architectural styles to characterize our places.

The American Southwest, for example, is seasoned with Pueblo Revival, Mission Revival, Pueblo Deco, and Spanish Colonial Revival architectural styles—all of which employ local materials and design techniques, such as adobe and stucco construction, rounded corners, low-pitched roofs with overhangs, inner courtyards, exposed timber beams, and thick external walls.[354] The East Coast is peppered with Georgian and Victorian architectural styles, among many others. Georgian architecture (which makes use of symmetry, gabled or hip roofs, quoins, two chimneys, and brick and stone) and Victorian architecture (characterized by steep roofs, porches, intricate moldings, and made of colorful wood or stone) both incorporate triangular pediments and reflect the availability of materials and historical attitudes. Another general example is the use of double windows, storm-windows and storm-doors, and tarpaper and burlap in the Northeast, the Midwest, and along the Great Lakes.

These permeations of climate, terrain, and physical environment show us that the human experience is innately spatial and shaped by the world around us. And rightly so. This adaptation to our surroundings is part of evolution and warranted by natural selection and survival. But there's a lot of things humans have built, and are continuing to build, that strip places of their individuality. Repetitive structures, monotonous housing communities, McMansions, stock floor plans, and cookie-cutter apartment complexes are just a few examples.

---

354 "The Features of the Southwestern Style Architecture," Santa Fe By Design, accessed April 11, 2020.

Most of this can be attributed to economics (via capitalism), principles of conformity, and patriarchal suppressions of design and individuality seen throughout American history. Large focus on the overall form of a building often takes attention away from other design details. Lack of consideration for material finishes, textures, lighting, colors, surfaces, and human-centered design in our environments is only hurting us. These details are typically value-engineered out, meaning developers strive to maintain functionality using the cheapest alternatives. As a result, we end up with impersonal touches and a brushing-off of surface-based cues (things like textures, colors, patterns, etc.) that actually contribute to our perception of space *more* than form-based cues (or the aggregate form of a building). This is because surface-based cues are more effective than form-based ones at eliciting inter-sensory and emotional responses, in that they involve neural pathways that touch our memory recall centers.[355]

Other economic factors, such as cost of construction, local zoning and building codes, fire codes, and profitability of mass production, play a role in why so many of our cities look alike. These were factors that resulted in tenement housing as well as suburban developments. Principles of conformity help explain why a property's value will increase if it resembles other properties around it in architectural style, age, condition, and size. As many before me have noted, architecture is not a neutral practice or occurrence in our lives; it either helps you or hurts you. And much of that has to do with embodied cognition.

---

355 Sarah Williams Goldhagen, *Welcome To Your World: How The Built Environment Shapes Our Lives* (New York: HarperCollins, 2017), 158.

Sarah Williams Goldhagen, a leading architecture critic and author of *Welcome to your World: How the Built Environment Shapes Our Lives* sets up the premise of embodied cognition: "[Humans] experienc[e] the world and the things in it according to conceptual categories, that are derived from their embodiment. Our cognitions are profoundly influenced, they're even structured by the fact of our human embodiment."[356]

* * *

In their 1979 book *Metaphors We Live By* George Lakoff and Mark Johnson highlight their breakthrough in cognitive linguistics and the significance of our physical interactions with our environment on our language, thoughts, and expressions. To put it briefly, the metaphors we use in our language are a reflection of our lived and embodied experiences. We associate our language and emotions with the movement and physiology of our bodies, both of which are undeniably related to the spaces and environments we inhabit and interact with.[357]

Some examples of this include saying "I'm on top of it," to express control over a situation, or "I feel trapped," when we're in a sticky situation, or "My mood sank," upon receiving bad news. These expressions stem from our physiological association of emotion with our physical bodies and environment, in what are called orientational metaphorical

356 Talks at Google, "Welcome to Your World | Sarah Williams Goldhagen | Talks at Google," June 15, 2017, video, 52:13.
357 Amanda Kolson Hurley, "This is Your Brain on Architecture," Bloomberg CityLab, July 14, 2017

concepts. The fact that we conceptualize our language based on our bodies and emotions represents a stark contrast from dualism—the theory that the mind and body are separate entities. In terms of the built environment, this is something we've encountered all our lives.

* * *

There's an intrinsic feeling you get when you're in a church, a movie theater, an office building, or even a concert hall. There's a different feeling you get when you're in a museum or art gallery as opposed to when you're at the doctor's office. The colors, acoustics, materials, layout, lighting, temperature, ventilation: it's all a concoction to make you feel a certain way. In a church or cathedral, the presence of high ceilings, long windows, ornamental design, and symmetry are just a few architectural properties that work together to invoke a sense of awe, which can foster religious openness, social cohesion, and gratitude.

These feelings help visitors position themselves in their larger communities and other prosocial behavior. Research also shows that feeling in awe increases belief in supernatural control, spiritual intention, subjective control, and availability of time.[358] In some newer healthcare facilities, the use of color is intentional and purpose-specific: ICUs have soft, neutral

---

358 Piercarlo Valdesolo, and Jesse Graham, "Awe, Uncertainty, and Agency Detection," *Psychological Science* 25, no. 1 (2014): 170-178; Patty Van Cappellen, and Vassilis Saroglou, "Awe Activates Religious and Spiritual Feelings and Behavioral Intentions," *Psychology of Religion and Spirituality* 4, no. 3 (2012): 223-236; Rudd, Melanie, Kathleen D. Vohs, and Jennifer Aaker, "Awe Expands People's Perception of Time, Alters Decision Making, and Enhances Well-Being," *Psychological Science* 23, no. 10 (2012): 1130-1136.

tones; waiting rooms have uplifting blue tones; and operating rooms have muted palettes of green and blue to help neutralize after-images of surgeons and assistants alike.

Another factor that plays into our experience is lighting, which impacts us even after we leave a space. Our circadian rhythm is responsible for our sleep and wake cycles, body temperature, productivity and wakefulness, and digestive systems. Part of our circadian rhythm is dictated by the presence of natural light. This is for two main reasons: Natural light is dynamic (meaning the color and intensity changes throughout the day) and is full spectrum. The different ranges and intensities of colors we see help send visual signals to our brains, where our suprachiasmatic nucleus (or SCN) sends a signal to our pineal gland (which regulates our hormones) to adjust accordingly.[359] This is why we are told to stay off our phones at night and have night-mode features on our phones, for the blue light emitted by our screens interfere with our natural secretion of melatonin, otherwise known as the sleep hormone.[360]

In buildings, it's critical to design lighting and spaces that aid occupant well-being. Exposure to daylight in office buildings, for example, has been proved to improve productivity, cognitive function, mood, and circadian rhythm.[361] In hospitals,

359 Adelah Nejati, "Lighting for Health and Well-Being: Circadian Rhythm Benefits," HMC Architects, accessed April 20, 2020.
360 "Blue Light has a Dark Side," Harvard Health Publishing, last modified July 7, 2020.
361 Boubekri, Mohamed, Ivy N. Cheung, Kathryn J. Reid, Chia-Hui Wang, and Phyllis C. Zee, "Impact of Windows and Daylight Exposure on Overall Health and Sleep Quality of Office Workers: A Case-Control Pilot Study," *Journal of Clinical Sleep Medicine* 10, no. 6 (2014): 603-611.

patients who have views to nature require lower dosage of medications and remain hospitalized for shorter amount of time.[362] Lastly, one study done on 21,000 elementary school-children found a 20 to 26 percent improvement in math and reading scores in classrooms with maximum daylight.[363] These connections between our well-being and the built environment have been well documented, and social design and thoughtful considerations for occupants offer ways to improve people's livelihoods.

Two other factors that contribute to our perception of a space is tactile and auditory simulation. Tactile simulation is the physiological response we receive from an object's touch, temperature, and texture. Beyond just physical touch, tactile stimulation can be invoked by simply looking at different textures and can offer benefits of enhanced learning and processing, especially for children. We can imagine the cold and rough feel of metal and concrete, just like we can feel the warmth and smooth feel of fur or silk.

Auditory stimulation is the physiological response we receive from sounds and vibrations in our surroundings. Architectural acoustics play a major role in auditory stimulation, in that they help control and facilitate cognitive performance, privacy, collaboration, energy levels, and sleep quality. This is why some highway corridors have sound walls (to deflect and absorb noise), libraries and coffee shops can be productive places to

362 R.S. Ulrich, "View Through a Window May Influence Recovery From Surgery," *Science* 224, no. 4647 (1984): 420-421.

363 Heschong, Lisa, Roger Wright, and Stacia Okura, "Daylighting Impacts on Human Performance in School," *Journal of the Illuminating Engineering Society* 31, no. 2 (2013): 101-114.

work (ambient sound provides sense of surroundings), and trying to listen to something underwater is extremely difficult.

Both these types of stimulation shape our perception of spaces we interact with. A loud and repetitive noise, such as a train track or construction sounds, can be distracting and disruptive. In contrast, natural sounds, such as birds chirping or water falling, can create a sense of peace and serenity. Likewise, a large industrial door sends a different signal than a clear, glass door. A building with windows and breakout spaces sends a different signal than a building covered in bricks and vines. Lastly, a neighborhood with large sidewalks, grassy parks, and visible markers of culture (such as art or food establishments) sends a different signal than a neighborhood with rocky potholes, decrepit buildings, and distorted echoes and loud acoustics.

Humans, as animals, are intrinsically drawn to patterns; they provide us with order, identification, and information. We also crave visual variety, so it's no surprise that complexity of pattern is important to engaging occupants. This plays a big part in why we find European cities to be so engaging, despite cultural differences and language barriers: There are constant streams of ornamentation, people, patterns, details, and land uses. I mention all this to point out that our physical surroundings play a pivotal role in how we perceive a space and conceive our thoughts, often traversing our sensory inputs without us consciously aware of it.

Another layer of our perception of space is related to how our bodies and senses react to them. This is made evident by paying close attention to our respiratory and immune system in certain buildings. In some cases, our buildings can literally make us sick, which primarily happens in two ways. Sick Building Syndrome (SBS) is when occupants suffer acute symptoms (such as headaches, irritation of the eyes, nose or throat, dizziness/nausea, and dry or itchy skin) after being in an unhealthy building. Building-Related Illness (BRI) is when occupants suffer clinically defined symptoms (such as muscle aches, persistent coughing, chest pain, fever, or chills) that may be similar to allergic reactions or infections. The difference between these two is that in SBS, symptoms subside after leaving the building whereas in BRI, symptoms are sustained.[364]

One of the biggest causations of SBS and BRI is indoor air quality (or IAQ). Poor air quality can result from insufficient ventilation or the presence of air contaminants, such as volatile organic compounds (VOCs, like formaldehyde), mold, ozone, particulate matter, dust or allergens, sulfur dioxide, nitrogen oxides, carbon monoxide, and carbon dioxide. These contaminants come from products, excess moisture, material finishes, as well as outside air. The EPA reports that IAQ can be two to five times worse than outdoor air, and a 1984 report from the World Health Organization found that up to 30 percent of new or remodeled buildings may have compromised IAQ.[365]

364 Sumedha M. Joshi, "The Sick Building Syndrome," *Indian Journal of Occupational and Environmental Medicine* 12, no. 2 (2008): 61-64.
365 "Sick Building Syndrome and Building Related Illness," Healthy Building Science, October 2, 2015; Jeff Flowers, "Why You (Probably) Have Poor Air Quality," Compact Appliance, February 16, 2015.

One critical component provided by buildings is the relationship between health and work, or social well-being and economic well-being. Occupational health has become increasingly relevant in the corporate world. The impact of workplaces has extensive ramifications on human health, particularly as relates to stress, rest, exercise, and mental health. Poor human health, despite the cause, can result in lost productivity—further straining the balance between people and profit. Numerous studies, like one out of Harvard and Syracuse Universities, find that healthy and well-ventilated buildings reduce SBS symptoms, reduces absenteeism (which translates to higher productivity and thus, revenue), and leads to healthier employees.[366] Therefore, it's no surprise that the link between human health and sustainable design is one to be valued and examined.

When I spoke to Goldhagen about how we treat design, she highlighted the contingency of health on architecture, saying, "We need to reframe the built environment and its design as a public health problem. Because it is, but people don't realize it is." Not only do we bear the brunt of physically unhealthy buildings, but our bodies and our brains hurt as well. Could it be that the mundane and repetitious nature of some neighborhoods (huge complexes, lack of variety in materials and colors, unkept streets, etc.) reinforces negative stereotypes about certain groups of people? Moreover, does the presence of "exciting design" in gentrified neighborhoods

---

366 Colleen Walsh, "Your Building Might Be Making You Sick. Joe Allen Can Help," Harvard Gazette, February 14, 2018; "The Impact of Green Buildings on Cognitive Function," Harvard University Sustainability, accessed April 21, 2020.

(public murals, greenery, outdoor seating, etc.) induce a halo effect of sorts?

* * *

Neglected communities and ghettos, as discussed in Chapter 8, have a specific look. The design and construction of buildings in disinvested neighborhoods differ immensely from affluent neighborhoods, creating a gap in user experience and perception. But aside from changes in socioeconomic data, neighborhoods that undergo gentrification, too, experience change in aesthetic and feel.

This gap has been studied by experts from a range of fields including policy, planning, neuroscience, and psychology. It turns out that science backs the feelings we have in these spaces. A 2011 study conducted by Colin Ellard, director of the Urban Realities Lab at the University of Waterloo, found subjects walking by bland, monotonous, and passionless buildings experienced a spike in cortisol (stress) than compared to buildings described as lively and busy.[367] Cortisol has repeatedly been linked to increased rates of heart disease, depression, and lower life expectancy, meaning that boring and unresponsive designs and cityscapes could very well be harming us over time.

Danish architect Jan Gehl, as well as many others, found that compared to active facades, people actually walk faster and with their heads down when walking past boring ones,

---

367 Jacob Urist. "The Psychological Cost of Boring Buildings," The Cut, April 12, 2016; Colin Ellard, "Streets with no game," AEON, September 1, 2015.

so as to escape the monotony. In fact, he recommends that city streets should be designed such that the average walker—moving at about five kilometers per hour—experiences a new sight every five seconds. But what does this mean for people in boring or repetitive neighborhoods? It could signify that folks in those areas—immersed in boredom and low states of arousal and physiological responses—are suffering from unhealthy architecture and design.

Ellard notes, "The holy grail in urban design is to produce some kind of novelty or change every few seconds. [...] Otherwise, we become cognitively disengaged."[368] Other studies and findings have shown that humans crave variety in building size and depth, green spaces, a sense of thrill, and that boringness even in small increments can cause stress.[369] Alas, all these things that we thought were insignificant become essential components of how we perceive the spaces we occupy.

* * *

Sense of place is essential for inclusivity and belonging in cities. Sometimes, this can be done by establishing and dedicating meanings to physical landmarks and structures that support an urban fabric, like the Black Heritage Trail and the Freedom Trail, which together connect over twenty-five landmarks and sites to shed light on the history of Boston,

---

368 Ibid.

369 Justin B. Hollander, and Ann Sussman, "Boring Cityscapes are Bad for Your Health," The Boston Globe, October 12, 2015; Merrifield, Colleen and James Danckert, "Characterizing the Psychophysiological Signature of Boredom," *Experimental Brain Research* 232 (2014): 481–491; "Are Cities Making Us Depressed?" November 5, 2015. In *WBUR*. Podcast, MP3 audio, 9:53.

or the Stonewall Inn in Greenwich Village, Manhattan (the site of the Stonewall Riots in 1969) which now stands as a beacon of LGBTQIA+ pride.

But for some places, place attachment and sense of belonging are severely lacking, especially in poverty-stricken, disinvested, and neglected neighborhoods. The barren design of ghettos—repetitive, characterless buildings, monotonous building styles and materials, lack of access to outdoor, green, and public spaces—is quite intentional, as is the very presence of ghettos themselves.

The realities of our physical presence and identities requires a balance of space and place: space to provide detachment, solitude, and reflection, and place to provide purpose, humility, and familiarity. Cities, as spaces, need to be adaptable and mobile in their physical presences. Places need to be able to promote dialogue, understanding, and compassion. A few examples of projects doing this well include the Women's Mobile Refuge Trailer and the Restorative Justice Center in the Bay Area, Paper Machine in New Orleans, and the Arcus Center for Social Justice Leadership in Kalamazoo.

This delicate balance between space and place is one of freedom and security, which various institutions and policies have long sought to disrupt. Gentrification is just another pawn in the effort to uphold the imbalance. But the things we now know about cognition and design require us to be more conscious and aware of the spaces and places around us.

11

EDUCATION
FOR JUST US

"In cities in the United States, we cannot pretend that all bodies have the freedom to move through, occupy, and enjoy public space."

ISIS FERGUSON[370]

Growing up, I rarely used the front door. When entering someone's crib, we always used the side or back door. Whatever it was—picking something up from a neighbor, getting water after playing in the park, or coming home from school—the back door was my rite of passage. It wasn't until I made white friends (when we moved to a bigger house) that I started using the front door. All my life, I've been opening and closing doors, yet I couldn't rationalize why we gravitated toward some doors more than others. Maybe it was

---

370 Diana Budds, "How Urban Design Perpetuates Racial Inequality—And What We Can Do About It," *Fast Company*, July 18, 2016.

because the back or side door was always more functional, and the front door was for more formal occasions. Or maybe it was because those entrances were more connected to the yard and neighbors. But I soon discovered this wasn't just a Northeast thing.

In the Jim Crow era, when many facilities were duplicated and segregated, some were coinhabited and separated. In these places, folks not only occupied different spaces inside, but also used different entrances. Black and colored folks were funneled through back and side doors at schools, theaters, and buses, as part of the post-war ethnographic patterns that dictated how different groups of people moved through a space.[371] This residual Jim Crow etiquette, in many ways, dictated how we as groups of people interact with spaces differently.

The things I learned in school were very focused on the Western world, and even then, were whitewashed and dismissive of Indigenous history, Black and Brown communities, women, and queer folks. It was attempted propaganda—from the Pledge of Allegiance to history curriculums and literature—that intentionally excluded vital parts of history and the world in an effort to brainwash students to believe a certain narrative. My time outside of the classroom was where I really learned, but unfortunately, not everyone shares that privilege.

---

371 Steven Hoelscher, "Making Place, Making Race: Performances of Whiteness in the Jim Crow South," *Annals of the Association of American Geographers* 93, no. 3 (2003): 657-686; Ronald L. F. Davis, "Racial Etiquette: The Racial Customs and Rules of Racial Behaviour in Jim Crow America," California State University, Northridge, accessed July 4, 2020.

* * *

NUTRITIONAL EDUCATION

The identity of cities can, again, undoubtedly be tied to certain foods and cuisines. The restaurants we frequent, in many ways, uphold our urban fabrics; they provide places for city dwellers to congregate, help support the local economy, and increase the social interactions that we associate with cities. But for many places across the country, lack of emphasis on food systems is decimating our communities, thus posing a huge threat to urban living.

As patterns of immigration and settlement divided the country, so too did the role of food. After all, it's the basic form of sustenance for our bodies and provides us with a sense of belonging and familiarity. Coinciding with the rise in car ownership, the popularity of fast food establishments has exploded across the country and even the world. Starting with White Castle in 1921, the fast food industry has evolved to incorporate bellhops, drive-thrus, and personal brandings. America maintains the top fast food industry in the world, a feat matched with equally concerning rates of high obesity and caloric intake.[372]

In fact, multiple studies have linked a disproportionate density of fast food restaurant in low-income and minority neighborhoods with increasing rates of obesity and similar health issues. For example, 45 percent of dining

---

372 Cheryl D. Fryar, and R. Bethene Ervin, "Caloric Intake From Fast Food Among Adults: United States, 2007–2010," NCHS Data Brief, No. 114. Hyattsville, MD: National Center for Health Statistics. 2013.

establishments in South Central LA (a majority Black and Latinx neighborhood) are fast food restaurants, compared to only 16 percent in the Westside neighborhood (a majority white neighborhood).[373] Furthermore, a 2017 study looked into the causes of nutritional inequality and found that 55 percent of zip codes with a median income of $25,000 (less than the threshold for poverty for a family of four) are food deserts. This is more than double the percentage of zip codes that classify as food deserts nationwide, signaling that food deserts typically coexist with poverty.

The study also looked into household food habits and found that higher-income households buy more of healthy food groups (fruits, vegetables, proteins, and fibers) and less of unhealthy food groups (sugars and saturated fats). One particularly interesting finding of the report was that even when new supermarkets opened up in low-income neighborhoods or when low-income residents move to better-served neighborhoods, low-income residents were more or less still buying the same, generally unhealthy, food groups.[374]

This sheds light on the fact that even though food deserts pose a barrier to food access, we—as a nation—need to do a better job on educating folks about nutrition. Furthermore, the divide between socioeconomic class between households of different incomes reveals itself in patterns of obesity, exercise,

---

373 Tami Abdollah, "A Strict Order for Fast Food," *LA Times*, September 10, 2007.

374 Allcott, Hunt, Rebecca Diamond, Jean-Pierre Dubé, Jessie Handbury, Ilya Rahkovsky, and Molly Schnell, "Food Deserts and the Causes of Nutritional Inequality," *The Quarterly Journal of Economics*, vol. 134, no. 4 (2018): 1793-1844.

car dependency, and well-being. Another study found that rural and suburban residents eat more, walk less, exercise less, and drive more than their urban counterparts.[375]

Recently, a farm-to-table trend has swept across the country. Farm-to-table dining represents a healthier and more sustainable approach to eating. First, it reduces the distance (and thus emissions) associated with the travel of our food, which is important considering these "food miles" can number in the hundreds for a typical American plate of food.[376] Second, shorter travel time and distance means that foods are less likely to be treated with hormones and waxy coatings for preservation, making them healthier and tastier. Along with farmer's markers, farm-to-table dining improves the awareness around and accessibility of nutritional education— allowing folks to understand where their food comes from and what's inside of it.

FINANCIAL EDUCATION (OR LACK THEREOF)

In a country where the average household debt is over $100,000, less than half the country requires high school students to learn about public finance or economics.[377] In a time of growing national debt, student loans, and higher

---

375 Richard Joseph Jackson, and Chris Kochlitzky, "Creating a Healthy Environment: The Impact of the Built Environment on Public Health," Center for Disease Control and Prevention, accessed May 19. 2020.

376 Molly Leavens, "Do Food Miles Really Matter?" Harvard University, March 7, 2017; Lindsay Wilson, "The Tricky Truth About Food Miles," Shrink That Footprint, accessed May 23, 2020; Jane Black, "What's in a Number?" Slate, September 17, 2008.

377 Grant Eckert, "Why Is Financial Education No Longer Part of The Curriculum?" National Debt Relief, April 15, 2019.

costs of education, the need to teach young people about finance is severely understated. Topics like credit, interest, and investing are directly tied to bigger issues, such as housing, wealth accumulation, and retirement. Things like budgeting, credit, loans, and taxes are inexorably a part of our lives—so why aren't we being taught this information?

There is a false understanding that personal finance isn't taught in K-12 education curriculums due to lack of funding. But this misconception is inherently flawed, mostly because personal finance is essentially a branch of mathematics. The same principles that students learn to determine things like half-lives and rates of change are the same used to determine things like mortgages and interest rates—it's a matter of exponents and basic mathematical principles. A 2015 study published in the Journal of Human Resources found that financial education was much more effective when taught in math, economics, and social science courses than in standalone financial literacy classes (which were actually found to have almost no impact on one's financial success).[378]

In addition, an increased emphasis on standardized testing (coupled with decreased federal funding) has prompted school districts and teachers to focus more on subjects and content that will be tested, such as English and math. (Generally speaking, math tested on the SAT and ACT doesn't touch on financial concepts.) A report published by the National Endowment for Financial Education found that almost 90

---

378 Cole, Shawn, Anna Paulson and Gauri Kartini Shastry, "High School Curriculum and Financial Outcomes: The Impact of Mandated Personal Finance and Mathematics Courses," *Journal of Human Resources* 51, no. 3 (June 2016): 656-698.

percent of K-12 teachers believe that students should learn financial literacy in order to graduate. Yet only 30 percent of teachers are actually teaching these topics, 64 percent feel unqualified to properly use their state's resources, less than 40 percent have taken a personal finance course themselves, and less than 20 percent feel competent enough to teach any of the six topics surveyed: risk management, insurance, saving, investing, financial responsibility, and decision making.[379]

There's a strong correlation between the saving and financial habits of parents and their children. Given that Americans are collectively some of the worst savers in the world and hold an insurmountable amount of debt, many children aren't being exposed to smart saving and financial habitats from their parents. And if students aren't learning in the classroom or at home, then there's almost no hope that children will be taught these things. But for those who don't fully learn the importance of things like investing and saving, they end up suffering when it comes time to apply for credit cards, loans, housing, and insurance.[380]

ARCHITECTURAL EDUCATION

In a city, pretty much everything you see and interact with has been designed and manufactured: buildings, cars, lights,

---

379 Wendy L. Way, and Karen Holden, "Teachers' Background & Capacity to Teach Personal Finance: Results of a National Study," National Endowment for Financial Education, 2010.

380 Megan Lowry, "New Report Finds K-12 Teachers Face New Expectations and More Demands; Training and Workforce Changes Could Help," The National Academies of Sciences, Engineering, and Medicine, February 12, 2020; "Why Isn't Personal Finance Taught in School?" National Financial Educators Council, accessed June 19, 2020.

materials, art, even the positioning of trees and plants. Designers of our physical world—architects, planners, engineers, and so on—are fundamental in shaping our external experiences. In an increasingly diverse world, it's crucial that these designers are diverse themselves, and are able to design for all populations.

But such a task is difficult considering the field's underrepresentation of women and minorities, especially in leadership positions. Of the registered architects in America, less than 2 percent are Black, less than 8 percent are Latinx, less than 6 percent are Asian, and less than 15 percent are women; and the retention rates of these communities are even more alarming.[381] The last census survey by the Planning Accreditation Board on degrees awarded found that over 80 percent of American planners are white, and about 60 percent were men.[382] And of all bachelor's engineering degrees awarded every year, less than a quarter of recipients identify as women, less than 5 percent Black, and about 11 percent Hispanic.[383] These fields have long histories and reputations of being reserved for white men, and while there has been tremendous growth in the enrollment and graduation rates, there's still work to be done.

These values are the result of a few things. First, low-income and minority populations are already less likely to finish high

381 Toni L. Griffin, and Esther Yang, "Inclusion in Architecture," J. Max Bond Center on Design for the Just City at the Bernard and Anne Spitzer School of Architecture at The City College of New York, September 14, 2015.

382 Cassie Owens, "Urban Planning Faces Possible Diversity Setback," NextCity Foundation, November 12, 2015.

383 Joseph Roy, "Engineering By The Numbers," American Society of Engineering Education, last modified July 15, 2019.

school, enroll in higher education, and graduate. This has to do with income and wealth disparities and access to things like quality education, social and public services, positive role models and representations in media, and disenfranchised communities as a whole. A lack of representation in design fields reduces awareness of these professions in underserved communities, and a lack of education programs means that of the opportunities that do exist, few end up reaching under-represented groups.[384]

Second, the notion of selective programs and unpaid internships disproportionately affects minority and low-er-income students. Many lower-income and minority students cannot afford to go unpaid for their efforts—meaning they lose out on valuable industry experience. In turn, wealthier applicants who can afford unpaid intern-ships get more experience and thus can further develop their skills and portfolios, attracting better opportunities in the long run. Combine this with the costly and lengthy education process of becoming a licensed architect (about eleven years), and you end up with major barriers and underrepresentation.[385]

Lack of diversity in design is problematic for a number of reasons. It has been proven that increased diversity also increases creativity, productivity, dialogue, perspectives, and team problem-solving abilities. It also prevents income

---

384 "Diversity in the Profession of Architecture," American Institute of Architects, 2015; Kelsey Landis, "Growth in Racial Diversity Among Architects is Slow, but Experts Say the Conversation Continues," Insight Into Diversity, September 16, 2019.

385 Mimi Kirk, "Why Architecture?" *Architect Magazine*, February 7, 2018.

and wealth generation of minority groups, and leads to one-tracked products and innovations that only serve part of the population.

* * *

In terms of architectural education itself, there have been a few large criticisms of common pedagogy and approaches. First, the failure of instructors and institutions to enforce a practical sense of reality ends up placing burdens on employers to teach graduates about the working nature of architecture. Things like budgets, regulations, limitations, and client pressure are often missing from student projects. So too is fundamental background knowledge about construction and engineering processes and materials.[386] Many instructors pride themselves on not teaching the practicality of architecture, but rather how to think. And while this is incredibly important and heroic, students also need to be well-versed in the true intricacies of architecture as a profession.

Second, there's widespread use of hierarchal teaching environments. At many institutions, instructors transfer information in a way they see fit, in which their interests and opinions are cast onto the class. This model promotes a patriarchal and hierarchal learning environment in which students' voices and opinions aren't valued or considered

---

386 Andrew Hawkins, "Top 4 Concerns with Current Architectural Education," Hawkins Architecture, August 26, 2011; Phil Bernstein, "Architectural Education is Changing: Let's Hope the Profession Can Keep Up," Common Edge, January 22, 2018; Dou Dickinson, "Architectural Education Will Have to Change or Risk Becoming Irrelevant," Common Edge, January 4, 2018.

until the instructor deems them worthy (diminishing the possibility of partnership and mutual collaboration between professor and student).[387]

Architect and educator Peter Zellner points this flaw out in his interviews: "If you look at the sciences or medicine, senior researchers and graduate students are coworkers on projects. In architecture, we have this very antique model—and again it's mostly patriarchal—of information and ideas being handed down from elder to young people. The expectation is a kind of servitude in a way and I think that's pretty backwards."[388] This model fails to hold both parties accountable and fails to give students autonomy and responsibility in articulation and practice. In 2016, Zellner launched the Free School of Architecture as a way to revolutionize architectural pedagogy. His teaching model is one where "the student isn't simply a recipient of, let's say, 'approved' knowledge but rather acts as a co-researcher with the teacher and has a responsibility to make new knowledge."[389]

Third, when it comes to teaching architectural history, there tends to be a focus on more recent European, colonial, and post-colonial styles (beaux arts, neoclassicism, modernism, etc.). Moreover, there are even subliminal

---

387 Sherry Ahrentzen and Linda N. Groat, "Rethinking Architectural Education: Patriarchal Conventions & Alternative Visions From The Perspectives of Women Faculty," *Journal of Architectural and Planning Research* 9, no. 2 (1992): 95-111.

388 Diana Budds, "Architecture Schools Are Failing. This Designer Is Calling For a Revolution," Fast Company, October 5, 2016.

389 Gretchen Von Koenig, "Peter Zellner's New Architecture School: No Tuition & a Radical Curriculum," *Metropolis Magazine*, December 15, 2016.

racial biases in building visualizations, with an over-whelming amount of white and able-bodied scale figures in architectural renderings. Not only does this dismiss the existence of folks outside the prescribed norm, but it's rare to see elements of other cultural architectural styles (ancient African, Eastern, Indo-Islamic, etc.), thereby reinforcing the idea that these styles and people are not worthy of being served. In reality, global and diverse styles can help students understand the complexity and various approaches to design and help expand their palettes to include various methods, forms, and ideas.

Overall, architects and students need to be cognizant of the political, economic, and social ramifications of design. Yes, architecture is an art, but it also encompasses a great deal of science, engineering, culture, and philosophy. It requires a deep understanding of these contexts and how each con-tributes to the experience and function of design. Topics of cognitive science, accessibility, race, and health—especially now that we know about their roles in our perception and experience—need to become more of a focal point in archi-tectural education and curriculums.

* * *

The intersection of race and architecture is critical for mov-ing our world forward. Much of the cities we live in has been constructed and divided because of race, and we are still seeing how race informs traditional power structures and struggles today. Weaponization of design and planning in cities has decimated the vitality of certain communities and thus requires not only a dismantling of these power structures, but a strengthening of communal and societal bonds in cities.

One of the first times I saw the results of a lack of diversity in design was when I realized the inability of automatic hand sensors to pick up my dark skin—something that persists in almost every public restroom I enter. I eventually learned that these sensors weren't broken, but that they only worked when I showed the inside of my hands or a white paper towel. This is the result of racial bias in technology and design, which corrupts user experience for thousands of Americans and has huge implications in the fields of security and facial recognition. What good is automation and technology if it's going to uphold the same racist and oppressive attitudes that already exist in the world?

* * *

The Design Justice movement offers a rethinking and reworking of traditional design processes by focusing on sustaining, healing, and empowering communities marginalized by design. This intersection of race and space, history and architecture, and equity and design are the base of the movement. There is an emphasis on connecting community members with larger societal issues and on sharing knowledge and resources within a community.[390] Design Justice also calls for reallocated public funding, an end to the carceral state, redefined models of affordability and financing for neighborhoods, and self-determination for communities.[391]

---

390 "Design Justice Network Principles," Design Justice Network, last modified summer 2018.

391 "Design Justice for Black Lives," Colloqate Design, accessed May 21, 2020.

Design Justice organizations, such as Colloqate Design, Allied Media Projects, and Algorithmic Justice League, have formed to call for more just and representative approaches to design. An example of Design Justice is the Claiborne Innovation District in New Orleans, in which the space underneath a highway that previously segregated the community was converted into a public market and cultural performance space as a way to reconnect and heal community members.

As alluded to in the introduction, public and civic spaces are the most democratic ones we can inhabit. But other spaces—offices, institutional spaces, supermarkets, etc.—need to be democratic as well. One place to start would be to understand the intersections that exist in our world to enhance user-centered design and social justice in everyday life.

ENVIRONMENTAL RACISM

The ongoing climate crisis presents an equally pervasive issue for us all. For cities, especially those located on a coast, climate change will disrupt the majority of urban centers as we know them, displacing and creating millions of "climate migrants."

As mentioned in Chapter 6, the placement and proximity of toxic waste and treatment facilities, landfills, and hazardous incinerators near Black and Brown neighborhoods have serious ramifications on community health. This is the same story as Cancer Alley in Louisiana, the Flint Water Crisis, and the fact that twice as many Black students in Detroit—or 82 percent—went to schools in the most polluted parts of the city compared to white students. All of these fall under the umbrella of environmental racism, which states that under-lying causes of climate injustice are race-based.[392]

A study out of the University of Minnesota found that Black and Latinx folks are exposed to 56 percent and 64 percent more pollution when compared to their own rates of consumption.[393] In fact, race, more than income, location, age, or anything else, is the single biggest factor in determining one's exposure to pollution.[394] And as Ron Sims, Former Deputy Secretary of HUD, states, "A zip code is not just an address. It is a life determinant."[395]

Almost every city in America (and the world) experiences something called the Urban Heat Island (UHI) effect, a phe-nomenon in which urban centers are much warmer than their surrounding areas. This occurs because there are typi-cally more paved surfaces, traffic and congestion, and waste heat in cities—all of which work to decrease air and water quality. And in many metropolitan areas, such as LA, there is a strong overlap between areas with high UHI effect and

---

392 Zoe Schlanger, "Choking to Death in Detroit: Flint Isn't Michigan's Only Disaster," *Newsweek Magazine*, March 30, 2016.

393 Tessum, Christopher W., Joshua S. Apte, Andrew L. Goodkind, Nicholas Z. Muller, Kimberley A. Mullins, David A. Paolella, Stephen Polasky, Nathaniel P. Springer, Sumil K. Thakrar, Julian D. Marshall, and Jason D. Hill, "Inequity in Consumption of Goods and Services Adds to Racial-Ethnic Disparities in Air Pollution Exposure," *Proceedings of the National Academy of Sciences* 166, no. 13 (March 2019): 6001-6006.

394 Zoe Schlanger, "Race is the Biggest Indicator in the US of Whether You Live Near Toxic Waste," *Quartz Magazine*, March 22, 2017.

395 Charles Ellison, "Urban Planning Can't Happen Without Black People in the Room—Yet it Does," Congress for the New Urbanism Public Square, May 18, 2017; Jonathan Gang, "Ron Sims: How Where You Live Affects Your Health," Public Health Post, January 4, 2017.

lower-income neighborhoods (and vice versa), posing additional health and wealth barriers for vulnerable communities.[396] (Of course, this is also related to things like sprawl, larger lot sizes with bigger yards, less vegetation, denser housing areas, etc.)

A study mentioned in the previous chapter found heightened cortisol levels in those walking by boring and monotonous cityscapes. Well, it turns out there are recurring implications of urban design. Sims goes on to note,

> *"We realized that the built environment had significant epigenetic consequences for people. A neighborhood could either soothe them or it could bring a sense of wanting to escape or flee. If you look at cortisol levels, we see that flight response. If you have that flight response when you go to the classroom of a school, you can't learn because the information you're getting is being packaged differently than a student that comes in and is very relaxed."*[397]

The relationship between design and climate change should be automatic at this point. We need to embrace a future with more renewable energy, carbon neutral or negative designs, adaptive reuse, sustainable transit and development, building and transportation electrification, and carbon capture and sequestering technologies. But before and while we move to a more sustainable future, we need to

---

396 Angel Hsu, and Kim Samuel, "How Cities are Failing to be Inclusive - And What They can do About it," World Economic Forum, December 6, 2018.

397 Jonathan Gang, "Ron Sims: How Where You Live Affects Your Health," Public Health Post, January 4, 2017.

work constantly to promote racial equity and Indigenous sovereignty. Because without racial justice, there cannot be any climate justice.

* * *

FOOD

Food production doesn't always have to be limited to exurban land or rural parts of the country. The idea of food production and availability being central to urban communities has existed since ancient river civilizations (as seen in the Incan use of the Andes' Mountain for crop production). Recently, cities like Detroit, Cleveland, and Seattle have started to utilize their open land to promote urban agriculture, providing a more sustainable and efficient approach to food production. Along with community gardens, the two present a promising future that can alleviate burdens of food access, bring folks together, and educate the surrounding community on nutrition and the environment.

The Brooklyn Grange is a great example of using urban intensification for multiple purposes: it provides rooftop access for occupants, fresh food, and opportunities to learn in the city. In addition, hydroponics, aquaponics, and aeroponics present ways to grow food in water, mist, and air and in vertical farms—producing higher yields at a fraction of the time, money, and space.

Furthermore, nonprofits and community-owned grocery stores, such as the Mandela Co-op in West Oakland, CA, are a form of public partnership that intentionally benefits local farmers, residents, workers, and businesses in the area. Research shows that these types of supermarkets are more likely to succeed, as they prioritize community involvement.[398] Supporting local farmers and food production is better for the community as well: 90 percent of the money spent on food at farmer's markets are paid to farmers, compared to just 7.8 percent of commercially bought food. And of the money we spend at local businesses, 68 percent is recirculated back into our community, compared to just 43 percent from chain stores and corporations.[399]

FINANCE

In terms of financial education, there needs to be more conversation about its importance, both at home and in the classroom. It's also important to cultivate a sense of responsibility among young people to learn about financial literacy (through online blogs, books, projects, videos, etc.). For caretakers and educators, it's imperative to start talking about basic concepts, such as budgeting and saving, ultimately progressing to more complicated ones like mortgages, investing, and risk assessment.

Starting this education at a younger age will help students grasp the fundamentals and workings of the financial system. Caretakers must also demand and hold lawmakers and

---

398 Catherine Brinkley, "Why Community-Owned Grocery Stores Are the Best Recipe for Revitalizing Food Deserts," NextCity Foundation, September 13, 2019.

399 Caitlin Dewey, "Why Farmers Only Get 7.8 Cents of Every Dollar Americans Spend on Goods," *The Denver Post*, last modified May 2, 2018; "Small Business Saturday Statistics" Grasshopper (blog), accessed May 23, 2020.

educators accountable for teaching financial literacy. When they demand changes in the curriculum, policymakers and educators listen (as seen with technology and computer literacy reform).[400] Lastly, lawmakers need to increase funding for education as a whole and give teachers the salaries and resources they deserve.

DESIGN

There's always concern that good or sustainable design is too expensive and time-consuming to pursue for all projects and communities, but that's just incorrect. The difference between good design and bad design lies in the amount of thought and care given to the process, people, and planet. Sustainable design is a matter of using local and sustainable materials and expertise, and progressive technology and strategies, to decrease long-term operating costs and payoff periods.

We need to increase access to things like architecture and design as well as STEM fields to people of color and low-income communities. Educating young folks—especially those from marginalized communities—will create a promising path to more equitable and diverse environments. The Project Pipeline Initiative by the National Organization of Minority Architects and the Pre-Collegiate Initiative by the National Society of Black Engineers are great examples of educational and interactive programs. More awareness of and training around racial biases is needed in tech and design fields at large.

---

400 Olaf Jorgenson, "Why Curriculum Change Is Difficult and Necessary," National Academy of Independent Schools, Summer 2006; "Empowering Parents Through Technology," Digital Opportunity for Youth, Vol. 7, October 2010.

I urge all architects, designers, engineers, and planners to really think about what they design and for whom. Part of this requires pushing clients and contractors to see the value and necessity of diversity, culturally significant architecture, and sustainable design. If ethical reasons don't cut it, then the economic and social benefits will. As the guardians of the built environment, we have to continually advocate for diversity and inclusion. This means spreading opportunities, recognizing and using non-Eurocentric architectural styles, protecting the place of all communities, and being intentional about spaces to unite, create, gather, and heal.

Black, queer, Indigenous, minority, immigrant, marginalized, and women's spaces should be preserved, protected, and created—using the lexicon and communities themselves as a guiding force. One of the most beautiful projects that demonstrates this power is the National Museum of African American History and Culture in Washington, DC. Under the leadership of Lonnie Bunch, the museum was intentional in bringing together design teams that demonstrated diversity and embodied the museum's principles. Another example of this is the Feel It, Speak It open mic movement in Boston, which was started by architect and activist Jha D Williams as a space for LGBTQIA+ communities of color to express and connect via spoken word.

In terms of architectural education and representation, more efforts to increase and retain enrollment of minorities and women are needed. Some things that can help are more funding, scholarships, representation amongst educators, and better assistance for professionals returning to work after extended absences. This goes hand-in-hand with better mentorship programs, clear and written criteria for workplace promotions, and better community outreach and K-12 education.

High schools like the Charter High School for Architecture and Design (CHAD) and the Architectural Foundation of San Francisco's Build Institute are great examples of strengthening the pipeline for minority communities into design fields. Schools like this see almost 40 percent of their students go on to pursue architecture in college, and the rest continue into other STEM fields.[401]

For local officials and policymakers, I urge you all to start treating architecture and design like the public health issue it is. Consciously reworking patterns of development and transportation networks can help to more evenly spread access, opportunities, and systems of care. I also recommend learning more about the offerings of smart cities, just sustainabilities, community ownership, tactical urbanism, and design justice. Look into how they can improve a city.

CONNECTION
Social issues faced by urban residents rarely make it to the design or decision table. A public meeting informing residents of a proposed project is not community engagement, nor is retroactive engagement, tokenism, or one-sided information transfers. It is imperative that residents and those in urban networks have a more democratic role in the future development of their cities.

---

401 "Not Enough: A Lack of Diversity May Kill Architecture," The Thinking Architect, December 19, 2015.

In order to truly engage with a community, more power and ownership need to be diverted into their hands. This includes taking stock of residents and businesses in an area and understanding the cultural talent, knowledge, and expertise that lie in the community. Things like public-private partnerships, equitable development, co-operative facilities, and co-creation are a few examples of engagement strategies that promote two-way communication and collaboration. Developers and designers can partner with local artists, activists, businesses, and residents to inspire and cultivate change from within. Neighborhood organizations and centers can be formed and strengthened as a place for community members—and to cultivate a sense of pride and connection to place.

Because so much of this country and world is tainted by injustice, hatred, and suffering, there has never been a better opportunity to improve life for all. We are at a time when we know so much about so many things, yet we lack the will to transform that energy into action. For cities to become more inclusive, equitable, and just, they must start by acknowledging their histories and listening to marginalized communities. This should be followed by deployment of funds, investments, education, and resources to underserved neighborhoods.

They can also start exploring gender-mainstreaming approaches to decisions involving planning, policy, and budgeting, in order to consider and work out any results that might perpetuate gender inequalities.[402] Lastly, cities,

---

402 "Gender Mainstreaming," UN Women, accessed June 14, 2020.

companies, and governments in general should align themselves with the 17 Sustainable Development Goals (SDGs) put forth by the United Nations in 2015, which call for global advances in health, economic and environmental sustainability, and equality and equity for all. Above all, cities and those in power need to show they care—about others, about the planet, and about their communities.

* * *

In the words of architect and design justice advocate Bryan C. Lee:

> *"Language is important. Architecture is a language. And Architecture, like all languages, allows us to tell a story.*
>
> *Stories are important. Buildings tell our stories. And diverse stories come from diverse cultures.*
>
> *Culture is important. Culture is the consequence of persistent circumstances and immediate conditions. Our cities, our neighborhoods, our blocks incubate this culture.*
>
> *And for people of color in America, there is power in the places and spaces where our culture is recognized, where our stories are told, where our language is valued."*[403]

---

403 Design Plus Diversity, "Design Justice: Colloquial design for a just city | Bryan Lee | Design + Diversity Conference 2017," November 27, 2017, video, 35:23.

Readjusting the center of design to create inclusive, accessible environments should be at the forefront of every designer's mind. This requires not only a well-versed and educated designer, but a well-versed and educated user. After all, it's important to ask ourselves—who, or *what*, are we designing for?

12

EPILOGUE

"You can't escape the role you play in displacement any more than a white person can escape their whiteness, because those are both subject to systemic processes that have created your relevant status and assigned its consequences."[404]

Cities are magical places. But they have their baggage. And before you fix something, you must first figure out what's wrong. This book started as I was thinking about why I felt cities and design fail people. Cities—and people—are complex. As hell. While this book has some resolutions, it doesn't have all the answers, or even all the *problems* for that matter. It is merely a 30,000-foot view, packed with bits and pieces of information, insight, and wonder.

The magnetic draw between cities and people isn't excused from our notions of change. Our feelings, perceptions, and conceptions of spaces and places are transient and organic. They factor into the character and identity of a place. Decades'

---

404 Daniel Hertz, "There's Basically No Way Not to Be a Gentrifier," Bloomberg CityLab, April 23, 2014.

worth of discriminative policies and institutions that brought us to this point have become muddled and faded, and the inability to identify them has fostered a sense of complacency and jadedness within our communities and cities.

On the topic of gentrification, of which I, too, believed was a widespread issue, I learned just how complex something like neighborhood change is. Different places experience different types of change, which is largely due to their different histories. Gentrification does happen but, again, not as much as we think it does. Displacement of residents and businesses was where I drew my frustration from. But I realized my energy fared better addressing topics like housing policies, capitalism, discrimination, and exploitation, and focusing on the root causes of things like crime, poverty, and injustice.

* * *

Throughout history, the link between identity and community has provided a framework for how we view the world. As Europeans colonized the Americas, they brought with them their ways of thinking—appearing in food, culture, architecture, and language. In fact, the social, cultural, and economic shifts over the past 400 years have become so location-specific that we still maintain pretexts about parts of our country. Therein lies the setting for the Diaspora, where desire to Belong has been etched into the world around us. Just as social bonds were critical for the evolution of *Homo sapiens*, the need to belong is critical to our health and well-being.[405]

---

405 Roy Baumeister, and Mark Leary, "The Need to Belong: Desire for Interpersonal Attachments as a Fundamental Human Motivation," *Psychological Bulletin* 117, no. 3 (1995): 497–529.

Up until the mid-eighteen hundreds things like slavery, the gold rush, immigration patterns, and colonial differences were active in assigning identity to places. After the Civil War and Reconstruction, Jim Crow and the Great Migration were instrumental in creating the social atmosphere and interactions we live in today. By the nineteen hundreds, however, cities were forming and growing faster than ever before, and these shifts were central to things like housing shortages, mass transit, unemployment, and escalating racial tensions.

In the 1930s and 40s, as the country recovered from the Great Depression, a slew of new agencies and programs forged an institutional divide between different communities via redlining, restrictive covenants, zoning, predatory lending, and housing projects. By the 1950s, postwar attitudes had surrounded and engulfed the American landscape. The advent and adoption of the interstate highway system, suburbs, consumerism, and automobiles deepened the spatial segregation that was always present in America, and urban renewal, although present in the early nineteen hundreds, cemented those effects for decades to come.

The 1960s and 70s saw multiple liberation and counterculture movements, and a new presidential initiative unleashed a new wrath of institutionalized racism. By this time, cities across the country had already changed as a result of white flight, blockbusting, and public works; communities were touched by ghettoization, anchor institutions, houselessness, and poverty.

By the year 2000, cities saw trends related to population, mobility, and economics—some even experiencing an inundating flush of capital, newcomers, and gentrification. Since then, the impact of tech and innovation hubs have become more pronounced, as are those from housing shortages, high costs of living, and residential spillovers. If I am one to predict, the impacts of the climate crisis and climate migration will be the next inflection point for cities across America.

* * *

The role of economics (as both an underlying and overarching theme) presents a constant cause-and-effect relationship with cities. Gentrification tends to be as much an economic phenomenon as it is cultural, social, and psychological. This is to say, changes in a neighborhood are reflected in many, many ways. The more pressing matter, and the one we're not focusing enough on, is widespread poverty in America. The inability to comfortably maintain a modest standard of living—one that includes housing, food, transportation, healthcare, and basic resources and services—is one shared by Americans of all ethnicities and identities.

Within topics of economics and poverty lies an alarming wealth and resource gap between different groups of people—mostly enabled by a fraudulent collective of racist institutions and incompetent policymakers and officials. Our perception of poverty and crime is deeply flawed, our approach to rehabilitation and the prison system grossly skewed, and our barriers to equal and just housing, transportation, healthcare, education, wealth, and opportunities are persistently present.

Where we live and spend our time can say a lot about us. Most cities have handfuls of enclaves or cultural districts. These are the Chinatowns, Little Italies, Koreatowns, and Greektowns across America. Some cities also have gay villages, such as Greenwich Village in Manhattan, Provincetown in Massachusetts, and the Castro District in San Francisco. In all of these cases, the common identities, cultures, establishments, business, and even language create a place of pride and refuge, strengthening the sense of community among residents. Oftentimes, these districts are populated via chain migration and self-selection; they embody the essence of place-making and place-keeping.

The way we feel about a space is not only a testament to our individual character and identity, but reflective of the space we occupy. The architecture and design of our buildings and neighborhoods is not and should not be a neutral component in the human experience. Things like lighting, materials, ventilation, textures, shapes, and acoustics all contribute to our feelings, behavior, and productivity. And as our external environments inform our internal cognitions, we need to be intentional and deliberate about making all neighborhoods—not just business and tourist districts—inviting, purposeful, and vibrant.

Lastly, our knowledge is greater than our education, yet both would benefit from an expanded understanding of the world around us. For most of us, access to education is largely determined by where we live and our family's economic status. But even with access, there are still gaps in attainment between public and private schools, wealthy students and low-income students, and urban students and rural students. The need for comprehensive nutritional and financial education should be mandated and invested in as a supplement to traditional K-12 topics. Education cannot remain a partisan issue.

This means that things like climate change, Indigenous histories, sex education, non-white and queer literature, and global and current events should be taught to all students. Without education, we fail ourselves. And an uneducated public is destined to succumb to the bullies of the world. The role of architects, engineers, planners, and designers (not to mention accompanying professions in real estate, banking, business, healthcare, etc.) underline the world we experience, and it's time we provide a more holistic training of professionals, who can then provide a more transformational living experience.

* * *

This journey has taught me so much about things I thought I knew, but the more I learn and think I know, the more I realize how much I *don't* know. (Shoutout to Aristotle, Socrates, and Einstein for the validation). Despite all the hundreds of reports, journals, articles, publications, studies, books, lectures, interviews, and experts I've consulted, there's so much still to be explored regarding our cities, history, and communities—things like smart cities, busing, sundown towns, wars, social welfare, tribalism, drugs, environmental psychology, and popular culture. But my primary goal for this book was to open the conversation about how history is memorialized in our built environment. For me, it has created a sense of hyperawareness and intensified my information-induced anxiety, but I'd say that's a small price to pay. The world is an intricate and complicated web, and I don't mind getting caught in it.

* * *

The history of this country is rooted in hatred, discrimination, marginalization, and injustice. My call to action to anyone reading is to start thinking, learning, advocating, and investing. This goes hand-in-hand with listening, observing, and getting involved in your local communities.

OBSERVE

Start thinking about the spaces and places you frequent. What is it about a place that makes you feel welcome; is it the lighting, the ceiling heights, or the wall colors? Is it the textures, the furniture, or air circulation? Think about the spaces that make you feel cold and alienated. What does that tell you about the purpose of design? What lets you know that you are safe, or that you belong? How can you improve a space? How can you preserve a place?

EDUCATE

Explore the history of places. Learn the finance and economics behind everyday things. Learn about the forces and people that shape a society. Spark your curiosity, engage in discussions (both sanctioned and challenging), and push yourself and those around you to do better.

ADVOCATE

The data and the stories behind cities paint very delicate images. It's difficult to not fall victim to the finger-pointing at gentrification. Just because you are able to acquire a position in a neighborhood (regardless of external privilege) doesn't mean you should be drowned in the guilt of changing the neighborhood identity. There's talk in the field of how not to be a gentrifier, which points to seemingly irrelevant and minuscule actions to help rid ourselves of guilt and pat ourselves on the back. But as my friend and urban planner Wendell Joseph puts it, "If you're trying to do 'good' gentrification ... What even is that?"

There are ways to use your privilege to advocate, educate, and communicate. Moving into a previously disenfranchised community gives you an outside perspective. City officials may not listen to other residents, but they might listen to you, especially if you carry any of the racial or other socioeconomic privileges they answer to. Use your skills, join forces, and expand knowledge of those around you to lift the community. Communicate your struggles, address your privilege, and demand your local government and housing agencies to employ equitable practices.

INVEST

Invest your time, money, and resources to improve your surroundings. Support local businesses, volunteer your skills, and amplify voices within your community. Don't sacrifice your power to big corporations and corrupt politicians. The social and economic capital you hold is paramount, and you can choose to circulate that capital within your community.

ENGAGE

Get to know (and challenge) your local officials. Seek out or start neighborhood associations. Advocate for things like rent control, affordable housing, better transit options, and equitable policies. Respect and connect with your neighbors and community members. Get involved in local politics and city initiatives. Understand institutionalized racism and what resources are available to spread awareness and action.

* * *

In a conversation with architect Jha D Williams, planner Danicia Malone walks us through a line of questioning that addresses the seemingly constant evolution of knowledge and priorities when it comes to inclusivity and advocacy:

"It's time to go from community engagement to partic-ipatory design. Are the two different? Or are we just looking for kind of another slice, right like it used to be. [...] Are you diverse? [...] And then it was, are you inclu-sive? And then it was, are you culturally competent?"[406]

Or as architect Mabel O. Wilson puts it:

"Race in modern architecture is not about being inclu-sive. It's about questioning racial concepts, how we think racially, how that is embedded in the very things, the tools, the discourse through which we learn and understand architecture."[407]

406 Lourenzo Giple. "DAYLIGHT Podcast | Season 2 Episode 1 | Inclusion," March 21, 2019. In *Daylight*. MP3 audio, 1:18:00.
407 Syrkett, Asad, Tanay Warerkar, and Patrick Sisson, "16 Architects of Color Speak Out About the Industry's Race Problem," Curbed, February 22,

But a key point through it all remains how to properly honor and serve all communities through design. This realization poses questions about our advancements as a species and our capabilities to care for others. Because we *are* capable of building inclusive environments. We *are* capable of connecting neighborhoods and helping communities. We *are* capable of fixing the wrongdoings of the past. The answers, solutions, and methods are already out there; we just have to amplify them.

The Diaspora of Belonging represents many things at once. It is a call for people everywhere to look more critically at the spaces around them. Sure, there have been strides toward equality and equity—but there's also a growing divide between rich and poor. There are great contradictions in our cities and our country, all existing in the same Diaspora. The scattering of humans, both in and out and within this country, has demanded reflections in the built environment. Whether these migrations and calls for Belonging were welcomed or contested, reactions are sketched in stone, steel, and streets.

The histories of these twelve cities have seen tremendous amounts of change, from colonial settlements to gentrification, from wartime antics to economic strongholds. As cities adapt (either proactively or reactively) there are reminders that the sense and need to belong is innately human. Design is a language; a vehicle; a power. It holds the values of stories, cultures, and peoples. There are stones in the road, but good design takes time. Good systems require iterations to improve. Our cities need time, and our people need a place to grow.

2017.

But we need to start seeding. Because it's time for urban living to refocus on connection—with our environment, with the world, and with each other.

ACKNOWLEDGMENTS

———

Writing a book is hard. It all started with a DM from Eric Koester (aka, the GOAT).

During our first call, he convinced me into thinking I could write a book. I agreed. But I'll admit, at the time, I didn't know what the fuck I had gotten myself into. I thought this would a nice little side project. But it wasn't.

Naturally, the course of the book changed over the course of a year. The version you've read is quite different than what I had in mind. At times, I was so submerged in the sea of information (and in my head) that I forgot what I was doing in the first place. Luckily, I had some real ones to keep me grounded.

First, big shoutout to *all* the dandy folks at New Degree Press. I still don't how y'all do it.

Shoutout to my DE, Cassandra, for bringing this book the structure it needed and for the affirmation. Shoutout to my MRE, Paige, for being so trusting and for keeping it a buck.

Shoutout to Eric, Brian, Amanda, Emily, Srdjan, Michelle, and the rest of the team for the tons of support, guidance, and wisdom. (Sorry I skipped some of our meetings.)

Shoutout to the all the interviewees, experts, and smart people I spoke to. Thanks for letting me pick your brains. Shoutout to the fam. Thanks for giving me space. Lastly, shoutout to these fine folks who pre-ordered a copy. Thank you for the backing, support, feedback, and love.

Karen Hubbard	Jayson P. Albuerme
Adrienne Guyton	Montana Heise
Jacob Cottrell	Alviss Phua
Nick Corneilson	Justin Brown
Tamar Daniel *	Ally Thatcher
Vincent Tarpo	Justice Stuart
Noah Smith	Chris Lee
Michelle Nguyen	Meena Sharma *
Aaron Banks	Arjun Sharma *
Aruzhan Bazylzhanova	Rebecca Maloney
Assata Gilmore	Rebecca Keys
Anuj Gupta	Thomas Walsh
Zurum Okereke	Nicholas Collins
Anthony Waikel	Ruby Green
Tyler Lamar	Denise Caceres
Saida Osman *	Cyan Cosby
Carly Rose Roy	Karma Tashi
Jasmin Delva	Connor Bryan
Carolina Tornesi	Anadil Allawalaana
Victoria Miller-Browne	Eric Koester
Alexandra Miller-Browne	Jillian McCarthy
Sean Palmer	Amrita Patil

Jeremy Mankins
Rushi Desai
Ryan P. Conner
Luke Baily-Zona
Michelle Watt
Monica Chaudhary *
Georgia Bowder-Newton
Griffin Fuller
Chizua Onua
Wendell T. Joseph ~
Talia Matarazzo
Matthew Stone
Tenzin Kunga *
Simona Miller
Sudarmadhi Rabindran
Katie Ross
Curtis Tuden
Khambrel Simpson
Michelle Buckles
Kasiemba Okeyo
Ann-Elizabeth Le
Christopher Ellis
Andrew Santos
Jahna MacNamee
Everett Tu
Jasmine Walker
Annette Watters
Keme Etta
Camila Ribeiro
Tenzin Phunkhang
Nneoma Mbakogu
Liwam Beraki

Vincent Tran
Talia Broekers
Jaden Gladden
Ying Yang
Jason Chang
Tamara Brisibe
Tyler Cody
William Colin Mixon
Joshua Gregory
Brenden Drinkard
Fazana Afroz
Jordan Boileau
Shaurya Sinha
Enitan Adebonojo
Dare Adebonojo
Emma deRosas
Paul Dawley
Teah-Elyse Grupee
Lise Mansaray
Kyle Massa
Mark D'Aloia
George Damaa
Marcus Mazzotti
Jaylon Tucker
Iragi Nkera
Brianna Smyles
Rhiannon Arnold
Gurkriti Ahluwalia
Jordan Howard
Prince Kumar
Kara Hinton
Peter Ntala

Nate Bowser
Omozafe Udegbe
Heather Ren
Guransh Singh
Brandon J Wells
Patrick Trahey
Jonathan Chitamber
Selena Nadav
Loring Nies
Owen Bailey
Adam Williams
Julie Jesiek
Sara Volmar
Paul Corneilson
Beth McCuskey
Andrew Milne
Amrita Gill
Hayayine JeanMarie
Sabrina Singh
Ateev Nahar
Shalea Schriver
Abby Abel
Steve Wilson
Tayana Settles-Austin
Andres Carrillo
Jillian McCarthy
Katie Sermersheim *
Matthew Alexander
Cesar Montenegro
Nyla Gilbert
Dane Chapman
Amanda Warnock

DeMario Webb
Abdullahi Akorede
Sheyenne Harris
Jacqueline Christon
Seyi Akinwumi
Carl Kleifgen
Alyson Grigsby
Djata Nyaawie
Kori M Maxie
Humza Syed
Caitlinn Lineback
Shelbie Prater
Evan Williamson
Ava Richardson
Rohan Dighe
Roger Stewart *
Justin Thomas
Jordyn Tucker
Marina E Mehling
Medha Sthalekar
Laura Monies
Nathan Longo
Rayven Tate
Natalie Murdock
Barry Lewis
Zhao Ma

APPENDIX

———

0 AUTHOR'S NOTE

Buckingham, Cheyenne, and Joseph Gideon. "13 Cities Where People Are Proud of Their Communities." 24/7 Wall St. Last modified March 20, 2020. https://247wallst.com/special-report/2017/09/28/cities-where-people-are-proud-of-their-communities/.

Center for Sustainable Systems. "U.S. Cities Factsheet." University of Michigan, Pub. No. CSS09-06, September 2020. http://css.umich.edu/sites/default/files/US%20Cities_CSS09-06_e2020.pdf

Maciag, Michael. "Gentrification Report Methodology." *Governing*, January 31, 2015. https://www.governing.com/gov-data/gentrification-report-methodology.html.

Ratcliffe, Michael. "A Century of Delineating A Changing Landscape: The Census Bureau's Urban and Rural Classification, 1910 to 2010," U.S. Census Bureau. Accessed July 28, 2020. https://www2.census.gov/geo/pdfs/reference/ua/Century_of_Defining_Urban.pdf.

"Reflecting on an Act of Discrimination: County Council Recognizes Native American Expulsion Remembrance Day." King County, February 4, 2015. https://www.kingcounty.gov/council/news/2015/February/native_expulsion.aspx.

Saunders, Pete. "Detroit, Five years After Bankruptcy." *Forbes*, July 18, 2018. https://www.forbes.com/sites/pete-saunders1/2018/07/19/detroit-five-years-after-bankruptcy/#63854aeacfeb.

"The Most Loved Cities on Instagram," LendingTree. Accessed September 1, 2020. https://www.lendingtree.com/home/the-most-loved-cities/.

"Urban and Rural Areas," U.S. Census Bureau. Accessed July 28, 2020. https://www.census.gov/history/www/programs/geography/urban_and_rural_areas.html.

"2016 Community Well-Being Rankings." Gallup-Healthways Well-Being Index, March 2017. https://wellbeingindex.sharecare.com/wp-content/uploads/2017/12/2016-Community -Well-Being-Rankings-2017.pdf.

1 HOW WE SETTLED (OR BASE FARE)
1 MOBILITY IN SPACE

Andrews, Evan. "8 Ways Roads Helped Rome Rule the Ancient World." *History.com*. Last modified August 29, 2018. https://www.history.com/news/8-ways-roads-helped-rome-rule-the-ancient-world.

Brinkley, Alan. *American History: A Survey.* New York: McGraw-Hill College, 1995.

Encyclopaedia TimeMaps, Academic ed., s.v. "Hunter-Gatherers." Accessed May 25, 2020. https://www.timemaps.com/encyclopedia/hunter-gatherer/.

Encyclopaedia TimeMaps, Academic ed., s.v. "Origins of Civilization." Accessed May 25, 2020. https://www.timemaps.com/encyclopedia/origins-of-civilization/.

Geggel, Laura. "Humans Crossed the Bering Land Bridge to People the Americas. Here's What It Looked Like 18,000 Years Ago." LiveScience, February 15, 2019. https://www.livescience.com/64786-beringia-map-during-ice-age.html.

Shea, Matthew. "Exploration and Colonization of the North America." American Battlefield Trust. Accessed May 29, 2020. https://www.battlefields.org/learn/articles/exploration-and-colonization-north-america.

"Urbanization and the Development of Cities," Lumen Learning. Accessed May 25, 2020. https://courses.lumenlearning.com/boundless-sociology/chapter/urbanization-and-the-development-of-cities/.

2 CHESS, NOT CHECKERS

Beck, E.M and Tolnay, Stewart. "Black Flight: Lethal Violence and the Great Migration, 1900–1930." *Social Science History* 14, no. 3 (Autumn 1990). doi:10.2307/1171355. JSTOR 1171355.

Bushman, Richard Lyman. "Markets and Composite Farms in Early America." *The William and Mary Quarterly* 55, no. 3 (1998). doi:10.2307/2674528.

"Civil Rights and Equal Protection." Judicial Learning Center, accessed May 39, 2020.

Craven, Jackie. "Guide to Colonial American House Styles From 1600 to 1800." ThoughtCo. Last modified August 23, 2019. https://www.thoughtco.com/guide-to-colonial-american-house-styles-178049.

Sorting Out the New South City: Race, Class, and Urban Development in Charlotte, 1875-1975 (Chapel Hill: The University of North Carolina Press, 1998), Chapter 3, Kindle.

Jacobs, Jane. *The Death and Life of Great American Cities*. New York: Vintage Books, 1992.

Kimball, Fiske. "Architecture in the History of the Colonies and of the Republic." *The American Historical Review* 27, no. 1 (1921). https://www.jstor.org/stable/1836919?seq=1#metadata_info_tab_contents.

Nelson, Megan Kate. "Urban Destruction During the Civil War." *Oxford Research Encyclopedia, American History* (June 2016). https://oxfordre.com/americanhistory/view/10.1093/

acrefore/9780199329175.001.0001/acrefore-9780199329175-e-
313?print=pdf.

"Rebuilding the South After the War." PBS, accessed June 1, 2020.

Sanso-Navarro, Marcos, Fernando Sanz, and María Vera-Cabello.
"The Impact of the American Civil War on City Growth." *Urban
Studies* 52, no. 16 (2015). https://www.jstor.org/stable/26146215.

Semuels, Alana. "'Segregation Had to Be Invented'." *The Atlantic*,
February 17, 2017.

Silva, Catherine. "Racially Restrictive Covenants History." University of Washington. Accessed June 5, 2020. https://depts.
washington.edu/civilr/covenants_report.htm.

Pinkerton, James P. "A Vision of American Strength: How Transportation Infrastructure Built the United States." American
Road & Transportation Builders Association, 2015.

Polino, Valerie Ann. "The Architecture of New England and
the Southern Colonies as it Reflects the Changes in Colonial Life." Yale-New Haven Teachers Institute. Accessed
June 3, 2020. https://teachersinstitute.yale.edu/curriculum/
units/1978/4/78.04.03.x.html.

3 SHOW ME THE $$$

"Audre Lorde." Poetry Foundation. Accessed in April 29, 2020. https://www.poetryfoundation.org/poets/audre-lorde.

Clark, Alexis. "Tulsa's Black Wall Street Flourished as a Self-Contained Hub in Early 1900s." History.com. Last modified January 2 2020, https://www.history.com/news/black-wall-street-tulsa-race-massacre.

Desjardins, Jeff. "Visualizing 200 Years of U.S. Population Density." Visual Capitalist, February 28, 2019. https://www.visualcapitalist.com/visualizing-200-years-of-u-s-population-density/.

Edmunds, Susan. "Accelerated Immobilities: American Suburbia and the Classless Middle Class." *American Literary History* 15, no. 2 (2003). http://www.jstor.org/stable/3567923.

"Equal Access for LGBT Individuals." National Housing Law Project. Accessed May 6, 2020. https://www.nhlp.org/initiatives/fair-housing-housing-for-people-with-disabilities/equal-access-for-lgbt-individuals/.

"The New Great Migration: Black Americans' Return to the South, 1965-2000." The Brookings Institution, Center on Urban and Metropolitan Policy, May 2004. https://web.archive.org/web/20130617212732/http://www.brookings.edu/~/media/research/files/reports/2004/5/demographics%20frey/20040524_frey.

Furth, Salim. "A Brief History of Zoning in America—and Why We Need a More Flexible Approach." Economics21, August 5, 2019. https://economics21.org/history-zoning-america-flexible-housing-approach.

Gregor, James. "Mapping the Southern Diaspora." The Great Depression in Washington State Project. Accessed June 4, 2020. https://depts.washington.edu/moving1/map_diaspora.shtml.

"Great Depression History." History.com, last modified February 28, 2020. https://www.history.com/topics/great-depression/great-depression-history.

Department of Administration & Information, last modified March 1, 2013. http://eadiv.state.wy.us/housing/Owner_0010.html.

Gross, Terry. "A 'Forgotten History' Of How The U.S. Government Segregated America." NPR, May 3, 2017. https://www.npr.org/2017/05/03/526655831/a-forgotten-history-of-how-the-u-s-government-segregated-america.

Hoffman, Abraham. *Unwanted Mexican Americans in the Great Depression: Repatriation Pressures, 1929-1939.* Tucson, Arizona: The University of Arizona Press.

"Housing Discrimination Against Racial and Ethnic Minorities 2012." U.S. Department of Housing and Urban Development Office of Policy Development and Research, June 2013. https://www.huduser.gov/portal/publications/fairhsg/hsg_discrimination_2012.html.

"Housing Discrimination Under the Fair Housing Act." U.S. Department of Housing and Urban Development, accessed May 6, 2020. https://www.hud.gov/program_offices/fair_housing_equal_opp/fair_housing_act_overview.

Hunter, Marcus Anthony. "Black America's Distrust of Banks Rooted in Reconstruction." *Chicago Reporter*, February 22, 2018. https://www.chicagoreporter.com/black-americas-distrust-of-banks-rooted-in-reconstruction/.

Hur, Johnson. "History of the 30 Year Mortgage—From Historic Rates to Present Time." BeBusinessEd.com. Accessed June 3, 2020. https://bebusinessed.com/history/history-of-mortgages/.

Hyman, Louis. "The New Deal Wasn't What You Think." *The Atlantic*, March 6, 2019. https://www.theatlantic.com/ideas/archive/2019/03/surprising-truth-about-roosevelts-new-deal/584209/.

Kopp, Carol M. "Balloon Payment." Investopedia. Last modified June 28, 2019. https://www.investopedia.com/terms/b/balloon-payment.asp.

Lorde, Audre. *Sister Outsider: Essays and Speeches*. Berkeley, CA: Crossing Press 2007.

Mitchell, Bruce. "HOLC "Redlining" Maps: The Persistent Structure Of Segregation And Economic Inequality." National Community Reinvestment Coalition, March 20, 2018. https://ncrc.org/holc/.

Moore, Robbie. "The Death of the American Mall and the Rebirth of Public Space." The International, February 26, 2013. https://www.academia.edu/2650284/The_Death_of_the_American_Mall_and_the_Rebirth_of_Public_Space.

Pinkser, Joe. "Why Are American Homes So Big?" *The Atlantic*, September 12, 2019. https://www.theatlantic.com/family/archive/2019/09/american-houses-big/597811/.

Public Works Administration, *America Builds: The Record of PWA*. Public Works Administration. Washington D.C: U.S. Government Printing Office, 1939.

"Public Works Administration (PWA), 1933-1943." The Living New Deal. Accessed June 11, 2020. https://livingnewdeal.org/glossary/public-works-administration-pwa-1933-1943/.

"Questions and Answers About HUD." U.S. Department of Housing and Urban Development. Accessed May 6, 2020. https://www.hud.gov/about/qaintro.

Rosenthal, Elisabeth. "The End of Car Culture." *New York Times*, June 29, 2013. https://www.nytimes.com/2013/06/30/sunday-review/the-end-of-car-culture.htm.

Roth, J.D. "A Brief History of U.S. Homeownership." Get Rich Slowly. Last modified February 23, 2020. https://www.getrichslowly.org/homeownership/.

Rothstein, Richard. *The Color of Law: A Forgotten History of How Our Government Segregated America*. New York: Liveright Publishing Corporation, 2017.

Smith, Erin A. "The Media, the Suburbs, and the Politics of Space." *American Quarterly* 54, no. 2 (2002). http://www.jstor.org/stable/30041936.

"STATE MOTOR VEHICLE REGISTRATIONS, BY YEARS, 1900 – 1995." U.S. Federal Highway Administration, April 1997. https://www.fhwa.dot.gov/ohim/summary95/mv200.pdf.

"The Rise of American Consumerism." *PBS*. Accessed June 10, 2020. https://www.pbs.org/wgbh/americanexperience/features/tupperware-consumer/.

Tomer, Adie. "America's Commuting Choices: 5 Major Takeaways from 2016 Census Data," The Brookings Institute, October 3, 2017. https://www.brookings.edu/blog/the-avenue/2017/10/03/americans-commuting-choices-5-major-takeaways-from-2016-census-data/.

Weingroff, Richard F. "Original Intent: Purpose of the Interstate System 1954 - 1956)." Federal Highway Administration. Last modified June 27, 2017. https://www.fhwa.dot.gov/infrastructure/originalintent.cfm.

2 REGIONAL DIFFERENCES
4 THE NORFEAST

"A Region Divided: The State of Growth in Greater Washington, D.C." The Brookings Institute, 1999. https://www.brookings.edu/wp-content/uploads/2016/06/DCRegion.pdf.

"An Affordable Continuum of Housing ... Key to a Better City." Coalition for Nonprofit Housing & Economic Development, 2010. https://www.dropbox.com/s/fzs2zl74z91w13u/Continuum%20of%20Housing%20Report.pdf.

Berke, Carly. "People Before Highways: A discussion with Dr. Karilyn Crockett." Boston University Initiative on Cities. Accessed June 13, 2020. http://www.bu.edu/ioc/people-before-highways/.

Byrnes, Mark. "40-Year-Old Images Show East Boston Grappling With an Expanding Logan Airport." Bloomberg CityLab, May 6, 2013. https://www.bloomberg.com/news/articles/2013-05-06/40-year-old-images-show-east-boston-grappling-with-an-expanding-logan-airport.

Charlie Surrel. "Why Did The U.S. Let Highways Ruin Its Cities, And How Can We Fix It?" FastCompany, May 31, 2016. https://www.fastcompany.com/3060340/why-did-the-us-let-highways-ruin-its-cities-and-how-can-we-fix-it.

"Cities During the Progressive Era." Library of Congress. Accessed April 8, 2020. https://www.loc.gov/classroom-materials/united-states-history-primary-source-timeline/progressive-era-to-new-era-1900-1929/cities-during-progressive-era/.

Crowder, Kyle and Scott J. South. "Spatial Dynamics of White Flight: The Effects of Local and Extralocal Racial Conditions on Neighborhood Out-Migration." *American Sociological Review* 73, no.5 (2008). 10.1177/000312240807300505.

Dawkings, Caset and Rolf Moeckel. "Transit-Induced Gentrification: Who Will Stay, and Who Will Go?" University of Maryland, October 18, 2014. https://drum.lib.umd.edu/bitstream/handle/1903/21508/tod_gentrification_v3.pdf?sequence=1&isAllowed=y.

Edward L. Glaeser, Hyunjin Kim and Michael Luca. "Nowcasting Gentrification: Using Yelp Data to Quantify Neighborhood Change." NBER Working Paper No. w24010, 2017, quoted in Dina Gerdeman. "How to Know If Your Neighborhoods Is Being Gentrified." Harvard Business Review, May 23, 2018. https://hbswk.hbs.edu/item/how-to-know-if-your-neighborhood-is-being-gentrified.

Fayyad, Abdallah. "The Criminalization of Gentrifying Neighborhoods." *The Atlantic*, December 20, 2017. https://www.theatlantic.com/politics/archive/2017/12/the-criminalization-of-gentrifying-neighborhoods/548837/.

Gaspaire, Brent. "Blockbusting." Blackpast, January 7, 2013. https://www.blackpast.org/african-american-history/blockbusting/.

Ikonomova, Violet. "Report: Gentrification Not a Problem in Detroit." Deadline Detroit, April 24, 2019. https://www.deadlinedetroit.com/articles/22193/report_gentrification_not_a_problem_in_detroit.

Jones, Robert P., Daniel Cox, Rob Griffin, Molly Fisch-Friedman and Alex Vandermaas-Peeler. "American Democracy in Crisis: The Challenges of Voter Knowledge, Participation, and Polarization." PRRI. 2018. https://www.prri.org/research/American-democracy-in-crisis-voters-midterms-trump-election-2018.

Kennedy, David and Lizabeth Cohen. *The American Pageant: A History of the American People, 15th (AP) edition*. Stamford, CT: Cengage Learning, 2013.

Kye, Samuel H. "The Persistence of White Flight in Middle-Class Suburbia." *Social Science Research* 72 (May 2018). https://www.sciencedirect.com/science/article/abs/pii/S0049089X17305422.

Laniyonu, Ayobami. "Coffee Shops and Street Stops: Policing Practices in Gentrifying Neighborhoods." *Urban Affairs Review* 54, no. 5 (January 2017). https://doi.org/10.1177/1078087416689728.

Miriam, Zuk, Ariel H. Bierbaum, Karen Chapple, Karolina Gorska, Anastasia Loukaitou-Sideris, Paul Ong, Trevor Thomas. "Gentrification, Displacement and the Role of Public Investment: A Literature Review." Community Development Investment Center and Federal Reserve Bank of San Francisco, Working Paper 2015-05 (August 2015). https://www.frbsf.org/community-development/files/wp2015-05.pdf.

Misra, Tanvi. "Yes, 311 Calls Nuisance Calls Are Climbing in Gentrifying Neighborhoods." Bloomberg CityLab, October 18, 2018. https://www.bloomberg.com/news/articles/2018-10-18/in-new-york-city-gentrification-brings-more-311-calls.

Pyke, Alan. "Top Infrastructure Official Explains How America Used Highways to Destroy Black Neighborhoods." Think Progress, March 21, 2016. https://archive.thinkprogress.org/top-infrastructure-official-explains-how-america-used-highways-to-destroy-black-neighborhoods-96c1460d1962/.

Richardson, Jason, Bruce Mitchell, and Jad Edlebi. "Gentrification and Disinvestment 2020." National Community Reinvestment Coalition, June 2020. https://ncrc.org/gentrification20/.

Salvador, DeAndrea. "Can Curbing Gentrification Help Stop the Climate Crisis?" The Week, February 18, 2017. https://theweek.com/articles/680154/curbing-gentrification-help-stop-climate-change.

Sarachan, Sydney. "The Legacy of Robert Moses." *PBS*, January 17, 2013. https://www.pbs.org/wnet/need-to-know/environment/the-legacy-of-robert-moses/16018/.

Saul, John. "When Brooklyn Juries Gentrify, Defendants Lose." *New York Post*, June 16, 2014. https://nypost.com/2014/06/16/brooklyn-gentrification-is-changing-juries-who-decide-cases/.

Schweitzer, Ally. "How To Limit Gentrification Along The Purple Line, According To Housing Advocates." *NPR*, December 12, 2019. https://www.npr.org/local/305/2019/12/12/787445618/how-to-limit-gentrification-along-the-purple-line-according-to-housing-advocates.

Shaver, Katherine. "Suburbs Seeking Transit Look for Ways to Keep Residents from Being Priced Out." *The Washington Post*, November 28, 2016. https://www.washingtonpost.com/local/

trafficandcommuting/suburbs-seeking-transit-look-for-ways-to-keep-residents-from-being-priced-out/2016/11/28/110d5b6c-b01d-11e6-840f-e3ebab6bcdd3_story.html.

Shoenfeld, Sarah Jane. "How segregation shaped DC's northernmost ward." Greater Greater Washington, September 14, 2017. https://ggwash.org/view/64764/how-segregation-shaped-dcs-north-ernmost-ward-4-petworth-brightwood-takoma-shepherdpark.

"The Big Dig: Project Background." Mass.gov, accessed May 29, 2020. https://www.mass.gov/info-details/the-big-dig-project-background.

"The Rise of the City." Lumen Learning, accessed April 16, 2020. https://courses.lumenlearning.com/boundless-ushistory/chap-ter/the-rise-of-the-city/.

Thompson, Nicole Akoukou. "The Williamsburg Effect: The Gentrification of Brooklyn Is Being Reflected in the Court System." Latin Post, June 17, 2014. https://www.latinpost.com/articles/14961/20140617/williamsburg-effect-gentrification-brooklyn-being-reflected-court-system.htm.

Turrentine, Jeff. "When Public Transportation Leads to Gentri-fication." National Resources Defense Council, June 1, 2018. https://www.nrdc.org/onearth/when-public-transporta-tion-leads-gentrification.

"Urban and Rural Populations in the United States." Our World in Data. Accessed June 3, 2020. https://ourworldindata.org/grapher/urban-and-rural-populations-in-the-united-states.

Violette, Zachary J. "Nineteenth-Century Working-Class Housing in Boston and New York." Society of Architectural Historians. Accessed May 24, 2020. https://sah-archipedia.org/essays/TH-01-ART-003.

von Hoffman, Alexander. "A Study in Contradictions: The Origins and Legacy of the Housing Act of 1949." *Housing Policy Debate* 11, no. 2 (2000). https://www.innovations.harvard.edu/sites/default/files/hpd_1102_hoffman.pdf.

von Hoffman, Alexander. "The Origins of American Housing Reform." Harvard University Joint Center for Housing Studies, August 1998. https://www.jchs.harvard.edu/sites/default/files/von_hoffman_w98-2.pdf.

"Washington Post-Kaiser Family Foundation Poll." *Washington Post*, accessed May 16, 2020. https://www.washingtonpost.com/wp-srv/metro/documents/postkaiserpoll_052911.html.

"2019 U.S. Population Estimates Continue to Show the Nation's Growth Is Slowing." U.S. Census Bureau, December 30, 2019. https://www.census.gov/newsroom/press-releases/2019/popest-nation.html.

"38b. The Underside of Urban Life." U.S. History. Accessed April 8, 2020, https://www.ushistory.org/us/38b.asp.

5 THE SOUTH

Abrams, Amanda. "Using Preservation to Stop Gentrification Before It Starts." Bloomberg CityLab, December 14, 2016. https://www.bloomberg.com/news/articles/2016-12-14/historic-preservation-can-stop-gentrification-before-it-starts.

Andrews, Eve. "Why do Cities Keep Building All this New Stuff for Cars?" *Grist*, April 17, 2019. https://grist.org/article/why-do-cities-keep-building-all-this-new-stuff-for-cars/.

Bertolet, Dan. "When Historic Preservation Clashes with Housing Affordability." Sightline Institute, December 19, 2017. https://www.sightline.org/2017/12/19/when-historic-preservation-clashes-with-housing-affordability/.

Bolois, Justin. "8 Common Soul-Food Myths, Debunked." First We Feast, April 23, 2015. https://firstwefeast.com/eat/2015/04/soul-food-myths-debunked-adrian-miller.

Bridges, Roger D. "Codes." Northern Illinois University Libraries. Accessed June 7, 2020. https://www.lib.niu.edu/1996/iht329602.html.

Brones, Anna. "Food Apartheid: The Root of the Problem with America's Groceries." *The Guardian*, May 15, 2018. https://www.theguardian.com/society/2018/may/15/food-apartheid-food-deserts-racism-inequality-america-karen-washington-interview.

Campanella, Richard. "What Makes Architecture 'Creole'?" Nola.com. Last modified July 19, 2019. https://www.nola.com/

entertainment_life/home_garden/article_3e9f4d3a-6ae3-59b-d-9e49-b5dc8300fef1.html.

Chang, Alvin. "We Can Draw School Zones to Make Class-rooms Less Segregated. This is How Well Your District Does." *Vox.* Last modified August 27, 2018. https://www.vox.com/2018/1/8/16822374/school-segregation-gerrymander-map.

"Climate Gentrification: Fact or Fiction?" We Sell NOLA, May 16, 2020. https://www.wesellnola.com/what-climate-gentrifica-tion-means-for-new-orleans/.

Cooper, Christopher A. and H. Gibbs Knotts. "Defining Dixie: A State-Level Measure of the Modern Political South." *American Review of Politics* 25 (Spring 2004). https://1library.net/docu-ment/zwoxejly-defining-dixie-state-level-measure-modern-political-south.html.

Cruse, Kevin M. "The Barrier Wall: The Berlin Wall of Atlanta in 1962." ArcGIS, 2005. https://www.arcgis.com/apps/Cascade/index.html?appid=c6e0344494c7452c9e36a71626846fd1.

Davidson, Ethan. "History of the Atlanta Beltline Project in Public Roads Magazine." *Atlanta Beltline*, December 2, 2011. https://beltline.org/2011/12/02/history-of-atlanta-beltline-project-in-public-roads-magazine/.

Denton. Jack. "Is Landmarking a Tool of Gentrification or a Bulwark Against It?" *Pacific Standard*, July 3, 2019. https://psmag.com/economics/is-landmarking-a-tool-of-gentrifica-tion-or-a-bulwark-against-it.

"Edgehill NCZO Design Guidelines." Metropolitan Historic Zoning Commission, accessed June 28, 2020. https://www.nashville.gov/Portals/0/SiteContent/MHZC/docs/Whats%20New/Edgehill%20NCZO.pdf.

"Edgehill State of Emergency." The Edgehill Story Project. Accessed June 28, 2020. https://edgehillstateofemergencyreport.files.wordpress.com/2016/11/edgehill-report_11-16-16.pdf

Gustafson, Seth. "Displacement and the Racial State in Olympic Atlanta," *Southeastern Geographer* 53, no. 2 (Summer 2013).

Hanlon, Bernadette. "Beyond Sprawl: Social Sustainability and Reinvestment in the Baltimore Suburbs." In *The New American Suburb*, edited by Katrin B. Anacker. New York: Routledge, 2018.

Hatfield, Katherine H. "How The Music City is Losing Its Soul: Gentrification in Nashville and How Historic Preservation Could Hinder the Process." (master's thesis, Middle Tennessee State University, May 2018). https://jewlscholar.mtsu.edu/handle/mtsu/5676.

Hauer, Matthew E. "Migration Induced by Sea-Level Rise Could Reshape the US Population Landscape." Nature Climate Change 7 (April 2017). https://doi.org/10.1038/nclimate3271.

Hilmers, Angela, David C. Hillmers, and Jayna Davis. "Neighborhood Disparities in Access to Healthy Foods and Their Effects on Environmental Justice." *Am J Public Health* 109, no. 9 (2012). https://www.ncbi.nlm.nih.gov/pmc/articles/PMC3482049/.

Holliman, Irene V. "Techwood Homes." Georgia Encyclopedia. Last modified August 26, 2020. https://www.georgiaencyclo-pedia.org/articles/arts-culture/techwood-homes.

"Hurricane Katrina: A Nation Still Unprepared." Washington DC: U.S. Government Printing Office, 2006. https://www.govinfo.gov/content/pkg/CRPT-109srpt322/pdf/CRPT-109srpt322.pdf.

Ignaczak, Nina. "Metro Detroit Gets Ready to Grow with Transit-Oriented Development." Metromade Detroit, January 16, 2014. https://www.secondwavemedia.com/metromode/features/Transit-OrientedDevelopment%200329.aspx.

Immergluck. Dan. "Sustainable for Whom? Green Urban Development, Environmental Gentrification, and the Atlanta Beltline." *Urban Geography* 39, no. 4 (August 2017). https://doi.org/10.1080/02723638.2017.1360041.

Jackson, Richard J., and Chris Kochtitzky. "Creating A Healthy Environment: The Impact of the Built Environment on Public Health." Centers for Disease Control and Prevention. Accessed July 1, 2020. https://www.cdc.gov/healthyplaces/articles/Creating%20A%20Healthy%20Environment.pdf.

"Key Statistics & Graphics." USDA Economic Research Service. Last modified September 9, 2020. https://www.ers.usda.gov/topics/food-nutrition-assistance/food-security-in-the-us/key-statistics-graphics.aspx.

Lee, Trymaine. "Cancer Alley: Big Industry, Big Problem." *MSNBC*. Accessed May 19, 2020. http://www.msnbc.com/interactives/geography-of-poverty/se.html.

Leinberger, Christopher B. "The WalkUP Wake-Up Call: Atlanta." The George Washington University School of Business, 2013. http://www.cumberlandcid.org/wp2/wp-content/uploads/WalkUP_Atlanta_final-small.pdf.

Lind, J.R. "Historic Buildings in Nashville's Black Neighborhoods Are Disappearing." *The Nashville Scene*, September 24, 2020. https://www.nashvillescene.com/news/cover-story/article/21143499/historic-buildings-in-nashvilles-black-neighborhoods-are-disappearing

Little, Becky. "How the US Got So Many Confederate Statues." History.com. Last modified June 12, 2020. https://www.history.com/news/how-the-u-s-got-so-many-confederate-monuments.

Maciag, Mike. "Vehicle Ownership in U.S. Cities Data and Map." Governing, November 28, 2017. https://www.governing.com/gov-data/car-ownership-numbers-of-vehicles-by-city-map.html.

Maddock, Jay. "These Five Charts Help Explain Why the South Is So Unhealthy." *Vice*, February 8, 2018. https://www.vice.com/en_us/article/59kb4b/why-is-the-south-less-healthy.

Mariano, Willoughby, Lindsey Conway, Anastaciah Ondieki. "How the Atlanta Beltline Broke Its Promise of Affordable Housing." AJC, December 13, 2017. https://www.ajc.com/news/local/how-the-atlanta-beltline-broke-its-promise-affordable-housing/oVXnu1BlYCoIbA9U4u2CEM/.

Mazza, Sandy. "South Nashville Community Bitterly Split Over Plan to Restrict Development." *The Tennessean*. Last modified August 3, 2018. https://www.tennessean.com/story/

news/2018/08/02/nashville-edgehill-community-bitter-ly-split-over-plan-restrict-development/882358002/.

McCabe, Brian J. and Ingrid Gould Ellen. "Does Preservation Accelerate Neighborhood Change? Examining the Impact of Historic Preservation in New York City." *Journal of the American Planning Association* 82, no. 2 (2016). DOI: 10.1080/01944363.2015.1126195.

McClain, Dani. "Former Residents of New Orleans's Demolished Housing projects Tell Their Stories." *The Nation*, August 26, 2015. https://www.thenation.com/article/archive/for-mer-residents-of-new-orleans-demolished-housing-proj-ects-tell-their-stories/.

"Measuring Sprawl 2014." Smart Growth America, April 2014. https://www.smartgrowthamerica.org/app/legacy/documents/measuring-sprawl-2014.pdf.

"Messages from Mission 2: Partisan Gerrymander." USC Annen-berg, accessed May 15, 2020. http://www.redistrictinggame.org/learnaboutmission2.php.

Middleton, Stephen. *The Black Laws: Race and the Legal Process in Early Ohio.* Athens, Ohio: Ohio University Press, 2005.

Ness, Michelle. "A Short History of Edgehill." The Edgehill Neigh-borhood Coalition, January 2015. https://edgehillcoalition.org/edgehill-a-short-history/.

Olson, Siri Mackenzie. "Overlapping Historic Preservation and Affordable Housing: Successful Outcomes in New York City and San Francisco." (master's thesis, Columbia University, May 2018).

Orfield, Gary and Erica Frankenberg. "Brown at 60: Great Progress, a Long Retreat and an Uncertain Future." The Civil Rights Project, May 15, 2014. https://www.civilrightsproject.ucla.edu/research/k-12-education/integration-and-diversity/brown-at-60-great-progress-a-long-retreat-and-an-uncertain-future/Brown-at-60-051814.pdf.

Petti, Jeanette. "Rigging Elections: A Spatial Statistics Analysis of Political and Unintentional Gerrymandering." Cornell Policy Review. October 18, 2017. http://www.cornellpolicyreview.com/rigging-elections-spatial-statistics-analysis-political-unintentional-gerrymandering/.

Plazas, David. "Is Nashville in an Urban Crisis?" The Tennessean, last modified January 10, 2019. https://www.tennessean.com/story/opinion/columnists/david-plazas/2017/05/28/nashville-urban-crisis/342963001/.

Plyer, Allison, Elaine Ortiz, Margery Austin Turner, and Kathryn LS Pettit. "Housing Production Needs: Three Scenarios for New Orleans." Greater New Orleans Community Data Center and The Urban Institute, November 2009. (https://gnocdc.s3.amazonaws.com/reports/GNOCDCHousingProduction-Needs2009.pdf.

Powel, Lawrence N. "Unhappy Trails in the Big Easy." Southern Spaces, January 17, 2012. https://southernspaces.org/2012/unhappy-trails-big-easy-public-spaces-and-square-called-congo/.

Randall, Morgan. "The Storytelling Ironwork of New Orleans." Atlas Obscura, August 24, 2017. https://www.atlasobscura.com/articles/ironwork-new-orleans-french-quarter-pontalba-adinkra.

"Report: 'Food Desert' Gets a Name Change in Response to Baltimore Community Feedback." John Hopkins Center for A Livable Future, January 17, 2018. https://clf.jhsph.edu/about-us/news/news-2018/report-food-desert-gets-name-change-response-baltimore-community-feedback.

Rolinson, Mary G. "Atlanta Before And After the Olympics." Perspectives on History, November 1, 2006. https://www.historians.org/publications-and-directories/perspectives-on-history/november-2006/atlanta-before-and-after-the-olympics.

Rotenberk, Lori. "Can Historic Preservation Cool Down a Hot Neighborhood?" Bloomberg CityLab, June 20, 2019. https://www.bloomberg.com/news/articles/2019-06-20/when-historic-preservation-can-curb-gentrification.

Schouten, Cory. "'Climate Gentrification' Could Add Value to Elevation in Real Estate." CBS News, last modified December 28, 2017. https://www.cbsnews.com/news/climate-gentrification-home-values-rising-sea-level/.

Sisson, Patrick "Atlanta's Beltline, a Transformative Urban Redevelopment, Struggles with Affordability." *Curved*, October 3, 2017. https://www.curbed.com/2017/10/3/16411354/beltline-atlanta-affordable-housing-development-high-line.

"The Black Law of Connecticut (1833)." Yale University Gilder Lehrman Center for the Study of Slavery, Resistance, & Abolition.

Accessed June 7, 2020. https://glc.yale.edu/sites/default/files/files/The%20Black%20Law%20of%20Connecticut%281%29.pdf.

Thysell, Joseph R. "Race Gerrymandering in Louisiana." *International Social Science Review* 77, no. 3/4 (2002). http://www.jstor.org/stable/41887102.

Van Mead, Nick. "A city cursed by sprawl: can the BeltLine save Atlanta?" *The Guardian*, October 25, 2018. https://www.the-guardian.com/cities/2018/oct/25/cursed-sprawl-can-beltline-save-atlanta.

Wagner, Steven. "Evidence and Implications of Gerrymandering in Louisiana." University of Notre Dame. Accessed June 8, 2020. http://sites.nd.edu/sisi-meng/files/2019/05/Wagner-Final-Poster.pdf.

"Wherever You Want to Go, Atlanta Beltline Takes You There." *Atlanta BeltlLine*. Accessed June 14, 2020. https://beltline.org/the-project/project-goals/.

"Whose Heritage? Public Symbols of the Confederacy." Southern Poverty Law Center, February 1, 2019. https://www.splcenter.org/20190201/whose-heritage-public-symbols-confederacy.

Worley, Sam. "Where Soul Food Really Comes From." EpiCurious, June 29, 2018. https://www.epicurious.com/expert-advice/real-history-of-soul-food-article.

Zepp, George. "Slave Market Included Auction Blocks, Brokers Offices in Downtown Nashville." *The Tennessean*, April 30, 2003. https://www.newspapers.com/newspage/112668696/.

"7 Things to Know About Redistricting." Brennan Center. Last modified July 3, 2017. https://www.brennancenter.org/our-work/analysis-opinion/7-things-know-about-redistricting.

6 THE MIDWEST

Alder, Simeon, David Lagakos, and Lee Ohanian. "The Decline of the U.S. Rust Belt: A Macroeconomic Analysis." Center for Quantitative Economic Research, August 2014. https://www. frbatlanta.org/-/media/documents/cqer/publications/working-papers/cqer_wp1405.pdf.

"American Neighborhood Change in the 21st Century: Gentrification and Decline." University of Minnesota, accessed May 13, 2020. https://www.law.umn.edu/institute-metropolitan-opportunity/gentrification.

Badger, Emily. "The Bipartisan Cry of 'Not in My Backyard'." *New York Times*, August 21, 2018. https://www.nytimes. com/2018/08/21/upshot/home-ownership-nimby-bipartisan. html.

Bartik, Timothy J. and George Erickcek. "The Local Economic Impact of 'Eds & Meds'." Metropolitan Policy Program at Brookings Institute, December 2008. https://community -wealth.org/sites/clone.community-wealth.org/files/down-loads/report-bartik-erichcek.pdf.

Beyer, Scott. "Why Has Detroit Continued To Decline?" *Forbes*, July 31, 2018. https://www.forbes.com/sites/scottbeyer/2018/07/31/ why-has-detroit-continued-to-decline/.

Boustan, Leah P., and Robert A. Margo. "A Silver Lining to White Flight? White Suburbanization and African-America Home-ownership, 1940-1980." Boston University, August 2013. http:// www.bu.edu/econ/files/2010/10/Pages-from-YJUEC-D-11-00201R31.pdf.

Boustan, Leah Platt. "Was Postwar Suburbanization 'White Flight'? Evidence From the Black Migration." National Bureau of Economic Research, October 2007. https://www.nber.org/papers/w13543.pdf.

Bradley, Bill. "The Evolving Role of Eds and Meds." NextCity, October 14, 2013. https://nextcity.org/daily/entry/interview-omar-blaik-eds-and-meds.

Buchta, Jim. "Already-Low Homeownership Rates of Twin Cities Minorities Fall Further." *StarTribune*, August 10, 2017. https://www.startribune.com/already-low-home-ownership-rates-of-twin-cities-minorities-fall-fur-ther-down/441087863/.

Budds, Diana. "Will Upzoning Neighborhoods Make Homes More Affordable?" *Curbed,* January 30, 2020. https://www.curbed.com/2020/1/30/21115351/upzoning-definition-affordable-hous-ing-gentrification.

Burke, Barlow D. *Understanding the Law of Zoning and Land Use Controls.* Newark: LexisNexus, 2002.

Chen, James. "Rust Belt." Investopedia, last modified August 25, 2020. https://www.investopedia.com/terms/r/rust-belt.asp.

"Chicago Fire of 1871." History.com, last modified August 21, 2018. https://www.history.com/topics/19th-century/great-chicago-fire.

"Contract Buying and Blockbusting." The Newberry, accessed May 12, 2020. http://publications.newberry.org/digital_exhibitions/

exhibits/show/civil-war-to-civil-rights/segregated-chicago/
contract-buying-blockbusting.

Darden, Joe T. "Black Access to Suburban Housing in America's
Most Racially Segregated Metropolitan Area: Detroit." University of Toronto, Centre for Urban and Community Services,
June 27, 2014. http://www.urbancentre.utoronto.ca/pdfs/hous-
ingconference/Darden_Black_Access_Housing.pdf.

"Data Comparison: Minneapolis, MN & St. Paul, MN." DataUSA.
io, accessed May 20. 2020. https://datausa.io/profile/geo/min-
neapolis-mn?compare=st.-paul-mn.

Darity, William Jr., Darrick Hamilton, Mark Paul, Alan Aja, Anne
Price, Antonio Moore, and Caterina Chiopris. "What We Get
Wrong About Closing the Racial Wealth Gap." Samuel Dubois
Cook Center on Social Equity, April 2018. https://socialequity.
duke.edu/wp-content/uploads/2020/01/what-we-get-wrong.
pdf.

Delegard, Kirsten. "'Gentiles Only.'" Historyapolis, March 6, 2015.
http://historyapolis.com/blog/2015/03/06/gentiles/.

Ehlenz, Meagan M., and Eugenie L. Birch. "The Power of Eds
and Meds." University of Pennsylvania Institute for Urban
Research, July 2014. https://penniur.upenn.edu/uploads/media/
Anchor-Institutions-PRAI-2014.pdf.

Erickson, Jim. "Targeting Minority, Low-Income Neighborhoods
for Hazardous Waste Sites," *University of Michigan News,*
January 19, 2016. https://news.umich.edu/targeting-minority
-low-income-neighborhoods-for-hazardous-waste-sites.

"Growing Detroit's African-American Middle Class." Detroit Future City, February 2019. https://detroitfuturecity.com/middleclassreport/#AA-Middle-Class-Section.

Guerrieri, Vince. "On The 40th Anniversary Of Youngstown's Black Monday." An Oral History." *BeltMag*, September 19, 2017. https://beltmag.com/40th-anniversary-youngstowns-black-monday-oral-history/.

Harkavy, Ira and Harmon Zuckerman. "Eds and Meds: Cities' Hidden Assets." The Brookings Institution, Center on Urban & Metropolitan Policy, August 1999. https://www.brookings.edu/wp-content/uploads/2016/06/09_community_development_report.pdf.

Holland, Jesse J. "Hundreds of Black Deaths During 1919's Red Summer are Being Remembered." *PBS*, July 23, 2019. https://www.pbs.org/newshour/nation/hundreds-of-black-deaths-during-1919s-red-summer-are-being-remembered.

Holmes, Thomas J., and James A. Schmitz. "Competition and productivity: A review of evidence." *Annual Review of Economics* 2, no. 1 (2010).

Johnson, David. "These American Cities Have the Best Public Park Systems in the Country." *Time*, May 25, 2018. https://time.com/5291562/best-parks/.

Jones, Hannah. "In 1930 Minneapolis, not just anyone got to be white." CityPages, July 24, 2018. http://www.citypages.com/news/in-1930s-minneapolis-not-just-anyone-got-to-be-white/488931381.

Krysan, Maria, and Michael D. M. Bader. "Racial Blind Spots: Black-White-Latino Differences in Community Knowledge." *Social Problems* 56, no. 4 (2009). doi:10.1525/sp.2009.56.4.677. https://www.jstor.org/stable/10.1525/sp.2009.56.4.677?seq=1.

Lintelman, Joy K. "Swedish Immigration to Minnesota." MNOpedia, last modified October 7, 2019. https://www.mnopedia.org/swedish-immigration-minnesota.

McPhillips, Deirdre. "A New Analysis Finds Growing Diversity in U.S. Cities." *US News*, January 22, 2020. https://www.usnews.com/news/cities/articles/2020-01-22/americas-cities-are-becoming-more-diverse-new-analysis-shows.

Molomo, Khanyi. "The Unique Challenges Faced By Black Business Owners." Big Cartel (blog). February 18, 2020. https://blog.bigcartel.com/the-unique-challenges-faced-by-black-business-owners.

Ohanian, Lee E. "Competition and the Decline of the Rust Belt." Federal Reserve Bank of Minneapolis, December 20, 2014. https://www.minneapolisfed.org/article/2014/competition-and-the-decline-of-the-rust-belt.

Perry, Andre and David Harshbarger. "The Rise of Black-Majority Cities." The Brookings Institute, February 26, 2019. https://www.brookings.edu/research/the-rise-of-black-majority-cities/.

Perry, Andre M., Jonathan Rothwell, and David Harshbarger. "Five-Star Reviews, One-star Profits: The Devaluation of Businesses in Black Communities." Brookings Institute, February

18, 2020. https://www.brookings.edu/research/five-star-reviews-one-star-profits-the-devaluation-of-businesses-in-black-communities/.

Saltzman, Amy. "New Research Illustrates the Struggles Facing Black Entrepreneurs in the South." ProspertyNow, July 20, 2017. https://prosperitynow.org/blog/new-research-illustrates-struggles-facing-black-entrepreneurs-south.

Schindler, Kurt H. "Zoning and Police Power Ordinances are not the Same, and Should Not be Mixed Together." Michigan State University Extension, June 19, 2014. https://www.canr.msu.edu/news/zoning_and_police_power_ordinances_are_not_the_same_and_should_not_be_mixed.

Sharoff, Robert. "University of Chicago Works on Its Neighborhood." *New York Times*, October 23, 2012. https://www.nytimes.com/2012/10/24/realestate/commercial/university-of-chicago-helps-revitalize-53rd-street-retail-district.html.

Silver, Christopher. "The Racial Origins of Zoning in American Cities." Arizona State University. Accessed May 15, 2020. https://www.asu.edu/courses/aph294/total-readings/silver%20--%20racialoriginsofzoning.pdf.

Spigarolo, Francesca. "A Tale of Two Cities: Detroit, Between Collapse and Renaissance." August 29, 2016. Laboratory for the Governance of the City as a Commons, August 29, 2016. https://labgov.city/theurbanmedialab/a-tale-of-two-cities-detroit-between-collapse-and-renaissance/.

Taylor, Kimberly Hayes. "Gentrification of Detroit Leaves Black-Owned Businesses Behind." *NBC News*, November 1, 2015. https://www.nbcnews.com/news/nbcblk/gentrification-detroit-leaves-black-residents-behind-n412476.

"The Great Migration." History.com, last modified January 16, 2020. https://www.history.com/topics/black-history/great-migration.

"The Negro and His Home in Minnesota." The Governor's Interracial Commission, June 1, 1947. https://www.leg.state.mn.us/docs/pre2003/other/I540.pdf.

Trounstine, Jessica. "The Geography of Inequality: How Land Use Regulation Produces Segregation." *American Political Science Review* 114, no. 2 (May 2020). doi:10.101/S0003055419000844.

"What are Covenants?" Mapping Prejudice, accessed April 29, 2020. https://www.mappingprejudice.org/what-are-covenants/index.html#what.

Williams, Joseph P. "A Tale of Two Motor Cities." *U.S. News*, January 22, 2020. https://www.usnews.com/news/cities/articles/2020-01-22/amid-detroits-rebirth-many-african-americans-feel-left-behind?src=usn_fb/

Wiltse-Ahmad, Alyssa. "Study: Gentrification And Cultural Displacement Most Intense in America's Largest Cities, And Absent From Many Others." National Community Reinvestment Coalition, March 18, 2019. https://ncrc.org/study-gentrification-and-cultural-displacement-most-intense-in-americas-largest-cities-and-absent-from-many-others/.

7 THE WEST

Allen, James P. and Eugene Turner. "Ethnic Change and Enclaves in Los Angeles." American Association of Geographers, March 3, 2013. http://news.aag.org/2013/03/ethnic-change/.

Balk, Gene. "Hate Crime Reports Against Blacks, LGBT People Double in Seattle." *Seattle Times*. Last modified June 24, 2016. https://www.seattletimes.com/seattle-news/data/hate-crimes-against-blacks-lgbt-people-double-in-seattle/.

Balk, Gene. "Seattle is Less White Than it has Ever Been in Modern History, New Census Data Show." *Seattle Times*. Last modified September 14, 2017. https://www.seattletimes.com/seattle-news/data/seattle-is-less-white-than-it-has-ever-been-in-modern-history-new-census-data-show/.

Bernardi, Monica. "The Impact of AirBnB on Our Cities: Gentrification and 'Disneyfication' 2.0." Laboratory for the Governance of the City as a Commons, October 2, 2018. https://labgov.city/theurbanmedialab/the-impact-of-airbnb-on-our-cities-gentrification-and-disneyfication-2-0/.

Bhattacharjee, Riya. "San Francisco Unseats Zurich as City with Highest Salaries and Most Disposable Income." *NBC Bay Area*. Last modified May 22, 2019. https://www.nbcbayarea.com/news/local/san-francisco-unseats-zurich-as-city-with-highest-salaries-and-most-disposable-income/156672/.

Boone, Alastair. "There's New Research Behind the Contention that Airbnb Raises Rents." Bloomberg CityLab, August 2, 2017. https://www.bloomberg.com/news/articles/2017-08-02/new-data-finds-more-airbnb-listings-mean-higher-rent.

Brahinsky, Rachel. "The Story of Property: Meditations on Gentrification, Renaming and Possibility." *Environment and Planning: Economy and Space 52*, no. 5 (January 2020). https://journals.sagepub.com/doi/abs/10.1177/0308518X19895787.

Brown, Gregory Christopher, James Diego Vigil, and Eric Robert Taylor. "The Ghettoization of Blacks in Los Angeles: The Emergence of Street Gangs." *Journal of African American Studies* 16, no. 2 (2012). http://www.jstor.org/stable/43526688.

Brown, Gary. "Los Angeles Gangs: The Bloods and the Crips," Socialist Alternative. Accessed June 3, 2020. https://www.socialistalternative.org/panther-black-rebellion/los-angeles-gangs-bloods-crips/.

Brummet, Quentin and Davin Reed. "The Effects of Gentrification on the Well-Being and Opportunity of Original Resident Adults and Children." Federal Reserve Bank of Philadelphia, July 2019. https://doi.org/10.21799/frbp.wp.2019.30.

Buhayar, Noah and Christopher Cannon. "How California Became America's Housing Nightmare." Bloomberg CityLab, November 6, 2019. https://www.bloomberg.com/graphics/2019-california-housing-crisis/.

"Bussed Out: How America Moves Its Homeless." *The Guardian*, December 20, 2017. https://www.theguardian.com/us-news/ng-interactive/2017/dec/20/bussed-out-america-moves-homeless-people-country-study.

"California Gold Rush, 1848-1864." Learn California, accessed May 17, 2020. https://web.archive.org/web/20110727033216/http://www.learncalifornia.org/doc.asp?id=118.

Case, Steve. "Steve Case: The Complete History Of The Internet's Boom, Bust, Boom Cycle." *Business Insider*, January 14, 2011. https://www.businessinsider.com/what-factors-led-to-the-bursting-of-the-internet-bubble-of-the-late-90s-2011-1.

Chin, Corrine. "Culture Clash: 'We Came Here to Get Away From You,' Says Capitol Hill Art." *The Seattle Times*. Last modified March 13, 2015. https://www.seattletimes.com/photo-video/video/artists-message-to-woo-girls-in-capitol-hill-we-came-here-to-get-away-from-you/.

"Chinese Exclusion Act." African American Policy Reform. Accessed June 6, 2020. https://aapf.org/chinese-exclusion-act.

"Chinese Immigration and the Chinese Exclusion Acts," United States Depart of State, Office of the Historian. Accessed June 5, 2020. https://history.state.gov/milestones/1866-1898/chinese-immigration.

Constant, Paul. "I'm From Seattle. Here's What Amazon Will Do To New York City." *Buzzfeed News*, November 15, 2018. https://www.buzzfeednews.com/article/paulconstant/amazon-seattle-new-york-city-long-island-city-queens.

Cutler, David, Edward Glaeser, and Jacob Vigdor. "The Rise and Decline of the American Ghetto." National Bureau of Economic Research, accessed May 29, 2020. https://www.nber.org/digest/oct97/w5881.html.

De Witte, Melissa. "Tight Housing, Immigration are Shifting Pressure onto Seattle's Black Neighborhoods, Stanford Sociologist Finds." *Stanford News*, August 28, 2019. https://news.stanford.edu/2019/08/28/immigration-seattle-driving-urban-change/.

"Fillmore Timeline 1860 – 2001." *PBS*, accessed May 30, 2020. https://www.pbs.org/kqed/fillmore/learning/time.html.

Florida, Richard. "America's Leading Startup Neighborhoods." Bloomberg CityLab, June 14, 2016. https://www.bloomberg.com/news/articles/2016-06-14/urban-startup-neighborhoods-martin-prosperity-institute-report.

Florida, Richard. "Tech Made Cities Too Expensive. Here's How to Fix It." *Wired*, April 26, 2017. https://www.wired.com/2017/04/how-to-save-the-middle-class/.

Graff, Amy. "Boomtime: What San Francisco looked like at the end of the Gold Rush." *SF Gate*. Last modified October 3, 2019. https://www.sfgate.com/sfhistory/article/San-Francisco-1855-1856-incorporation-Gold-Rush-12958094.php.

Greene, David, Steve Inskeep, and Karen Grigsby Bates. "Connie Rice: Conscience Of The City." January 12, 2012. In *NPR Author Interviews*. Podcast, MP3, 7:19. https://www.npr.org/transcripts/145037734.

"Great Depression Poverty." United States History for Kids, accessed May 17, 2020. http://www.american-historama.org/1929-1945-depression-ww2-era/great-depression-poverty.htm.

Grodach, Carl, Nicole Foster, and James Murdoch III. "Gentrification and the Artistic Dividend: The Role of the Arts in
Neighborhood Change." *Journal of the American Planning
Association* 80, no. 1 (July 2014). https://doi.org/10.1080/0194
4363.2014.928584.

Harrouk, Christele. "Public Spaces: Places of Protest, Expression
and Social Engagement." ArchDaily, June 10, 2020. https://
www.archdaily.com/941408/public-spaces-places-of-protest-
expression-and-social-engagement.

Hayes, Adam. "Dotcom Bubble." Investopedia. Last modified June
25, 2019. https://www.investopedia.com/terms/d/dotcom-bub-
ble.asp.

"Homelessness in America." National Coalition for the Homeless. Accessed May 17, 2020. https://nationalhomeless.org/
about-homelessness/.

"Hoovervilles and Homelessness." University of Washington,
accessed May 17, 2020. https://depts.washington.edu/depress/
hooverville.shtml.

Howell, James C. and Elizabeth A Griffiths. "History of Gangs
in the United States," in *Gangs in America's Communities,
3rd Edition*. Thousand Oaks, California: SAGE Publications,
2019. https://www.sagepub.com/sites/default/files/upm-bina-
ries/43455_1.pdf.

Howell, James C, and John P. Moore. "History of Street Gangs in
the United States." National Gang Center Bulletin, May 2010.

https://www.nationalgangcenter.gov/content/documents/history-of-street-gangs.pdf.

"Immigration to the United States, 1851-1900." Library of Congress. Accessed June 4, 2020. https://www.loc.gov/classroom-materials/united-states-history-primary-source-timeline/rise-of-industrial-america-1876-1900/immigration-to-united-states-1851-1900/.

Lamar, Kendrick. Section.80, recorded 2011, Top Dawg Entertainment, compact disc.

Lee, Dayne. "How Airbnb Short-Term Rentals Exacerbate Los Angeles's Affordable Housing Crisis: Analysis and Policy Recommendations." *Harvard Law & Policy Review* 10 (February 2016).

Kennedy, Lesley. "Building the Transcontinental Railroad: How 20,000 Chinese Immigrants Made It Happen." History.com. Last modified April 30, 2020. https://www.history.com/news/transcontinental-railroad-chinese-immigrants.

Krásná, Denisa. "Metamorphosis of the West Coast Cities: Gentrification, Displacement, Homelessness, and Racial Discrimination." Reviews Magazine, September 15, 2019. http://reviewsmagazine.net/metamorphosis-of-the-west-coast-cities-gentrification-displacement-homelessness-and-racial-discrimination/.

Manson, Steven, Jonathan Schroeder, David Van Riper, and Steven Ruggles. IPUMS National Historical Geographic Information

System: Version 12.0 [Database]. Minneapolis: University of Minnesota. http://doi.org/10.18128/D050.V12.0.

Mars, Roman, and Selena Savic. "Unpleasant Design & Hostile Architecture." August 5, 2015. In *99% Invisible*. Produced by Mars Roman. Podcast, MP3 audio, 18:49. https://99percentinvisible.org/episode/unpleasant-design-hostile-urban-architecture/.

McCullough, Brian. "A Revealing Look at the Dot-Com Bubble of 2000—and How It Shapes Our Lives Today." TED Ideas, December 4, 2018. https://ideas.ted.com/an-eye-opening-look-at-the-dot-com-bubble-of-2000-and-how-it-shapes-our-lives-today/.

McNamee, Gregory Lewis. "Seattle." *Encylopædia Brittanica*. Last modified September 21, 2017. https://www.britannica.com/place/Seattle-Washington.

Moskowitz, Peter. "What Role Do Artists Play in Gentrification?" *Artsy*, September 11, 2017. https://www.artsy.net/article/artsy-editorial-role-artists-play-gentrification.

Nicas, Jack. "As Google Maps Renames Neighborhoods, Residents Fume." *New York Times*, August 2, 2018. https://www.nytimes.com/2018/08/02/technology/google-maps-neighborhood-names.html.

Obenzinger, Hilton. "Geography of Chinese Workers Building the Transcontinental Railroad." Stanford University, 2018. https://web.stanford.edu/group/chineserailroad/cgi-bin/website/virtual/.

"QuickFacts: Los Angeles County, California," US Census Bureau, accessed June 3, 2020. https://www.census.gov/quickfacts/losangelescountycalifornia.

Rao, Ankita. "Tech Giants Want to Solve the Housing Nightmare They Helped Create." Vice, January 25, 2019. https://www.vice.com/en/article/pand9v/tech-giants-want-to-solve-the-housing-nightmare-they-helped-create.

Rodrigo, Chris Mills. "Tech Firms Face Skepticism Over California Housing Response." *The Hill*, November 12, 2019. https://thehill.com/policy/technology/469989-tech-firms-face-skepticism-over-california-housing-response.

"San Francisco Gold Rush." SF Info. Accessed June 14, 2020. http://www.sf-info.org/history/d4/gold-rush.

"San Francisco." History.com. Last modified August 21, 2018. https://www.history.com/topics/us-states/san-francisco.

Sastry, Anjuli and Karen Grigsby Bates, "When LA Erupted in Anger: A Look Back At The Rodney King Riots," *NPR*, April 26, 2017. mhttps://www.npr.org/2017/04/26/524744989/when-la-erupted-in-anger-a-look-back-at-the-rodney-king-riots.

Sayej, Nadja. "'Forgotten by Society' – How Chinese Migrants Built the Transcontinental Railroad." *The Guardian*, June 18, 2019. https://www.theguardian.com/artanddesign/2019/jul/18/forgotten-by-society-how-chinese-migrants-built-the-transcontinental-railroad.

Schneider, Benjamin. "CityLab University: Understanding Homelessness in America." Bloomberg CityLab. Last modified July 6, 2020. https://www.bloomberg.com/news/features/2020-07-06/why-is-homelessness-such-a-problem-in-u-s-cities?in_source-=postr_story_3.

Schulman, Sarah. *The Gentrification of the Mind: Witness to a Lost Imagination.* Berkeley: University of California Press, 2012. http://www.jstor.org/stable/10.1525/j.ctt1pps9s.

Schwartzstein, Peter. "How Urban Design Can Make or Break Protests." *Smithsonian Magazine*, June 29, 2020. https://www.smithsonianmag.com/history/geography-protest-how-urban-design-can-make-or-break-people-power-180975189/.

Shelton, Kyle. "Protests, Public Space and the Remaking of Cities." Kinder Institute for Urban Research, June 15, 2020. https://kinder.rice.edu/urbanedge/2020/06/15/protests-public-space-transportation-inequalities-cities.

Slayton, Nicholas. "Number of Homeless People on Skid Row Spikes by 11%." *Los Angeles Downtown News*, August 12, 2019. http://www.ladowntownnews.com/news/number-of-homeless-people-on-skid-row-spikes-by/article_aa32fbda-bafb-11e9-849f-ab047fa8951a.html.

"The Great Arrival." Library of Congress, accessed June 6, 2020 https://www.loc.gov/classroom-materials/immigration/italian/the-great-arrival/.

"Urban Village Element." Seattle Comprehensive Plan, January 2005, https://www.seattle.gov/Documents/Departments/

OPCD/OngoingInitiatives/SeattlesComprehensivePlan/
UrbanVillageElement.pdf.

Wallenfeldt, Jeff. "Los Angeles Riots of 1992." *Encyclopædia Brittanica*. Last modified July 23, 2020. https://www.britannica.com/event/Los-Angeles-Riots-of-1992.

"When Big Businesses Attempt to Take Over and Rename Neighborhoods." *US News*, April 22, 2019. https://www.usnews.com/news/cities/articles/2019-04-22/when-big-businesses-attempt-to-take-over-and-rename-neighborhoods.

Wildermuth, John. "S.F. Neighborhoods Change Names to Map Out New Identity." *SF Gate*. Last modified March 23, 2014. https://www.sfgate.com/bayarea/article/S-F-neighborhoods-change-names-to-map-out-new-5341383.php#photo-6055400.

Yoon, Anna, Brian Lam, Gihoon Du, Jiang Wu, and Yurika Harada. "Mapping Race in Seattle/King Country 1920-2010." University of Washington, Spring 2017. http://depts.washington.edu/labhist/maps-seattle-segregation.shtml.

III SEAMS OF THE URBAN FABRIC
8 ECONOMICS PART 1: THE GROWING GRADIENT

"Best Practices For Using Crime Prevention Through Environmental Design in Weed and Seed Site." National Crime Prevention Council, 2009. https://www.ncpc.org/wp-content/uploads/2017/11/NCPC_BestPracticesCPTED.pdf.

Bhutta, Neil, Andrew C. Chang, Lisa J. Dettling, and Joanne W. Hsu. "Disparities in Wealth by Race and Ethnicity in the 2019 Survey of Consumer Finances." Federal Reserve Bank, September 28, 2020. https://www.federalreserve.gov/econres/notes/feds-notes/disparities-in-wealth-by-race-and-ethnicity-in-the-2019-survey-of-consumer-finances-20200928.htm.

Boule, Jamelle. "How We Built the Ghettos." *Daily Beast*. Last modified July 12, 2017. https://www.thedailybeast.com/how-we-built-the-ghettos?ref=scroll.

Brummet, Quentin, and Davin Reed. "The Effects of Gentrification on the Well-Being and Opportunity of Original Resident Adults and Children." Federal Reserve Bank of Philadelphia, July 2019. https://www.philadelphiafed.org/-/media/community-development/publications/discussion-papers/discussion-paper_the-effects-of-gentrification-on-the-well-being-and-opportunity-of-original-resident-adults-and-children.pdf?la=en.

Chingos, Matthew and Kristin Blagg. "How Do School Funding Formulas Work?" The Urban Institute, November 29, 2017, https://apps.urban.org/features/funding-formulas/.

Cortright, Joe and Dillon Mahmoudi. "Lost in Place: Why the Persistence and Spread of Concentrated Poverty—Not Gentrification—is Our Biggest Urban Challenge." CityObservatory, December 2014. https://cityobservatory.org/wp-content/uploads/2014/12/LostinPlace_12.4.pdf.

Currie, Elliot, Tim Goddard, Randolph R Myers. "The Dark Ghetto revisited: Kenneth B Clark's classic analysis as cutting edge criminology." *Theoretical Criminology* 19, no. 1 (2014): 5-22. https://journals.sagepub.com/doi/10.1177/1362480614553524.

Daniel B. Schwartz. "How America's Ugly History of Segregation Changed the Meaning of the Word 'Ghetto'." *Time*, September 24, 2019. https://time.com/5684505/ghetto-word-history/.

Donnelly, Patrick G. "Newman, Oscar: Defensible Space Theory." University of Dayton, eCommons, 2010. https://ecommons.udayton.edu/cgi/viewcontent.cgi?article=1026&context=soc_fac_pub.

Faber, Jacob, and Terri Friedline. "The Racialized Costs of Banking." NewAmerica. Last modified June 21, 2018. https://www.newamerica.org/family-centered-social-policy/reports/racialized-costs-banking/.

Freeman, Lance and Frank Braconi. "Gentrification and Displacement New York City in the 1990s." *Journal of the American Planning Association* 70, no. 1 (2004). DOI: 10.1080/01944360408976337.

Gonsalves, Kelly. "The 'Long, Hot Summer of 1967'." The Week, accessed April 15, 2020. https://theweek.com/captured/712838/long-hot-summer-1967.

Husain, Asma. "Reverse Redlining and the Destruction of Minority Wealth." Michigan Journal of Race & Law, November 2, 2016. https://mjrl.org/2016/11/02/reverse-redlining-and-the-destruction-of-minority-wealth/.

Hwang, Jackelyn and Robert J. Simpson. "Divergent Pathways of Gentrification: Racial Inequality and the Social Order of Renewal in Chicago Neighborhood." *American Sociological Review* 79, no. 4 (2014). https://journals.sagepub.com/doi/pdf/10.1177/0003122414535774.

Jan, Tracy. "Redlining was Banned 50 Years Ago. It's Still Hurting Minorities Today." *The Washington Post*, March 28, 2018. https://www.washingtonpost.com/news/wonk/wp/2018/03/28/redlining-was-banned-50-years-ago-its-still-hurting-minorities-today/.

Jargowsky, Paul. "Architecture of Segregation." The Century Foundation, August 7, 2015. https://tcf.org/content/report/architecture-of-segregation/.

Karma, Roge. "How Cities can Tackle Violent Crime Without Relying on Police." *Vox*, August 7, 2020. https://www.vox.com/21351442/patrick-sharkey-uneasy-peace-abolish-defund-the-police-violence-cities.

Karma, Roge. "We Train Police to be Warriors—and Then Send Them Out to be Social Workers." *Vox*, July 31, 2020. https://

www.vox.com/2020/7/31/21334190/what-police-do-defund-abolish-police-reform-training.

Kay, Jane Holtz. "Ghetto Architecture: An Exhibition of Makeshift Design." The Christian Science Monitor, October 7, 1983. https://www.csmonitor.com/1983/1007/100710.html.

La Vigne, Nancy, Jocelyn Fontaine, and Anamika Dwivedi. "How Do People in High-Crime, Low-Income Communities View the Police?" The Urban Institute, February 2017. https://www.urban.org/sites/default/files/publication/88476/how_do_people_in_high-crime_view_the_police.pdf.

Lee Jr, Bryan. "America's Cities Were Designed To Oppress." Bloomberg CityLab, June 3, 2020. https://www.bloomberg.com/news/articles/2020-06-03/how-to-design-justice-into-america-s-cities.

McKinnish, Terra, Randall P. Walsh, and Kirk, White. "Who Gentrifies Low Income Neighborhoods?" US Census Bureau Center for Economic Studies Paper No. CES-08-02, (January 2008). https://papers.ssrn.com/sol3/papers.cfm?abstract_id=1103055.

Mitchell, Bruce. "HOLC "Redlining" Maps: The Persistent Structure Of Segregation And Economic Inequality." National Community Reinvestment Coalition, March 20, 2018. https://ncrc.org/holc/.

Muñoz, Ana Patricia, Marlene Kim, Mariko Chang, Regine O. Jackson, Darrick Hamilton, and William A. Darity Jr. "The Color of Wealth in Boston." Federal Reserve Bank of Boston,

March 25, 2015. https://www.bostonfed.org/publications/one-time-pubs/color-of-wealth.aspx.

Newman, Oscar. "Creating Defensible Space." U.S. Department of Housing and Urban Displacement, April 1996. https://www.huduser.gov/publications/pdf/def.pdf.

Owens, Ann. "Income Segregation between School Districts and Inequality in Students' Achievement." *Sociology of Education* 91, no. 1 (2017). https://www.asanet.org/sites/default/files/attach/journals/jan18soefeature.pdf.

Pederson, Martin C. "Bryan C. Lee on Design Justice and Architecture's Role in Systemic Racism." Common Edge, June 18, 2020. https://commonedge.org/bryan-c-lee-on-design-justice-and-architectures-role-in-systemic-racism/.

"Quick Facts United States." US Census Bureau. Accessed June 14, 2020. https://www.census.gov/quickfacts/fact/table/US/PST120216#viewtop.

Ratcliffe, Caroline and Signe-Mary McKernan. "Childhood Poverty Persistence: Facts and Consequences." The Urban Institute, Brief 14, June 2010. https://www.urban.org/sites/default/files/alfresco/publication-pdfs/412126-Childhood-Poverty-Persistence-Facts-and-Consequences.PDF.

"REPORT OF THE NATIONAL ADVISORY COMMISSION ON CIVIL DISORDERS," New York: Bantam Books, 1968.

Reschovsky, Andrew. "The Future of U.S Public School Revenue From The Property Tax." Lincoln Institute of Land Policy, July

2017. https://www.lincolninst.edu/sites/default/files/pubfiles/
future-us-public-school-revenue-policy-brief_0.pdf.

Rothstein, Richard. "A Comment on Bank of America/Country-
wide's Discriminatory Mortgage Lending and Its Implications
for Racial Segregation." Economic Policy Institute, January
23, 2012. https://www.epi.org/publication/bp335-boa-country-
wide-discriminatory-lending/.

Rothstein, Richard. "Black Ghettos are no Accident—How State-
Sponsored Racism Shaped US Cities." Directed by Mark Lopez.
AEON, June 6, 2019. Video, 17:42 https://aeon.co/videos/black-
ghettos-are-no-accident-how-state-sponsored-racism-shaped-
us-cities.

"Ruth Glass and Coining 'Gentrification.'" The Bartlett, accessed
May 16, 2020. https://bartlett100.com/article/ruth-glass-and-
coining-gentrification.html.

Salviati, Chris. "The Racial Divide in Homeownership." Apartment List, August 21, 2017. https://www.apartmentlist.com/
rentonomics/racial-divide-homeownership/.

Sampson, Robert J., and Stephen W. Raudenbush. "Disorder in
Urban Neighborhoods— Does It Lead to Crime?" National
Institute of Justice: Research in Brief, February 2001. https://
www.ncjrs.gov/pdffiles1/nij/186049.pdf.

Sampson, Robert J., and Stephen W. Raudenbush. "Seeing Disorder:
Neighborhood Stigma and the Social Construction of 'Broken
Windows.'" *Social Psychology Quarterly* 67, no. 4 (2004). https://

journals.sagepub.com/doi/abs/10.1177/019027250406700401?s-source=mfc&rss=1.

Szto, Mary, "Real Estate Agents as Agents of Social Change: Redlining, Reverse Redlining, and Greenlining." *Seattle Journal for Social Justice* 12, 1 (2013). https://digitalcommons.law.seattleu.edu/cgi/viewcontent.cgi?article=1722&context=sjsj.

Turner, Cory, Reema Khrais, Tim Lloyd, Alexandra Olgin, Laura Isensee, Becky Vevea, Dan Carsen. "Why America's Schools Have A Money Problem." *NPR*, April 18, 2016. https://www.npr.org/2016/04/18/474256366/why-americas-schools-have-a-money-problem.

Vedantam, Shankar, Chris Benderev, Tara Boyle, Renee Klahr, Maggie Penman, Jennifer Schmidt. "How A Theory Of Crime And Policing Was Born, And Went Terribly Wrong." *NPR*, November 1, 2016. https://www.npr.org/2016/11/01/500104506/broken-windows-policing-and-the-origins-of-stop-and-frisk-and-how-it-went-wrong.

Vigdor, Jacob L. "Does Gentrification Harm the Poor?" Brookings-Wharton Papers on Urban Affairs (2002). doi:10.1353/urb.2002.0012.

Vorenberg, Justin. "The War on Crime: The First Five Years." *The Atlantic*, May 1972. https://www.theatlantic.com/past/docs/politics/crime/crimewar.htm.

Wagner, Peter, and Wanda Bertram. "'What Percent of the U.S. is Incarcerated?' (And Other Ways to Measure Mass Incarcera-

tion)." Prison Policy Initiative, January 16, 2020. https://www.
prisonpolicy.org/blog/2020/01/16/percent-incarcerated/.

"Wealth, Asset Ownership, & Debt of Households Detailed Tables:
2013." U.S. Census Bureau, 2013. https://www.census.gov/data/
tables/2013/demo/wealth/wealth-asset-ownership.html.

"What Drives the Cycle of Poverty." Stand Together Foundation, July
26, 2017. https://www.stand-together.org/drives-cycle-poverty/.

Yearwood, Lori Teresa. "Many Minorities Avoid Seeking Credit
Due to Generations of Discrimination. Why That Keeps Them
Back." *CNBC*. Last modified September 5, 2019. https://www.
cnbc.com/2019/09/01/many-minorities-avoid-seeking-credit-
due-to-decades-of-discrimination.html.

8.6 ECONOMICS PART 2: ARE WE MISSING SOMETHING?

Adler, Ben. "The Koch Brothers Just Kicked Mass Transit in the Face." Grist, February 3, 2015. https://grist.org/climate-energy/the-koch-brothers-just-kicked-mass-transit-in-the-face/.

Ahmad, Ali. "RIHA Releases New Report: Quantified Parking - Comprehensive Parking Inventories for Five Major U.S. Cities." Mortgage Bankers Association, July 9, 2018. https://www.mba.org/2018-press-releases/july/riha-releases-new-report-quantified-parking-comprehensive-parking-inventories-for-five-major-us-cities.

Andrews, Jeff. "10 Years After the Financial Crisis, is the Housing Market Still at Risk?" Curbed, August 29, 2018. https://www.curbed.com/2018/8/29/17788844/financial-crisis-2008-cause-housing-mortgage-lending.

Andrews, Rodney, Marcus Casey, Bradley L. Hardy, Trevon D. Logan. "Location Matters: Historical Racial Segregation and Intergenerational Mobility." Economic Letters 158 (September 2017). https://doi.org/10.1016/j.econlet.2017.06.018

Badger, Emily, and Quoctrung Bui. "Cities Start to Question an American Ideal: A House With a Yard on Every Lot." New York Times, June 18, 2019. https://www.nytimes.com/interactive/2019/06/18/upshot/cities-across-america-question-single-family-zoning.html.

Bailey, Giles. "How Europe's Free Public Transit Movement Tries to Rebalance Fare Use." Metro Magazine, October 23, 2019. https://www.metro-magazine.com/10007169/how-europes-free-public-transit-movement-tries-to-rebalance-fare-use.

Barter, Paul. "'Cars are Parked 95% of the Time'. Let's Check!" Reinventing Parking, February 22, 2013. https://www.reinventingparking.org/2013/02/cars-are-parked-95-of-time-lets-check.html.

Berg, Nate. "Lots to Lose: How Cities Around the World are Eliminating Car Parks." *The Guardian*, September 27, 2016. https://www.theguardian.com/cities/2016/sep/27/cities-eliminating-car-parks-parking.

Buehler, Ralph. "9 Reasons the U.S. Ended Up So Much More Car-Dependent Than Europe." Bloomberg CityLab, February 4, 2014. https://www.citylab.com/transportation/2014/02/9-reasons-us-ended-so-much-more-car-dependent-europe/8226/.

Bunten, Devin Michelle. "Untangling the Housing Shortage and Gentrification." Bloomberg CityLab, October 23, 2019. https://www.citylab.com/perspective/2019/10/neighborhood-gentrification-affordable-housing-california/598135/.

Capps, Kriston. "It's Time to Rewrite Fair Lending Rules. (Just Not Like This.)." Bloomberg CityLab, August 31, 2018. https://www.bloomberg.com/news/articles/2018-08-31/the-problem-with-this-community-reinvestment-act-update.

Capps, Kriston. "What Mike Bloomberg Got Wrong About Redlining and the Financial Crisis." Bloomberg CityLab, February 13, 2020. https://www.bloomberg.com/news/articles/2020-02-13/bloomberg-on-redlining-and-the-housing-crisis.

Charron, David. "Walkable Neighborhoods Provide Health, Environmental and Financial Benefits." *The Washington*

Post, October 9, 2017. https://www.washingtonpost.com/news/where-we-live/wp/2017/10/09/walkable-neighborhoods-provide-health-environmental-and-financial-benefits/.

Chetty, Raj, Nathanial Hendren, Patrick Kline, and Emmanuel Saez. "Where is the Land of Opportunity? The Geography of Intergenerational Mobility in the United States." *The Quarterly Journal of Economics* 129, no. 4 (2014). https://www.nber.org/papers/w19843.

Choi, Jung Hyun, Alanna McCargo, and Laurie Goodman. "Three Differences Between Black and White Homeownership that Add to the Housing Wealth gap." The Urban Institute, February 28, 2019. https://www.urban.org/urban-wire/three-differences-between-black-and-white-homeownership-add-housing-wealth-gap.

Coady, David, Ian Parry, Nghia-Piotr Le, and Baoping Shang. "Global Fossil Fuel Subsidies Remain Large: An Update Based on Country-Level Estimates." International Monetary Fund, May 2, 2019. https://www.imf.org/en/Publications/WP/Issues/2019/05/02/Global-Fossil-Fuel-Subsidies-Remain-Large-An-Update-Based-on-Country-Level-Estimates-46509.

Coleman, Clayton and Emma Dietz. "Fact Sheet: Fossil Fuel Subsidies: A Closer Look at Tax Breaks and Societal Costs." Environmental and Energy Study Institute, July 29, 2019. https://www.eesi.org/papers/view/fact-sheet-fossil-fuel-subsidies-a-closer-look-at-tax-breaks-and-societal-costs.

Cox, Daniel A. and Ryan Streeter. "The Importance of Place: Neighborhood Amenities as a Source of Social Connection and Trust." American Enterprise Institute, May 20, 2019. https://

www.aei.org/research-products/report/the-importance-of-place-neighborhood-amenities-as-a-source-of-social-connection-and-trust/.

"Consumer Expenditures—2019." U.S. Bureau of Labor Statistics, last modified September 9, 2020. https://www.bls.gov/news.release/cesan.nro.htm.

Cortight, Joe. "Why Carmaggedon Never Comes (Seattle Edition)." City Observatory, January 16, 2019. http://cityobservatory.org/seattle_carmaggedon/.

Cortright, Joe. "The 0.1 Percent Solution: Inclusionary Zoning's Fatal Scale Problem." CityObservatory, April 25, 2017. http://cityobservatory.org/the-0-1-percent-solution-inclusionary-zonings-fatal-scale-problem/.

DeMaria, Kyle and Alvaro Sanchez. "Accessing Economic Opportunity." Federal Reserve Bank of Philadelphia, December 2018. https://www.philadelphiafed.org/-/media/community-development/publications/special-reports/public-transit/accessing-opportunity.pdf.

Downs, Anthony. "Traffic: Why It's Getting Worse, What Government Can Do." Brookings Institute, January 1, 2004. https://www.brookings.edu/research/traffic-why-its-getting-worse-what-government-can-do/.

Ellsmoor, James. "United States Spend Ten Times More On Fossil Fuel Subsidies Than Education." *Forbes*, June 15, 2019. https://www.forbes.com/sites/jamesellsmoor/2019/06/15/united-states-

spend-ten-times-more-on-fossil-fuel-subsidies-than-educa-
tion/#488d4a0b4473

"Federal Poverty Level (FPL)." US Healthcare. Accessed June 17,
2020. https://www.healthcare.gov/glossary/federal-pover-
ty-level-FPL/.

Freeman, Lance and Jenny Schuetz. "Producing Affordable
Housing in Rising Markets." Federal Reserve Bank of Philadelphia, September 2016. https://penniur.upenn.edu/uploads/
media/Freeman-Schuetz_PennIUR-Philly_Fed_working_
paper_091616v2.pdf.

"Gasoline Prices, Liter, 21-Sep-2020." Global Petrol Prices, accessed
June 21, 2020. https://www.globalpetrolprices.com/gasoline_
prices/.

Glant, Aaron and Emmanuel Martinez. "Gentrifying Became Low-Income Lending Law's Unintended Consequence." *Reveal News*,
February 16, 2018. https://www.revealnews.org/article/gentrifica-
tion-became-low-income-lending-laws-unintended-consequence/.

"Greenhouse Gas Emissions from a Typical Passenger Vehicle." US
EPA. Accessed April 14, 2020. https://www.epa.gov/greenve-
hicles/greenhouse-gas-emissions-typical-passenger-vehicle.

Greene David. "IMF: Gas Prices Don't Reflect True Costs." *NPR*,
March 28, 2013. https://www.npr.org/2013/03/28/175550949/imf-
gas-prices-dont-reflect-true-costs.

Hess, Abigail. "Americans Spend Over 15% of Their Budgets on
Transportation Costs—These US cities are Trying to Make

It Free." *CNBC*. Last modified March 2, 2020. https://www.
cnbc.com/2020/03/02/free-public-transportation-is-a-reality
-in-100-citiesheres-why.html.

Hickey, Robert. "After the Downturn: New Challenges and Oppor-
tunities for Inclusionary Housing." Center for Housing Policy,
February 2013. https://nhc.org/wp-content/uploads/2017/10/
AfterTheDownTurn_InclusionaryReport201302.pdf.

"How Much Gasoline Does the United States Consume?" Energy
Information Administration. Last modified September 4, 2020.
https://www.eia.gov/tools/faqs/faq.php?id=23&t=10.

Humes, Edward. "The Absurd Primacy of the Automobile in
American Life." The Atlantic, April 12, 2016. https://www.the-
atlantic.com/business/archive/2016/04/absurd-primacy-of-the-
car-in-american-life/476346/.

Hymel, Kent. "Does Traffic Congestion Reduce Employment
Growth?" *Journal of Urban Economics* 65, no. 2 (March 2009).
https://doi.org/10.1016/j.jue.2008.11.002.

"Immigrants Create Billions For The US." Immigrant Business,
October 8, 2019. https://www.immigrantbiz.org/immi-
grants-creating-billions-for-the-us/.

"INRIX: Congestion Costs Each American 97 hours, $1,348 A Year."
INRIX, February 11, 2019. https://inrix.com/press-releases/
scorecard-2018-us/.

"Inventory of U.S. Greenhouse Gas Emissions and Sinks: 1990 –
2016." United States Environmental Protections Agency, April

12, 2018. https://www.epa.gov/sites/production/files/2018-01/documents/2018_complete_report.pdf.

Jacobs, Jane. *The Death and Life of Great American Cities*. New York: Vintage Books, 1992.

Jacobs, Jane. *Dark Age Ahead*. New York: Random House, 2005.

Jacobs, Tom. "American Idling: The Ecological Cost of Keeping The Engine Running." *PS Mag*, last modified June 14, 2017. https://psmag.com/environment/american-idling-ecological-engine-running-3771.

Jaffe, Eric. "Living Near Good Transit May Make You Happier." Bloomberg CityLab, September 12, 2013. https://www.bloomberg.com/news/articles/2013-09-12/living-near-good-transit-may-make-you-happier.

Johnson, Charlie and Jonathan Walker. "Peak Car Ownership Report." Rocky Mountain Institute, 2016. https://rmi.org/insight/peak-car-ownership-report.

Jonathan English. "Why Public Transportation Works Better Outside the U.S." Bloomberg CityLab, October 10, 2018. https://www.bloomberg.com/news/articles/2018-10-10/why-public-transportation-works-better-outside-the-u-s.

Kerr, Sari Pekkala, and William R. Kerr. "Immigrant Entrepreneurship in America: Evidence From the Survey of Business Owners 2007 & 2012." National Bureau of Economic Research. Last modified July 2019.https://www.nber.org/papers/w24494.pdf.

Khater, Sam, Len Kiefer, Ajita Atreya, Venkataramana Yanamandra. "The Major Challenge of Inadequate U.S. Housing Supply." FreddieMac, December 5, 2018.http://www.freddiemac.com/research/insight/20181205_major_challenge_to_u.s._housing_supply.page.

Knittel, Christopher R. and Elizabeth Murphy. "Generational Trends in Vehicle Ownership and Use: Are Millennials Any Different?" MIT Center for Energy and Environmental Policy Research, April 2019. http://ceepr.mit.edu/files/papers/2019-006.pdf.

Kosten, Dan. "Immigrants as Economic Contributors: Immigrant Entrepreneurs." National Immigration Forum, July 11, 2018. https://immigrationforum.org/article/immigrants-as-economic-contributors-immigrant-entrepreneurs/.

Kramer, Anna. "The Unaffordable City: Housing and Transit in North American Cities." Cities 83 (December 2018). https://doi.org/10.1016/j.cities.2018.05.013.

Lee, Changju, and John S. Miller. "Lessons Learned from the Rise, Fall, and Rise of Toll Roads in the United States and Virginia." Virginia Department of Transportation, accessed April 15, 2020. http://www.p3virginia.org/wp-content/uploads/2015/06/Rise-Fall-and-Rise-of-Toll-Roads-John-Miller-2015.pdf.

Leonhardt, David. "In Climbing Income Ladder, Location Matters." New York Times, July 22, 2013. https://www.nytimes.com/2013/07/22/business/in-climbing-income-ladder-location-matters.html?pagewanted=all&_r=0.

Levinson, David. "How To Make Mass Transit Financially Sustainable Once and for All." Bloomberg CityLab, June 5, 2014. https://www.bloomberg.com/news/articles/2014-06-05/how-to-make-mass-transit-financially-sustainable-once-and-for-all.

Mann, Adam. "What's Up With That: Building Bigger Roads Actually Makes Traffic Worse." Wired, June 17, 2014. https://www.wired.com/2014/06/wuwt-traffic-induced-demand/.

McArthur, Colin, and Sarah Edelman. "The 2008 Housing Crisis." Center for American Progress, April 13, 2017. https://www.americanprogress.org/issues/economy/reports/2017/04/13/430424/2008-housing-crisis/.

McCarty, Maggie. "Introduction to Public Housing." Congressional Research Service, January 3, 2014. https://fas.org/sgp/crs/misc/R41654.pdf.

"Millennials & Driving." ZipCar, February 27, 2013. https://www.slideshare.net/Zipcar_Inc/millennial-slide-share-final/3-2011_Key_Findings_In_2011.

Mironova, Oksana. "NYC Right to Counsel: First year results and potential for expansion." Community Service Project New York, March 25, 2019. https://www.cssny.org/news/entry/nyc-right-to-counsel.

"New Data Shows Immigrant-Owned Businesses Employed 8 Million Americans; Immigrants Wield $1.1 Trillion in Spending Power." New American Economy, March 12, 2019. https://www.newamericaneconomy.org/press-release/new-data-shows-immigrant-owned-businesses-employed-8-million-americans-immigrants-wield-1-1-trillion-in-spending-power/.

Ohern, Matt. "Minimum Lot Size: What is it Good for? Absolutely Nothing." Jefferson Policy Journal, July 21, 2010. http://www.jeffersonpolicyjournal.com/minimum-lot-size-what-is-it-good-for-absolutely-nothing/.

"Oil & Gas Subsidies: Myth vs. Fact." Oceana, accessed May 7, 2020. https://usa.oceana.org/oil-gas-subsidies-myth-vs-fact.

"Opportunity Zones Frequently Asked Questions." Internal Revenue Service. Accessed July 8, 2020, https://www.irs.gov/credits-deductions/opportunity-zones-frequently-asked-questions.

Poethig, Erika C. "Housing Assistance Matters Initiative." Urban Institute. Accessed June 3, 2020. https://www.urban.org/features/housing-assistance-matters-initiative.

Poon, Linda. "A Lesson from Social Distancing: Build Better Balconies." Bloomberg CityLab, April 20, 2020. https://www.citylab.com/life/2020/04/apartment-design-balcony-private-outdoor-space-zoning-laws/610162/.

Rascoe, Ayesha. "White House Touts Help For Poor Areas—But Questions Endure Over Who'll Benefit." NPR, July 8, 2019. https://www.npr.org/2019/07/08/736546264/white-house-touts-help-for-poor-areas-but-questions-endure-over-wholl-benefit.

Reed, Philip, and Nicole Arata. "What Is the Total Cost of Owning a Car?" NerdWallet, June 28, 2019. https://www.nerdwallet.com/article/loans/auto-loans/total-cost-owning-car.

Rob Warnock. "2019 Millennial Homeownership Report: More Millennials Are Preparing For A Life of Renting." ApartmentList, November 18, 2019. https://www.apartmentlist.com/ rentonomics/2019-millennial-homeownership-report/.

Sallis, James F., Heather R. Bowles, Adrian Bauman, Barbara E. Ainsworth, Fiona C. Bull, Cora L. Craig, Michael Sjöström, Ilse De Bourdeaudhuij, Johan Lefevre, Victor Matsudo, Sandra Matsudo, Duncan J. Macfarlane, Luis Fernando Gomez, Shigeru Inoue, Norio Murase, Vida Volbekiene, Grant McLean, Harriette Carr, Lena Klasson Heggebo, Heidi Tomten, Patrick Bergman. "Neighborhood Environments and Physical Activity Among Adults in 11 Countries." *American Journal of Preventative Medicine* 36, no. 6 (June 2009). https://doi.org/10.1016/j. amepre.2009.01.031.

Sawhill, Isabel V., and Joanna Venator. "Three Policies to Close the Class Divide in Family Formation." Brookings Institute, January 21, 2014. https://www.brookings.edu/blog/social-mobility-memos/2014/01/21/three-policies-to-close-the-class-divide-in-family-formation/.

Scally, Corianne Payton, Amanda Gold, and Nicole DuBois. "The Low-Income Housing Tax Credit." The Urban Institute, July 2018. https://www.urban.org/sites/default/files/ publication/98758/lithc_how_it_works_and_who_it_ serves_final_2.pdf.

Schloredt, Valerie. "Antidotes to Gentrification: Plans for Democratized, Affordable Housing." *Yes! Magazine*, February 19, 2020. https://www.yesmagazine.org/issue/world-we-want/2020/02/19/affordable-housing-gentrification/.

Schwartz, Mary, and Ellen Wilson. "Who Can Afford To Live in a Home?: A Look at Data from the 2006 American Community Survey." US Census Bureau, accessed April 30, 2020. https://www.census.gov/housing/census/publications/who-can-afford.pdf.

Simon, Morgan. "Opportunity Zones: We're Doing It Wrong." *Forbes*, September 3, 2019. https://www.forbes.com/sites/morgansimon/2019/09/03/opportunity-zones-were-doing-it-wrong/#2c04445456fa.

Simon, Morgan. "What You Need to Know About Opportunity Zones." *Forbes*, March 30, 2019. https://www.forbes.com/sites/morgansimon/2019/03/30/what-you-need-to-know-about-opportunity-zones/#18eed5a86ae2.

Sisson, Patrick, Jeff Andrews, and Alex Bazeley. "The Affordable Housing Crisis, Explained." *Curbed*. Last modified March 2, 2020. https://www.curbed.com/2019/5/15/18617763/affordable-housing-policy-rent-real-estate-apartment.

Stromberg, Joseph. "Highways Gutted American Cities. So Why did They Build Them?" *Vox*. Last modified May 11, 2016. https://www.vox.com/2015/5/14/8605917/highways-interstate-cities-history.

Stromberg, Joseph. "The Real Reason American Public Transportation is Such a Disaster." *Vox*. Last modified August 10, 2015. https://www.vox.com/2015/8/10/9118199/public-transportation-subway-buses.

Stromberg, Joseph. "The Real Story Behind the Demise of America's Once-Mighty Streetcars." *Vox*, May 7, 2015. https://www.vox.com/2015/5/7/8562007/streetcar-history-demise.

"The Basics on How Public Transit is Funded." Transportation for America. Accessed April 13, 2020. http://www.t4america.org/wp-content/uploads/2015/02/James-Corless-Indy-academy-5-14-15.pdf.

"The Community Reinvestment Act." National Community Reinvestment Coalition, December 2016. https://ncrc.org/wp-content/uploads/2016/12/cra_in_gentrifying_neighborhoods_web.pdf.

"The True Cost of Gasoline: $15 Per Gallon." Smart Cities Drive. Accessed May 4, 2020. https://www.smartcitiesdive.com/ex/sustainablecitiescollective/true-cost-gasoline-15-gallon/26284/.

"Toll Roads in the United States: History and Current Policy." US Department of Transportation, Federal Highway Administration, accessed April 15, 2020. https://www.fhwa.dot.gov/policyinformation/tollpage/documents/history.pdf.

Tomer, Adie. "America's Commuting Choices: 5 Major Takeaways from 2016 Census Data." The Brookings Institute, October 3, 2017. https://www.brookings.edu/blog/the-avenue/2017/10/03/americans-commuting-choices-5-major-takeaways-from-2016-census-data/.

"U.S. Average Retail Gasoline Prices in 2019 were Slightly Lower than 2018." Energy Information Administration, January 8, 2020. https://www.eia.gov/todayinenergy/detail.php?id=42435.

U.S. House of Representatives. *Toll Roads and Free Roads*. 76th
Cong., 1st sess., 1939. H. Doc. 272. http://www.virginiaplaces.
org/transportation/tollroadsfreeroads.pdf.

"United States Housing Act of 1937 as Amended by the Quality
Housing and Work Responsibility Act of 1998 as of 3/2/1999."
United States House of Representatives, March 2, 1999. http://
archives-financialservices.house.gov/banking/usha1937.pdf.

"Why and How to Fund Public Transportation." Arizona PIRG
Education Fund, March 2009. https://uspirgedfund.org/sites/
pirg/files/reports/Why-and-How-to-Fund-Public-Transpor-
tation.pdf.

Wittenberg, Alex. "The Biggest Problems With Opportunity Zones."
Bloomberg CityLab, June 25, 2020. https://www.bloomberg.
com/news/articles/2020-06-25/opportunity-zones-don-t-work-
can-they-be-fixed.

Young, Jay. "Infrastructure: Mass Transit in 19th- and 20th-Cen-
tury Urban America." Oxford Research Encyclopedia, March
2015. https://oxfordre.com/americanhistory/view/10.1093/acre-
fore/9780199329175.001.0001/acrefore-9780199329175-e-28.

"2 The Importance of Place and Connectedness." National Research Council. 2002. *Community and Quality of Life: Data Needs for Informed Decision Making.* Washington, DC: The National Academies Press. doi: 10.17226/10262. https://www.nap.edu/read/10262/chapter/5.

Alderman, Derek and Joshua Inwood. "Street Naming and the Politics of Belonging: Spatial Injustices in the Toponymic Commemoration of Martin Luther King Jr." *Social & Cultural Geography* 14, no. 2 (March 2013). 10.1080/14649365.2012.754488.

Abrahamson, Mark. "Urban Enclaves: Identity and Place in America." *Contemporary Sociology* 25, no. 6 (November 1996).

Busch, Akiko. "How To Disappear: Notes on Invisibility in a Time of Transparency." Penguin Press, 2019.

Cao, Xinyu (Jason). "Residential Self-Selection in the Relationships Between the Built Environment and Travel Behavior: Introduction to the Special Issue." *Journal of Transport and Land Use* 7, no. 3 (2014). http://www.jstor.org/stable/26202688.

"Changing Faces of Greater Boston." The Boston Foundation, May 2019. https://www.bostonindicators.org/-/media/indicators/boston-indicators-reports/report-files/changing-faces-2019/indicators-changing-facesf2web.pdf.

David, Bil. "Chris Rock MLK Blvd." January 14, 2015, video, 1:10. https://www.youtube.com/watch?v=7hJxWr1TKK8.

Douglas, Jen. "From Disinvestment to Displacement: Gentrification and Jamaica Plain's Hyde-Jackson Squares," *Trotter Review* 23, no. 1 (2016). https://scholarworks.umb.edu/cgi/viewcontent.cgi?article=1363&context=trotter_review.

Einstein, Katherine Levine, Maxwell Palmer, and David Glick. "Who Participates in Local Government? Evidence from Meeting Minutes." *Perspectives on Politics* 17, no. 1 (2018). https://doi.org/10.1017/s153759271800213x.

Gambini, Bert. "Love the Cook, Love the Food: Attraction to Comfort Food Linked to Positive Social Connections." University of Buffalo, March 27, 2015. http://www.buffalo.edu/news/releases/2015/03/052.html.

Godoy, Maria. "When Chefs Become Famous Cooking Other Cultures' Foods." *NPR*, March 22, 2016. https://www.npr.org/sections/thesalt/2016/03/22/471309991/when-chefs-become-famous-cooking-other-cultures-food.

Hall, Andrew B. and Jesse Yoder. "Does Homeownership Influence Political Behavior? Evidence from Administrative Data." Stanford University, March 26, 2019. http://www.andrewbenjaminhall.com/homeowner.pdf.

Higgins, Brian R. and Joel Hunt. "Collective Efficacy: Taking Action to Improve Neighborhoods." National Institute of Justice, May 1, 2016. https://nij.ojp.gov/topics/articles/collective-efficacy-taking-action-improve-neighborhoods.

Hymel, Kent. "Does Traffic Congestion Reduce Employment Growth." *Journal of Urban Economics* 65, no. 2 (March

2009). https://www.sciencedirect.com/science/article/abs/pii/
S0094119008001162.

Lind, Dara. "What 'Chain Migration' Really Means—and Why
Donald Trump Hates it so Much." *Vox*, December 29, 2017.
https://www.vox.com/policy-and-politics/2017/12/29/16504272/
chain-migration-family-how-trump-end.

LePan, Nicholas. "Form and Function: Visualizing the Shape of
Cities and Economies." VisualCapitalist, September 26, 2019.
https://www.visualcapitalist.com/form-and-function-the-
shape-of-cities-and-economies/.

Liu, Michael, and Kim Geron. "Changing Neighborhood: Ethnic
Enclaves and the Struggle for Social Justice." *Social Justice* 35,
no. 2 (112) (2008). http://www.jstor.org/stable/29768486.

Kay, Sara. "Yelp Reviewers' Authenticity Fetish Is White Supremacy in Action." Eater New York, January 18, 2019. https://
ny.eater.com/2019/1/18/18183973/authenticity-yelp-reviews
-white-supremacy-trap.

Malanga, Steven. "The Curse of the Creative Class." City-Journal,
Winter 2014. https://www.city-journal.org/html/curse-cre-
ative-class-12491.html.

Mercado, Paolo. "The Creative Economy Gay Index: Why Tolerant
Cities Attract Creative People." *Adobo Magazine*, June 18, 2018.

https://www.adobomagazine.com/the-magazine/the-cre-
ative-economy-gay-index-why-tolerant-cities-attract-cre-
ative-people/.

Misra, Tanvi. "The Remaking of Martin Luther King Streets." Bloomberg CityLab, November 23, 2015. https://www. bloomberg.com/news/articles/2015-11-23/the-ongoing-fight-to-revitalize-streets-named-after-martin-luther-king-jr.

O'Sullivan, Feargus. "The 'Gaytrification' Effect: Why Gay Neighborhoods are Being Priced Out." *The Guardian*, January 13, 2016. https://www.theguardian.com/cities/2016/jan/13/end-of-gaytrification-cities-lgbt-communities-gentrification-gay-villages.

Pager, Devah, and David S. Pedulla. "Race, Self-Selection, and the Job Search Process." *American Journal of Sociology* 120, no. 4 (2015). doi:10.1086/681072. https://www.jstor.org/stable/10.1086/681072.

Public Art Network Council. "Why Public Art Matters." Americans for the Arts, 2014. https://www.americansforthearts.org/by-program/reports-and-data/legislation-policy/naappd/why-public-art-matters-green-papero.

Public Art Network Council. "Why Public Art Matters 2018." Americans for the Arts, June 2018. https://www.americansforthearts.org/by-program/reports-and-data/legislation-policy/naappd/why-public-art-matters-2018.

Romm, Cari. "Why Comfort Food Comforts." *The Atlantic*, April 3, 2016. https://www.theatlantic.com/health/archive/2015/04/why-comfort-food-comforts/389613/.

Tebes, Jacob Kraemer, Samantha L. Matlin, Bronwyn Hunter, Azure B. Thompson, Dana M. Prince, and Nathanial Mohatt.

"Porch Light Program." Yale University School of Medicine, June 2015. https://medicine.yale.edu/psychiatry/consultation-center/Images/Porch_Light_Program_Final_Evaluation_Report_Yale_June_2015_Optimized_tcm798-218966.pdf.

Terzano, Kathryn. "Commodification of Transitioning Ethnic Enclaves." *Behavioral sciences (Basel, Switzerland)* 4, no. 4 (September 2014). doi:10.3390/bs4040341. https://www.ncbi.nlm.nih.gov/pmc/articles/PMC4287693/.

Trounstine, Jessica. "The Geography of Inequality: How Land Use Regulation Produces Segregation and Polarization." University of California, Merced, July 2018. https://polmeth.byu.edu/Plugins/FileManager/Files/Papers/Trounstine_polmeth.pdf.

"UNT Student Researches U.S. Streets Named for Martin Luther King Jr." *North Texas eNews*, January 5, 2011. http://www.ntx-e-news.com/cgi-bin/artman/exec/view.cgi?archive=42&num=66953&printer=1.

Wetherell, Sam. "Richard Florida Is Sorry." *Jacobin Magazine*, accessed June 16, 2020. https://jacobinmag.com/2017/08/new-urban-crisis-review-richard-florida.

10 WHAT'S THAT CALLED?

"Are Cities Making Us Depressed?" November 5, 2015. In *WBUR*. Podcast, MP3 audio, 9:53. https://www.wbur.org/hereand-now/2015/11/05/boring-cityscape-psychology.

"Blue Light has a Dark Side," Harvard Health Publishing. Last modified July 7, 2020. https://www.health.harvard.edu/staying-healthy/blue-light-has-a-dark-side

Boubekri, Mohamed, Ivy N. Cheung, Kathryn J. Reid, Chia-Hui Wang, and Phyllis C. Zee. "Impact of Windows and Daylight Exposure on Overall Health and Sleep Quality of Office Workers: A Case-Control Pilot Study." *Journal of Clinical Sleep medicine* 10, no. 6 (2014). doi:10.5664/jcsm.3780. https://www.ncbi.nlm.nih.gov/pmc/articles/PMC4031400/.

Ellard, Colin. "Streets with No Game." AEON, September 1, 2015. https://aeon.co/essays/why-boring-streets-make-pedestrians-stressed-and-unhappy.

Flowers, Jeff. "Why You (Probably) Have Poor Air Quality." Compact Appliance, February 16, 2015. https://learn.compactappliance.com/causes-of-poor-indoor-air-quality/.

Goldhagen, Sarah Williams. *Welcome To Your World: How The Built Environment Shapes Our Lives.* New York: HarperCollins, 2017.

Heschong, Lisa, Roger Wright, and Stacia Okura. "Daylighting Impacts on Human Performance in School." *Journal of the Illuminating Engineering Society* 31, no. 2 (2013). 10.1080/00994480.2002.10748396. https://www.researchgate.

net/publication/261618174_Daylighting_Impacts_on_Human_
Performance_in_School.

Hollander, Justin B. and Ann Sussman. "Boring Cityscapes are Bad
for Your Health." *The Boston Globe*, October 12, 2015. https://
www3.bostonglobe.com/opinion/2015/10/11/boring-cityscapes-
are-bad-for-your-health/mUeEkT43YGZr7pL1orrTNP/story.
html?arc404=true.

Hurley, Amanda Kolson. "This is Your Brain on Architecture."
Bloomberg CityLab, July 14, 2017. https://www.bloomberg.com/
news/articles/2017-07-14/this-is-your-brain-on-architecture.

Joshi, Sumedha M. "The Sick Building Syndrome." *Indian journal
of occupational and environmental medicine* 12, no. 2 (2008).
doi:10.4103/0019-5278.43262. https://www.ncbi.nlm.nih.gov/
pmc/articles/PMC2796751/.

Nejati, Adelah. "Lighting for Health and Well-Being: Circadian Rhythm Benefits." HMC Architects. Accessed
April 20, 2020. https://hmcarchitects.com/news/light-
ing-for-health-and-well-being-circadian-rhythm-bene-
fits-2019-04-10/.

Moser, Drew. "Space vs. Place [and Why it's Important to Know
the Difference]." DrewMoser.com (blog), July 12, 2016. https://
drewmoser.com/2016/07/12/space-vs-place-and-why-its-im-
portant-to-know-the-difference/.

Merrifield, Colleen and James Danckert. "Characterizing the psychophysiological signature of boredom." *Experimental Brain
Research* 232 (2014). https://doi.org/10.1007/s00221-013-3755-2.

Pedersen, Martin. "How Architecture Affects Your Brain: The Link Between Neuroscience and the Built Environment." ArchDaily, July 25, 2017. https://www.archdaily.com/876465/how-architecture-affects-your-brain-the-link-between-neuroscience-and-the-built-environment.

R.S. Ulrich. "View Through a Window May Influence Recovery From Surgery," *Science* 224, no. 4647 (1984). https://www.health-design.org/chd/knowledge-repository/view-through-window-may-influence-recovery-surgery.

Rudd, Melanie, Kathleen D. Vohs, and Jennifer Aaker. "Awe Expands People's Perception of Time, Alters Decision Making, and Enhances Well-Being." *Psychological Science* 23, no. 10 (2012). https://journals.sagepub.com/doi/10.1177/0956797612438731.

"Sick Building Syndrome and Building Related Illness." Healthy Building Science, October 2, 2015. https://healthybuilding-science.com/2015/10/02/sick-building-syndrome-and-building-related-illness/.

Talks at Google. "Welcome to Your World | Sarah Williams Goldhagen | Talks at Google." June 15, 2017, video, 52:13. https://www.youtube.com/watch?v=Y-4Oenywkog.

"The Impact of Green Buildings on Cognitive Function." Harvard University Sustainability. Accessed April 21, 2020. https://green.harvard.edu/tools-resources/research-highlight/impact-green-buildings-cognitive-function.

"The Features of the Southwestern Style Architecture." Santa Fe By Design. Accessed April 11, 2020. https://santafebydesign.com/design/features/.

Tuan, Yi-Fu. *Space and Place: The Perspective of Experience*. Minneapolis: University of Minnesota Press, 1977.

Urist, Jacob. "The Psychological Cost of Boring Buildings." *The Cut*, April 12, 2016. https://www.thecut.com/2016/04/the-psychological-cost-of-boring-buildings.html.

Valdesolo, Piercarlo and Jesse Graham. "Awe, uncertainty, and agency detection." *Psychological Science* 25, no. 1 (2014). https://journals.sagepub.com/doi/abs/10.1177/0956797613501884.

Van Cappellen, Patty and Vassilis Saroglou. "Awe Activates Religious and Spiritual Feelings and Behavioral Intentions." *Psychology of Religion and Spirituality* 4, no. 3 (2012). https://www.researchgate.net/publication/232598520_Awe_activates_religious_and_spiritual_feelings_and_behavioral_intentions.

Walsh, Colleen. "Your Building Might be Making You Sick. Joe Allen can help." *Harvard Gazette*, February 14, 2018. https://news.harvard.edu/gazette/story/2018/02/your-building-might-be-making-you-sick-joe-allen-can-help/.

11 EDUCATION FOR JUST US

Abdollah, Tami. "A Strict Order for Fast Food." *LA Times*, September 10, 2007. https://www.latimes.com/archives/la-xpm-2007-sep-10-me-fastfood10-story.html.

Ahrentzen, Sherry and Linda N. Groat. "Rethinking Architectural Education: Patriarchal Conventions & Alternative Visions From The Perspectives of Women Faculty." *Journal of Architectural and Planning Research* 9, no. 2 (1992). http://www.jstor.org/stable/43029068.

Allcott, Hunt, Rebecca Diamond, Jean-Pierre Dubé, Jessie Handbury, Ilya Rahkovsky, and Molly Schnell. "Food Deserts and the Causes of Nutritional Inequality." *The Quarterly Journal of Economics* 134, no. 4 (2018). https://www.nber.org/papers/w24094.

Bernstein, Phil. "Architectural Education is Changing: Let's Hope the Profession Can Keep Up." Common Edge, January 22, 2018. https://commonedge.org/architectural-education-is-changing-lets-hope-the-profession-can-keep-up.

Black, Jane. "What's in a Number?" *Slate*, September 17, 2008. https://slate.com/human-interest/2008/09/how-the-press-got-the-idea-that-food-travels-1500-miles-from-farm-to-plate.html.

Brinkley, Catherine. "Why Community-Owned Grocery Stores Are the Best Recipe for Revitalizing Food Deserts." NextCity Foundation, September 13, 2019. https://nextcity.org/daily/entry/community-owned-grocery-stores-revitalizing-food-deserts.

Budds, Diana. "How Urban Design Perpetuates Racial Inequality—And What We Can Do About It." Fast Company, July 18, 2016. https://www.fastcompany.com/3061873/how-urban-design-perpetuates-racial-inequality-and-what-we-can-do-about-it.

Budds, Diana. "Architecture Schools Are Failing. This Designer Is Calling For a Revolution." Fast Company, October 5, 2016. https://www.fastcompany.com/3064302/architecture-education-is-broken-this-architect-has-a-plan-to-fix-it.

Christopher W. Tessum, Joshua S. Apte, Andrew L. Goodkind, Nicholas Z. Muller, Kimberley A. Mullins, David A. Paolella, Stephen Polasky, Nathaniel P. Springer, Sumil K. Thakrar, Julian D. Marshall, and Jason D. Hill. "Inequity in consumption of goods and services adds to racial–ethnic disparities in air pollution exposure." *Proceedings of the National Academy of Sciences* 166, no. 13 (March 2019). DOI: 10.1073/pnas.1818859116.

Cole, Shawn, Anna Paulson and Gauri Kartini Shastry. "High School Curriculum and Financial Outcomes: The Impact of Mandated Personal Finance and Mathematics Courses." *Journal of Human Resources* 51, no. 3 (June 2016). doi:10.3368/jhr.51.3.0113-5410R1 http://jhr.uwpress.org/content/early/2015/11/20/jhr.51.3.0113-5410R1.abstract.

Davis, Ronald L. F. "Racial Etiquette: The Racial Customs and Rules of Racial Behaviour in Jim Crow America." California State University, Northridge. Accessed July 4, 2020. https://files.nc.gov/dncr-moh/jim%20crow%20etiquette.pdf.

Design Plus Diversity. "Design Justice: Colloquial design for a just city | Bryan Lee | Design + Diversity Conference 2017." November 27, 2017. Video, 35:23. https://www.youtube.com/watch?v=f8nwt6iQMQI&feature=emb_rel_end.

"Design Justice for Black Lives." Colloqate Design. Accessed May 21, 2020. https://colloqate.org/design-justice-for-black-lives.

"Design Justice Network Principles." Design Justice Network. Last modified Summer 2018. https://designjustice.org/read-the-principles.

Dewey, Caitlin. "Why Farmers Only Get 7.8 Cents of Every Dollar Americans Spend on Food." *The Denver Post*. Last modified May 2, 2018. https://www.denverpost.com/2018/05/02/farming-share-of-consumer-food-spending/.

Dickinsin, Dou. "Architectural Education Will Have to Change or Risk Becoming Irrelevant." Common Edge, January 4, 2018. https://commonedge.org/architectural-education-will-have-to-change-or-risk-becoming-irrelevant/.

"Diversity in the Profession of Architecture." American Institute of Architects, 2015. https://www.architecturalrecord.com/ext/resources/news/2016/03-Mar/AIA-Diversity-Survey/AIA-Diversity-Architecture-Survey-02.pdf.

Eckert, Grant. "Why Is Financial Education No Longer Part Of The Curriculum?" National Debt Relief, April 15, 2019. https://www.nationaldebtrelief.com/financial-education-not-part-of-curriculum/.

Ellison, Charles. "Urban Planning Can't Happen Without Black People in the Room—Yet it Does." Congress for the New Urbanism Public Square, May 18, 2017. https://www.cnu.org/publicsquare/2017/05/18/urban-planning-can't-happen-without-black-people-room—yet-it-does.

"Empowering Parents Through Technology." *Digital Opportunity for Youth* 7 (October 2010). http://www.digitalreadynow.com/wp-content/uploads/2015/07/TCP-ParentTech-Low-RezFinal.pdf.

Fryar, Cheryl D and R. Bethene Ervin. "Caloric Intake From Fast Food Among Adults: United States, 2007–2010." NCHS Data Brief, No. 114. Hyattsville, MD: National Center for Health Statistics. 2013. https://www.cdc.gov/nchs/products/databriefs/db114.htm.

Gang, Jonathan. "Ron Sims: How Where You Live Affects Your Health." Public Health Post, January 4, 2017. https://www.publichealthpost.org/profiles/ron-sims/.

"Gender Mainstreaming." United Nations Women. Accessed June 14, 2020. https://www.unwomen.org/en/how-we-work/un-system-coordination/gender-mainstreaming.

Griffin, Toni L. and Esther Yang. "Inclusion in Architecture." J. Max Bond Center on Design for the Just City at the Bernard and Anne Spitzer School of Architecture at The City College of New York, September 14, 2015. https://ssa.ccny.cuny.edu/wp-content/uploads/2015/12/InclusioninArchitectureReport_WebDec2015.pdf.

Hawkins, Andrew. "Top 4 Concerns with Current Architectural Education." Hawkins Architecture, August 26, 2011. http://hawkinsarch.com/top-4-concerns-with-current-architectural-education/index.html.

Hoelscher, Steven. "Making Place, Making Race: Performances of Whiteness in the Jim Crow South." *Annals of the Association of American Geographers* 93, no. 3 (2003). http://www.jstor.org/stable/1515502.

Hsu, Angel and Kim Samuel. "How Cities are Failing to be Inclusive - and What They can do About It." World Economic Forum, December 6, 2018. https://www.weforum.org/agenda/2018/12/how-global-cities-are-failing-to-be-inclusive/.

Jackson, Richard J., and Chris Kochlitzky. "Creating a Healthy Environment: The Impact of the Built Environment on Public Health." Center for Disease Control and Prevention. Accessed May 19. 2020. https://www.cdc.gov/healthyplaces/articles/Creating%20A%20Healthy%20Environment.pdf.

Jorgenson, Olaf. "Why Curriculum Change Is Difficult and Necessary." *National Academy of Independent Schools,* Summer 2006. https://www.nais.org/magazine/independent-school/summer-2006/why-curriculum-change-is-difficult-and-necessary/.

Kirk, Mimi. "Why Architecture?" *Architect Magazine*, February 7, 2018. https://www.architectmagazine.com/aia-architect/aiafeature/why-architecture_.

Landis, Kelsey. "Growth in Racial Diversity Among Architects is Slow, but Experts Say the Conversation Continues." Insight Into Diversity, September 16, 2019. https://www. insightintodiversity.com/growth-in-racial-diversity-among-architects-is-slow-but-experts-say-the-conversation-continues/.

Leavens, Molly. "Do Food Miles Really Matter?" Harvard University, March 7, 2017. https://green.harvard.edu/news/do-food-miles-really-matter.

Lowry, Megan. "New Report Finds K-12 Teachers Face New Expectations and More Demands; Training and Workforce Changes Could Help." The National Academies of Sciences, Engineering, and Medicine, February 12, 2020. https://www. nationalacademies.org/news/2020/02/new-report-finds-k-12-teachers-face-new-expectations-and-more-demands-training-and-workforce-changes-could-help.

"Not Enough: A Lack of Diversity May Kill Architecture." The Thinking Architect, December 19, 2015. https://thethinkingarchitect.wordpress.com/2015/12/19/not-enough-a-lack-of-diversity-may-kill-architecture/.

Owens, Cassie. "Urban Planning Faces Possible Diversity Setback." NextCity Foundation, November 12, 2015. https://nextcity. org/daily/entry/planning-accreditation-board-diversity-urban-planning.

Roy, Joseph. "Engineering By The Numbers." American Society of Engineering Education. Last modified July 15, 2019. https://ira.asee.org/wp-content/uploads/2019/07/2018-Engineering-by-Numbers-Engineering-Statistics-UPDATED-15-July-2019.pdf.

Schlanger, Zoe. "Choking to Death in Detroit: Flint Isn't Michigan's Only Disaster." *Newsweek Magazine*, March 30, 2016. https://www.newsweek.com/2016/04/08/michigan-air-pollution-poison-southwest-detroit-441914.html.

Schlanger, Zoe. "Race is the Biggest Indicator in the US of Whether You Live Near Toxic Waste." *Quartz Magazine*, March 22, 2017. https://qz.com/939612/race-is-the-biggest-indicator-in-the-us-of-whether-you-live-near-toxic-waste/.

"Small Business Saturday Statistics" Grasshopper (blog). Accessed May 23, 2020. https://grasshopper.com/resources/articles/small-business-saturday-statistics/.

Von Koenig, Gretchen. "Peter Zellner's New Architecture School: No Tuition & a Radical Curriculum." *Metropolis Magazine*, December 15, 2016. https://www.metropolismag.com/ideas/peter-zellners-new-architecture-school-promises-free-tuition-and-a-radical-curriculum-but-will-it-work/.

Way, Wendy L., and Karen Holden. "Teachers' Background & Capacity to Teach Personal Finance: Results of a National Study." National Endowment for Financial Education, 2010. https://www.fdic.gov/about/comein/mar3.pdf.

Wilson, Lindsay. "The Tricky Truth About Food Miles." Shrink That Footprint. Accessed May 23, 2020. http://shrinkthatfootprint.com/food-miles.

"Why Isn't Personal Finance Taught in School?" National Financial Educators Council. Accessed June 19, 2020. https://www. financialeducatorscouncil.org/why-isnt-personal-finance-taught-in-school/.

12 EPILOGUE

Baumeister, Roy and Mark Leary. The Need to Belong: Desire for Interpersonal Attachments as a Fundamental Human Motivation. *Psychological Bulletin* 117, no. 3 (1995). https://doi.org/10.1037/0033-2909.117.3.497.

Giple, Lourenzo. "DAYLIGHT Podcast | Season 2 Episode 1 | Inclusion." March 21, 2019. *In Daylight*. Podcast, MP3 audio, 1:18:00. https://peopleup.org/blogs/news/daylight-podcast-season-2-episode-2-inclusion.

Hertz, Daniel. "There's Basically No Way Not to Be a Gentrifier." Bloomberg CityLab, April 23, 2014. https://www.citylab.com/equity/2014/04/theres-basically-no-way-not-be-gentrifier/8877/.

Syrkett, Asad, Tanay Warerkar, and Patrick Sisson. "16 Architects of Color Speak Out About the Industry's Race Problem." *Curbed*, February 22, 2017. https://www.curbed.com/2017/2/22/13843566/minority-architects-diversity-architecture-solutions-advice.

CPSIA information can be obtained
at www.ICGtesting.com
Printed in the USA
BVHW090251211220
596044BV00005B/13